HOUSE
OF SPIES

ST ERMIN'S HOTEL
THE LONDON BASE
OF BRITISH
ESPIONAGE

PETER MATTHEWS

The
History
Press

To St Ermin's Hotel and its people and my
memories there of times past

First published 2016

This ediiton published 2017 by

The History Press
The Mill, Brimscombe Port
Stroud, Gloucestershire, GL5 2QG
www.thehistorypress.co.uk

© Peter Matthews, 2016, 2017

The right of Peter Matthews to be identified as the Author
of this work has been asserted in accordance with the
Copyright, Designs and Patents Act 1988.

British Library Cataloguing in Publication Data.
A catalogue record for this book is available from the British Library.

ISBN 978 0 75098416 4

Typesetting and origination by The History Press
Printed in Great Britain

CONTENTS

AUTHOR'S NOTE

The world of espionage is complex and so are the organisations that deal in it, therefore I have tried to simplify it a bit for the reader. The Soviet security organisation has gone through a number of transformations before it settled down into the format of KGB (Committee of State Security), which everyone seems to know. I have largely ignored the various transformations that it has gone through and stuck with the initials with which most people are familiar. I have taken the same view with MI6, which has not been its title since the 1950s. It is now the Secret Intelligence Service (SIS), but that is not the old familiar label that everyone knows so I have stuck with MI6 for at least most of the book, with an occasional reference to the service.

Peter Matthews
2016

FOREWORD

by Mark Birdsall

There are hundreds of buildings in London inextricably linked to monumental moments in the world of espionage and intelligence, perhaps none more so than St Ermin's Hotel. A perusal of documents linked to this aspect of the hotel hardly begins to touch upon the meetings and decisions made within its rooms that impacted so many people and changed history.

London is quite rightly known as the 'spy capital' of the world. Some of the oldest intelligence services were formed here and for centuries the greatest spies and their catchers played 'cat and mouse' on its city streets. Its reputation and links to intelligence go much deeper. One could argue that today's international intelligence services owe much to the pioneers often working from tiny offices, who a little over a century ago created services that would evolve into what we now know as MI5 (Security Service), MI6 (Secret Intelligence Service) and GCHQ (Government Communications Headquarters).

Every century brings new challenges for people who work in the shadows. For those London-based operators charged with intelligence collection and security at the outbreak of the First World War in 1914, managing and developing a dedicated spy service was truly a daunting task. The names of Cumming, Kell, Knight and Hall instantly spring to mind, but there were so many others, including ministers tasked with raising suitable finances. Thankfully the 'seeds' of what was initially known as the Secret Service

Bureau had been sown in 1909, thus when war did break out Britain had a hidden advantage.

It quickly became evident that defeat of Germany and the Kaiser would require implementation of both old and new intelligence techniques, including deception operations and ruses. The organisation and operation necessary became a complex affair. And whilst London planners successfully planted spies in Europe and elsewhere, it was evident they would need to counter tactics launched by Berlin. To compound matters further, propaganda became an integral 'ingredient' in the great game. Henceforth what emerged was an array of services and operations often linked to civilian concerns such as newspapers, broadcasters, film studios and even entertainers who could travel and report back observations. Many of these communications were written in code or secret inks, requiring the services of brilliant academics and analysts. And, of course, locations were required to plan, discuss, support and, yes, wine and dine the spies who were helping Great Britain in the Great War. Enter St Ermin's Hotel – close to Parliament and other places of importance, it was ideal for conducting business and taking moments to relax.

Britain and her allies defeated Germany but just two decades later the flames of war would consume Europe and other regions of the world again. However, this time the intelligence services of Britain would face a much tougher opponent and an equally cunning Abwehr (German Intelligence) headed by Admiral Canaris. In London, Churchill soon recognised MI6 had but a scant network of agents on the Continent to fight what was going to be a very dirty war. Thus he gathered a number of trusted associates and soon the emergence of a pseudo-military intelligence organisation emerged – the Special Operations Executive (SOE). MI6 hierarchy were not happy but the men and women of the SOE charged with 'setting Europe ablaze' soon proved their worth. To compound matters, the intelligence directorate and offices of the SOE were based in St Ermin's Hotel – just opposite a suite of rooms occupied by MI6 planners! Obviously many other buildings in London and beyond were used by British Intelligence and the SOE, but the hotel became a hub of divergent intelligence activity. As this uneasy truce continued, at least MI6 and the SOE forged ahead with developing their tradecraft, and the creative wings of both organisations produced an array of gadgets, bombs, maps, containers, secret cameras, etc … Then the Americans arrived in London and soon its version of the SOE, the Office of Strategic Services (OSS), began occupying various buildings. It was also during this haunting period that a number of guests and visitors to St Ermin's began their careers in the Foreign Office and intelligence. Some of these characters have been quite rightly described as 'infamous'. Several were already in the pay of spymasters in faraway Moscow.

In 1945, as the war theatres of Europe and the Far East fell silent, there was optimism around the world that a lasting peace would lead to a greater understanding between peoples. Not a chance. Russia refused to pull back its troops and half of Europe was consumed behind what Churchill dubbed an 'Iron Curtain' in 1946. The Cold War had begun and with it an enduring spy saga that continues to this day.

I am, of course, referring to the great game played out between the West and East involving spies, agents, counter-espionage officers, subversives, controllers and even assassins. For more than a century agencies such as MI6, MI5 and their friends at the CIA (born from the embers of the OSS), have been engaged in a secret war involving intelligence collection. And many of the operators have plied their trade on the streets of London.

There have been thousands of books written on the activities of spies and intelligence people who were based in London. Some were written by the operators themselves, including the likes of MI5's Peter Wright of *Spycatcher* fame, but most contain materials sourced from archives from the secret spy wars, particularly from the twentieth century.

Peter Matthews, a highly respected intelligence historian and author of note, was fortunate to work in various intelligence sectors and lived through momentous events, and at close quarters – not as a bystander, but as an active participant. He is a library of intelligence knowledge and has woven together a book that not only identifies key intelligence figures, operations and events in history, but intimately exposes the 'spylore' of London. He cleverly threads together decades of intelligence activities and operations such as Venona, the D-Day landings, the work of Room 40 codebreakers and the famous characters who will forever be embedded in British Intelligence history. Also included in this book are little-known operations and events that had global implications, and more importantly, his personal recollections of the events spanning many decades. Thankfully these elements of history have been documented and will be an important tool for scholars and amateur historians alike.

Even those who work in the closed world of secrets must have a base of operations, and what better place to hide in plain sight than the iconic and elegant St Ermin's Hotel. I hesitate to guess the number of people connected to intelligence and covert activities that have passed through the foyer of the hotel through the years, or walked its secret corridors on to the streets of London. However, Peter's research into the actual building and location reveals a fascinating period that dates back well before the creation of the Secret Service Bureau and contains a 'nugget' of intrigue in an absorbing chapter in the history of London.

Peter worked and operated in a very different world to ours today, forged by incredible endeavours of many people who worked in locations not for the faint-hearted. During his long career he made both mental and archive records of many 'intelligence gems' gleaned from the fascinating characters he encountered in disparate locations across the city, from dingy attics and basements where secret work was performed to the rooms of St Ermin's Hotel.

The author has written a time capsule of momentous intelligence events, which in truth can be sourced one way or another to London and the 'players' and 'operators' who for various reasons found themselves engaged in a world of spies. A few years ago I had the good fortune to meet Peter at St Ermin's. His brilliant book, *SIGINT*, had been short-listed for the prestigious St Ermin's Intelligence Book of the Year award. As we watched the activities, Peter smiled and said, 'If only walls could talk.'

For the intelligence connoisseur, the pages of *House of Spies* are more than echoes of conversations and the fading footprints of spies; they describe in plain language the many incredible events, people, monumental decisions and operations associated with St Ermin's Hotel and British Intelligence. Some of those walls have at last given up their secrets …

ACKNOWLEDGEMENTS

My thanks go to the select group of people who helped me to research and write my book and get over the troubles that I had in the battle against Windows 10, which caused me much grief.

Mark Beynon and Naomi Reynolds, my editors, who left me alone when I had troubles with my computer and encouraged me when I did not.

Mark Birdsall, who has stamped his authority on the book gained through the years of editing his magazine dedicated to revealing the secrets of the covert world of espionage. I am also indebted to him for the selection of images from his huge collection of photographs used to illustrate this book.

Paul Baumont, my friend who instructed me in the mysteries of 'Number Stations' and introduced me to intelligence lectures at the Imperial College of Science and Technology, which gave me new avenues of research.

Mike Grant, who managed to save an important part of the manuscript for me and probably still does not know how grateful I am to him for his help when the pressure was intense.

Tim Fordham-Moss, who helped to focus my thoughts over lunches and tea at St Ermin's, gave me a new slant on the functions of the hotel and showed me some of its secrets.

Ian Hunter, who has been my rock in surviving the storms and tempests of a crisis in computer technology when his calm counsel on what to do saved much grief and despair.

Anthony Kay, who was my principal researcher in finding relevant newspapers and other documentation that helped with the text and led to several new avenues of research.

Chris Northcott, whose expertise on the period before and during the First World War helped me enormously, as did him then reading those chapters.

The Imperial War Museum in London and its staff, particularly those that maintain the exhibits of the Secret War Galleries, which gave me a 'feel' of the equipment and weapons that the SOE agents used in their adventures. The Public Records Office (National Archives, Kew) where many obliging staff helped me to find what few documents of the beginning of the SOE survived the great 'tidy up' after the war. Tunbridge Wells Library, without whom I would never have had access to the wide range of books that they obtained for me to help my research. Westminster Abbey and its staff in the ancient Minument Rooms, which were a treat to visit for an archivist such as myself, with historic manuscripts and documents in every cranny of their ancient archives and for the image of the St Ermin's statue in the Abbey.

I left the best to last, which is my wife Carole, who has lived with the writing of my books and ran the house around me while I spent my waking hours sitting in front of an unfriendly computer.

Thank you all.

PREFACE

When I was commissioned to write this book about dear old St Ermin's it was like revisiting an old friend. The hotel and its locality had been a part of my youth, I was a daily visitor to Victoria Street and its environs as the war drew to an end. I joined A. Pauling & Co, which had offices at 28 Victoria Street on the site of what is now Scotland Yard, the headquarters of the Metropolitan Police. Pauling's were civil engineers and had a global reputation in Britain's civil engineering industry. They had been a main contractor in the construction of the Mulberry harbours, built to supply the Allied armies during the 1944 landings in Normandy.

As a very junior engineer I worked for Sir John Gibson, the charismatic managing director of the company, who was a leading figure in the construction of the harbours. He still maintained contact with his large team of engineers, most of whom had worked with him on the harbours, so there were plenty of wartime stories retold in the bar for me to hear. The offices at No. 28 were always bustling with men, some of whom were still in British Army uniform, sporting the insignia of the Royal Engineers.

The building was one of the few surviving office buildings at the Parliament Square end of Victoria Street, which had been largely occupied by civil engineering contractors of repute. Those buildings had a real Dickensian quality about them as they were built at the beginning of the nineteenth century when British civil engineering was the envy of the world. They were still anchored firmly in the early part of the previous century, and it was beginning to show. For instance, the lift serving the five storeys of the building was counterweight-driven with no motor to operate it. You did that by pulling hard on a rope that ran through the centre of the lift compartment. The rope had to be pulled hard to make it go up but less hard in the reverse downward direction. The lift attendant (or rope-puller) was a lady of uncertain age and temper called May who steadfastly refused to allow any junior members of staff – who she always treated with undisguised contempt – to ride in her lift.

The offices were as dated as the lift and filled with huge drawing boards, crouched over by ageing draftsmen labouring over exquisitely hand-drawn engineering drawings, often of very large scale. Their work was stored in the expansive drawers of polished wood cabinets that were already full of drawings of the components of the Mulberry harbour.

Victoria Street was occupied almost entirely by civil engineering companies clustering together largely because of their part in the growth of the railway system, and for that reason it was known as 'Engineers Alley'. During the 1850s every railway development required a Private Act of Parliament so every civil engineering firm working on a railway project needed an office close to the House of Commons to brief its sponsoring member of parliament.

The City of London was not the only area of London that burned in the Blitz unfortunately, most of the engineering offices in Engineers Alley were burned out, charred and gutted shells after the war. The German bombers had taken their toll on the rows of Victoria Street's combustible old buildings; they disappeared in an inferno one night, just before Christmas in 1941.

The German Luftwaffe had scattered its incendiary bombs over Westminster, so for some time after the war the street was flanked by rows of ruined shells of buildings. Later they were demolished to provide the footings for the large, modern office blocks we see today. Engineers Alley vanished, leaving only a couple of interesting historical buildings that remain today. St Ermin's is one of them and it was destined to provide an important venue for the intelligence community during the rest of the war and into the Cold War that followed.

The bombed ruins had to be demolished to provide footings for the large office blocks on the site of those old Victorian offices, and it was sad to watch No. 28 being demolished along with the others, to be replaced by the New Scotland Yard building. Another of those knocked down was Britannia House, which had escaped destruction. It was approached by an imposing flight of steps flanked by two large and impressive stone lions. The building was said to have been the German Kaiser's house in London before the First World War and part of his considerable investment in property in the Victoria Street area. I have yet to do the research to establish if the Kaiser's money went into the building of St Ermin's Mansions before it became a hotel.

Number 28 survived the flames to later fall victim to the developers' demolition ball, but in the meantime it became a meeting place for veterans of the Mulberry harbours' construction presided over by Sir John. He involved the company in the Ground Nut Scheme in Africa, so veterans of the harbour project would arrive, all bronzed and confident, to pay their respects to Sir John and try to find a role for themselves in the new scheme. When they had settled whatever business they had to do at No. 28 they usually repaired to the bar at St Ermin's, where they would tell and retell tales of derring-do about the harbour, which often became enriched with the telling.

One that had the ring of truth in it (some did not), concerned the respites from the backbreaking work they had to undertake in building and maintaining the Mulberry harbour. During what little rest they had they would enjoy nothing better than to lie in the sun in the sand dunes watching German prisoners as they came down to the boats to be shipped over to England. As they were marched down to the seashore, the vista of a major harbour with ships unloading the supplies for a growing and victorious army that had begun fighting its way into France became evident. Our group would explode with laughter as one or the other of them recalled the looks on the faces of the German prisoners when they viewed the panorama of a busy harbour full of ships coming and going that had not been there only days before.

My time with Pauling's went by and I was called to the colours, as most young men in Britain were at that time. Soon my regiment was posted to Berlin, just as the airlift that supplied that beleaguered city began. The Cold War had begun, with its use and misuse of intelligence in the struggle between the Western Allies and Communism and the skulduggery centred on Berlin where I served as a very small cog in the huge espionage machine. We all played our part in gathering military intelligence for the Anglo-American army, while the KGB did the same for the Russian armies that drove the Cold War.

At the end of my military service I was back in Victoria Street, this time in Artillery Mansions where MI6 had a base, of which more later. I found civil engineering not to my taste in the way that it had been before so I found myself involved in the pursuit of intelligence once again. It took me into interesting corners, such as working with SO6 in Scotland Yard and then across to America for a brush with the CIA (Central Intelligence Agency), and the camaraderie of MI6 men (rarely women then), many of who took their leisure in St Ermin's Caxton Bar. Some of these experiences I have put into my books and articles and I have joined a fairly exclusive club of intelligence 'buffs' who enjoy delving into the 'missing dimension' in our country's (and the world's) military history.

Public access to the history of intelligence and particularly signals intelligence, which is my interest, only began in 1972 when J.C. Masterman's book, *The Double Cross System in the War 1939–1945*, was published. The secret was blown wide open two years later when F.W.Winterbotham's book, *The Ultra Secret*, was launched – anything published before then was usually in the form of memoirs of different operations.

By the 1980s the academic world began to take the 'missing dimension' in history seriously and so did the book publishers. Bletchley Park's marketing operation began to roll and reached an apex in 1984, in the form of *The Missing Dimension: Governments and Intelligence Communities in the Twentieth Century* by Christopher Andrew.

The role played by intelligence in the Second World War was revealed in these books, showing that military history had to be virtually rewritten. There was little time to do it, as the generation that had fought their intelligence battles was fading fast, and a serious move to introduce academic discipline to the subject emerged. Two academic journals were founded to underpin the discipline – *The Intelligence and National Security Journal* and the *International Journal of Intelligence and Counter-intelligence* ensured a growth in historical and theoretical treatments of intelligence studies in universities.

The study of the subject's structure began to reveal how multi-faceted the study of intelligence really was and academia began to address its breakdown into a number of general headings:

Archival evidence – using primary source archival evidence.
History and biography – producing case study-based accounts that tend to be either memoir or archive based.
Functional matters – emphasising activities and processes rather than historical examples that focus on deeper abstract issues.

Structural focuses – on the organisation of intelligence agencies.

Political aspects – concentrating on the formation of policy and control mechanisms.

Perspectives – using case and other studies to test theoretical hypotheses.

Civil liberties – examining projects designed to look at how the activities of intelligence agencies impinge on the public and sectors of it.

The press – and the changing relationship of the intelligence community with the media and its servants (which is one of my interests).

Popular culture – which considers such topics as the way the public sees the intelligence community through such popular figures as James Bond, etc.

There are, therefore, a wide variety of ways that the study of intelligence can be approached. Britain did this predominantly as history, although there was the abstract aspect in cryptology. In the United States, intelligence academic studies are mainly approached from a political science point of view and less as a historical subject, with greater emphasis on theoretical deliberations. American university studies concentrate on the function of policy making and foreign policy but British intelligence studies focus more on historical aspects, to the extent that American academics specialising in the discipline refer to the 'British School of Intelligence', which they (probably rightly) regard as historically based. The half dozen or so universities in the UK that offer a degree course or module in the subject approach it from a variety of directions.

My first book on the subject was published by The History Press, entitled *SIGINT: The Secret History of Signals Intelligence in the World Wars* and, of course, follows the British school of study. That book was intended to show some of the achievements of signals intelligence from its inception in 1914; this book includes a little of my own experience around the edges of political intelligence as we exchanged a hot war for a cold one.

ONE

THE FIRST WORLD WAR

CABLES AND CODES

It is generally believed that the British Secret Service's domination of the intelligence conflict between itself and Germany began in 1939 in Bletchley Park – it did not. The whole saga began quietly enough almost exactly a century ago in 1914 in the Admiralty Buildings, not more than a mile from St Ermin's Hotel. Years before the war began, the Committee for Imperial Defence in Whitehall had made plans to cut German communications in an action that would lay the foundations for making British intelligence a world-class service that would last for half a century.

As war was declared and hostilities began against Germany in 1914 the committee's plan was quietly put into action in an undramatic way. At the time, international communications were based almost entirely on undersea cables whose network spread like a spider's web under the oceans to connect the great cities of the world. The telegraphic messages were mainly intended to carry information and data concerned with international trade, but political and military communications messages rapidly took an increasing slice of the transmissions on the busy cable network.

Telephones and telegraph networks had changed the nature of international commerce, and even diplomacy, in the decade before the war but now it would also change the nature of war beyond imagining. Instructions and reports from the German Kaiser's embassies, and orders and reports from

German warships and garrisons in German West Africa, all kept the cable network busy. The British were well aware of the system's importance because they were leaders in the use of undersea cable technology. They used the cable messaging system extensively themselves with speedy communications that were at the heart of the maintenance, administration and control of the diverse and distant parts of their great empire.

Britain's initial actions at the beginning of the war were directed against the enemy's network of cables that connected Berlin with its friends, embassies and forces around the world. Cable telegraphy was far more important at the time than wireless signalling, which was only just beginning to reach its workable technical capability. Even so, two orders were transmitted by wireless telegraphy as well as cable from the Admiralty on 3 August 1914. The first was sent to all commands of the British fleet with the priority 'Most Immediate', which takes precedence over all other messages. The signal, sent in the Admiralty naval code (which the German *Kriegsmarine* had broken) and transmitted at 11.21 a.m. read 'XIlTO SSZKAP ACAAP SZBEC SXUYZ'. All the ships of the fleet received and decoded it as 'Commence hostilities at once with Germany'. The signal was sent from aerials that can still be seen above the domed roof of the Admiralty Buildings.

The second message, transmitted within hours of the first, was sent to a cable ship in clear language to execute a 'war reserve' standing order of the Committee of Imperial Defence. The secret order was to sever Germany's international undersea cables, which the cable ship carried out just a couple of days after war was declared (the vessel may have been the *Telconia* or the *Alert*, the records are unclear).*

The ship slipped her moorings in Harwich Harbour and steamed out into the North Sea, setting a course for the German coast near the town of Emden to dredge up five of the main telegraphic cables and slice them through. The cables they were to cut ran down the English Channel and connected Germany to France, neutral Spain, and the German colonies in Africa, as well as her many friends in North and South America. A few days later the *Telconia*

---

* References are confused as to which ship carried out the action but the author's preference is the *Telconia* because of an entry in Lloyd's register at the time. The ship's name *Telconia* is used in the following account because of that preference.

returned and with second thoughts dredged up several more thousands of feet of cable just to make sure that the damage was irreparable.

Cable links between Europe and North America had been laid more than a decade before and became a well-established part of Germany's international communication system. Wireless technology, however, was emerging fast and Germany had just managed her first long-range transmission in 1913 from the wireless station at Nauen, near Berlin, to Togo in Germany's West African colony. The transmission was barely audible compared with that of a cable message, which would have been clear and distinct, so wireless telegraphy still had some way to go to be a reliable form of communication.

Following the *Telconia*'s exploits, one of the war's earliest actions by British troops was to raid and destroy the German cable station at Lomé in West Africa. The destruction of their communications isolated German naval units in the waters of the South Atlantic, as without their cable connections the German cruiser squadrons could only receive wireless signals. They could be overheard by others and also, in responding to Berlin's signals, a vessel ran the risk of giving its position away to an enemy's listening and tracking station. Not that the British had much in the way of listening equipment in that early stage of the war, although listening stations began to quickly sprout along the coasts of the world's oceans just as soon as they found there were signals to intercept.

The need for interception and interpretation of wireless signals practised so well by Bletchley Park in the Second World War began with the *Telconia*'s action in 1914 in the North Sea. It fundamentally changed the signals intelligence battleground, although neither the Committee of Imperial Defence nor the Imperial German High Command could have foreseen its implications. At a stroke German maritime communications had been deprived of their reliance on cable telegraphy for orders and reports of all kinds as well as diplomatic dispatches. This would later prove to be fatal to the Kaiser's war objectives, particularly in the war at sea.

The first indication of the vulnerability of wireless transmissions in Morse code soon became evident almost as the *Telconia* returned to harbour. Navies of the world had grasped the opportunities for communicating with their ships by wireless at an early stage in the development of the technology, and among the first to do so was Britain's Royal Navy. It made the first ship-to-ship transmission of a message during fleet manoeuvres in 1909, although reception was far from perfect. By the time the war began five years later every major vessel in the navies of world was equipped with radio transmitter and receiver sets, and the trained operators to operate them.

Even so, for the British Navy the first indication of transmissions intercepted from the German High Sea Fleet (*Hochseeflotte*) base was discovered by radio amateurs. They brought their message pads to the Admiralty within days of the declaration of war and Admiral Henry Oliver, the Director of Naval Intelligence, was given the first copies of wireless interceptions – the trouble was, they were in code. First Lord of the Admiralty Winston Churchill ordered Oliver to set up a wireless intercept service and also establish a decoding facility at the Admiralty, and so Room 40 in the Admiralty Old Building was allocated for their use.

Britain's new intelligence bureau was destined to do great things in the war at sea and would later expand to provide an intelligence centre of wider dimensions. It would substantially influence the conduct of the war and even play a major part in ending it.

ROOM 40

With Room 40 OB, as it was designated, now the new home of his bureau, Admiral Oliver wanted the equivalent of an Alan Turing, the code breaker at Bletchley Park, to break the Imperial German Navy's coded transmissions. Oliver was lucky to have an old friend in Sir Alfred Ewing, who had an interest in codes and ciphers, and he invited Ewing to lunch at the United Services Club (now the Institute of Directors) in Pall Mall.

Ewing was offered the job of head of Room 40, which he immediately accepted; it turned out to be an inspired choice for the new intelligence bureau. He began a review of the various techniques of coding in the British Library, the British General Post Office and any other institutions that were able to help him. It soon became obvious that he would need a multi-talented team to help him tackle the difficult task that was beginning to emerge.

German transmissions were coming thick and fast from amateurs as well as naval wireless telegraphy personnel, who were now monitoring all transmissions in a disciplined manner in a chain of listening stations. They were quickly created up and down the eastern coast of England and Scotland to intercept and record German wireless transmissions using a device first developed by the army, which they called the 'wireless compass'. The apparatus could indicate the direction from which the wireless transmission came and, using the chain of direction finding (DF) stations that used the naval version of the wireless compass, two or more DF stations could take a reading on a transmission source. Where two or more direction finding readings converged would indicate the transmitter's location, and the DF station could estimate (sometimes quite accurately) where a U-boat or naval shore station transmitter was located when sending a signal.

DF stations were manned by trained wireless telegraphists who were organised by 'watches' around the clock in a way that missed little in the way of enemy transmissions. The network of listening stations and DF stations' techniques developed in the First World War was widely used in much the same way that 'Y' stations were in the Second World War.

Meanwhile, Ewing in Room 40 was not only beginning to crack the codes of some of the German wireless transmissions but also beginning to recruit others with similar code-breaking talents; he made some appointments that were as inspired as his own.

Oliver and Ewing decided that the team needed to have a variety of skills. German speakers were an obvious necessity, as was an understanding of naval procedures, practice and terminology, but there needed to be an overriding talent for understanding codes and ciphers. Ewing therefore looked first for candidates among naval personnel, and an early recruit was Commander Alistair Denniston, who was teaching German at Osbourne Naval College. Denniston thought that his appointment was a short-term one, but it was to become his life's work, enabling him to gain immense experience and become a leading figure in the intelligence community.

He was appointed to the Room 40 team, where he served until the end of the war and then he was appointed head of the bureau to lead it through the lean interwar years. Denniston led his small but experienced code-breaking team into Bletchley Park as war was declared in 1939, and, with its expertise gained during the First World War, it contributed substantially to 'the Park's' huge success in the second.

This was not the only link to British intelligence work made during the war, because Churchill served his apprenticeship in overseeing intelligence gathering and application in his supervision of Room 40. His experience in directing its activities in the First World War enabled him to see the value of intelligence and so he appreciated and supported his young intelligencers in the Second World War.

Churchill did not repeat the mistake in the Second World War that he had made in the management of Room 40, which was to allow the naval head of the agency, Admiral Oliver's, concern for secrecy to constrain the distribution and effect of the intelligence valuations. Oliver was allowed, in the early stages of Room 40's development, to keep his cards too close to his chest as he was unable to delegate work or responsibility for intelligence evaluations. Thus, the sharing of information with his colleagues was limited because Oliver's obsession was that he alone was absolutely essential to the operation of Room 40.

As he was unable to escape the heavy responsibility for his work and felt unable to share it with anyone, he would never leave the Admiralty War Room, day or night, for almost two years. He insisted on seeing everything and signing all correspondence himself; it is not an uncommon fault among intelligence officers, where the need for secrecy increases the burden a senior officer bears.

I have witnessed the effect that this can have on an individual. It can lead to every single aspect of his life and work being unnecessarily secret. I was aware of an intelligence officer who was warned that a senior government minister he was going to see did not have the necessary clearances for certain subjects to be discussed.

The intelligence systems management would change for the better later on in the war when another admiral, William 'Blinker' Hall, replaced Oliver, who was given a sea command. Ewing also later retired as he was worn out and exhausted from the service to his country. He had created a world-class interception and decoding organisation that would dominate the enemy in the art of intelligence. Methods of intercepting and decoding enemy wireless traffic had developed extraordinarily quickly from a standing start in the first months of the war where no organisation had existed previously. The Admiralty's intelligence bureau had gathered a hugely talented team, but what it now needed was what any code breaker needs and that was luck – and Room 40 found that in abundance.

The cryptologists in Room 40 were making slow but steady progress in understanding and penetrating the enemy's codes and ciphers as the code breakers gradually worked out how the keys of the encoded messages functioned. Many of the secret clues were held in books and papers that the enemy desperately wanted to keep safe and secure.

Encryption of messages into coded form is a science and like so many scientific disciplines has its roots in the culture of ancient Greece. The word 'cryptography' comes from the Greek *kryptos* (secret) and *graphos* (writing). The science divides into two aspects of the 'black art' of enciphering and deciphering messages. There is a difference between codes and ciphers – a code can be any form of prearranged signal, such as the array of flags that Nelson used in sending a message to his fleet, or dots and dashes indicating a particular letter in the Morse code. Sailors in particular were more at home with codes because they were simpler than ciphers (as long as you had the code book). A cipher is the substitution of one letter for another using a method that the recipient already knows and so will be able to reconstruct the message, but to do that they must have the cryptographic 'key'.

Julius Caesar used a code based on a Polybius square, which he used as a key, similar to that shown below:

	1	2	3	4	5
1	A	B	C	D	E
2	F	G	H	I/J	K
3	L	M	N	O	P
4	Q	R	S	T	U
5	V	W	X	Y	Z

The table was a simple construct and as long as the recipient had the table as a key he could easily decode the text. The letter A is represented by the number 11 and the letter Z as 55, thus to spell out the word 'war' would be ciphered as '25/11/24'.

The Polybius square was the basis of a coding method widely used in the trenches of northern France in the First World War, more than 2,000 years after the Romans first used it. Caesar also used a simple substitution code that took the letter A and substituted it for D, three places further on in the alphabet. B became E, and so on, so that the word 'Caesar' would be encoded as 'FDHVDU'. The decrypt was pretty easily worked out as long as you knew your alphabet backwards. This form of substitution cipher is called the

Caesar Shift Code and represents one of the basic forms of today's modern encryption systems.

Codes that were being worked on by Room 40 were far more complex than those described above and the lights often burned late into the night in the Admiralty. Code breakers working on encoded German wireless transmissions needed a 'crib', and in the early days of the war they were soon to get not one but four. The first lucky strike occurred on the other side of the world in Australian waters. The German steamship *Hobart* was one of the few ships that had not installed a wireless set and so the captain was unaware that war had broken out. He was not alarmed when a party of sailors of the Royal Australian Navy boarded his vessel on what he assumed was a routine inspection, until the Australian Navy began to search his ship.

Secret papers issued by the *Admiralstab* (the German equivalent of the British Admiralty) were found, among which was the *Handelsverkehrsbuch* (HVB) code book used to communicate with German merchant ships. A copy was immediately dispatched to Room 40 and enabled staff to read the coded German transmissions sent to the ships of her merchant fleet. Why was a ship with no wireless set carrying books to encode signals?

At about the same time a small force of German cruisers were patrolling in the cold misty eastern Baltic Sea, in the waters of the Gulf of Finland close to the Russian coast. A dense fog separated the ships of the flotilla and the German cruiser *Magdeburg* alone was sighted by a Russian cruiser squadron patrolling the seas around their base in Konigsberg. They engaged and sank her, after which the Imperial Russian Navy sent down divers into the ship's signals cabin to recover the *Admiralstab*'s most secret *Signalbuch der Kaiserlichen Marine* (SKM) code book.

The Russian Navy listened to German coded transmissions just to make sure that the German Navy was still using the code book in signals sent to its own ships. Having confirmed the value of the code book by making sure that it was still in use, it generously sent a copy to the British Admiralty. The original copy of the SKM code book resides in the British Public Records Office in Kew, while the HVB copy is on show in the National Archives and Records Office in Victoria, Australia.

The third incredible stroke of luck occurred in the North Sea. A strong force of British warships was shelling German troops advancing along the Belgian coast when a flotilla of German destroyers appeared. They were all immediately engaged and sunk, and as the ships went down their secret papers were put into a lead-lined chest and thrown overboard, as was normal in such a disastrous situation. Some weeks later a British trawler netted a mysterious lead-lined box with a German inscription on it so the crew promptly sent it to the Admiralty for the staff of Room 40 to open. Among the contents was the *Verkehrsbuch* (VB) code book.

So, the complete trilogy of code books of the Imperial German Navy was now in the possession of Room 40. Finding the complete set of German Navy code books was roughly the First World War equivalent of Bletchley Park being handed the Enigma machine in 1939 by the Polish cryptanalysts of the Second World War.

Naval coded messages were not the only ones of interest to Room 40. Diplomatic messages carried a different level of intelligence to that of the military and naval material and contained mainly political information. It was a diplomatic message that, to all intents and purposes, ended the war, but more of that later. Diplomatic codes were generally more complex and difficult to crack than *Admiralstab* ones, so a section was formed in Room 40 specifically to decrypt diplomatic messages. However, the new team was having trouble decoding messages.

The solution to breaking the German diplomatic codes came, at least in part, in Persia in the spring of 1915 as Herr Wassmuss, a German diplomat, was sent out there to try and blow up the Anglo-Persian oil pipeline. The oil fuelled the British Navy's ships in the Mediterranean and was a highly strategic target. Wassmuss was given away by fellow diplomats and was about to be arrested by the British military police, but managed to escape with so little time to spare that he left his luggage piled up outside his hotel. The disappointed British soldiers gathered up his suitcases and sent them to London, where they were searched by Room 40 staff. They found the keys to the German diplomatic ciphers wrapped in the long johns of Herr Wassmuss. This extraordinary series of strokes of good fortune gave the bureau a solid foundation on which to build an incredibly successful intelligence organisation.

These intelligence coups allied to Room 40's technical proficiency enabled it to read almost 20,000 encoded wireless signals and capture or intercept written material (a great deal of German mail was read) from 1915 right up to the end of the war. The majority of the decrypted material was fed into a huge bank of information maintained in a massive card index in the Admiralty War Room by a large staff of men (and just a few women) who stored the huge intelligence database in handwritten form. They were backed up by a small army of telegraphists on a 24/7 watch, manning the wireless sets at the listening stations on the coast and alert for signals crossing the airways of Europe. Intercept service personnel needed a special kind of dedication to do the close and demanding work required of them in their long days of vigilance.

The war at sea was the one battle that Britain could not afford to lose in either the First World War or the Second and one that the British Navy came close to losing on both occasions. At one time in the First World War one in four of all British ships leaving port were sunk and the sinkings were almost as severe in the Second. The drain on maritime resources was enormous, so the Admiralty had the idea of using 'Q' ships that were reconditioned old merchant ships with powerful guns hidden under deck structures and manned by Royal Navy crews. Up to this time single vessels not sailing in convoy were intercepted by U-boats, which surfaced and gave the crew time to take to the boats before sinking the ship with gunfire or boarding her to lay explosive charges. A Q ship that was intercepted in this way would let half her crew take to the boats and appear to abandon her, simulating panic, and when the boats were clear the submarine would close to point-blank range to sink her by gunfire or explosives. As the U-boat closed on the Q ship, mock deck cabins or tarpaulins disguising the guns would be whipped away and before the U-boat could escape it would be sunk. U-boat captains liked to surface and sink unarmed merchantmen in this manner as it saved their torpedoes for richer targets in escorted convoys or even warships. The scheme was working well for the British and every U-boat that had intercepted a Q ship had been sunk, so the German Navy was sorely puzzled at the increasing losses in her submarine fleet.

The ruse was working until a German spy gave the game away. A German national named Jules Silber, who worked as a double agent in a branch of the British intelligence system when he really still owed his allegiance to his German homeland, revealed the secret. He was in America when war broke out but had worked in South Africa for the British and had a certificate to prove it. He arrived in Britain after travelling through Canada to get his papers registered as a Commonwealth citizen.

With no evidence of contact with German intelligence or any training in the espionage scene it appears he had no training as an agent. He came to Liverpool and applied for a job in the Postal Censorship Department on the strength of his speaking several languages and was put into a group that censored the mail to and from Holland. The Netherlands was neutral but had the reputation for being a hotbed of spies. Silber was allocated the southern region of Holland and was responsible for censoring letters addressed to that region. He soon found himself able to read information in the letters that would be valuable to his mother country, Germany.

He could not communicate the intelligence to the German government directly so he selected an address from the 'suspect list' of people in Holland who were thought by British security to be active in espionage. Silber wrote to one of these Dutch addresses offering his services to the German authorities and letting them know the kind of information to which he had access. The Germans agreed to co-operate, as they had nothing to lose, and so a flow of very valuable intelligence began that was sent by a simple but clever method. Silber would write a quite innocent letter to an address that he covered in Holland and posted it in London knowing that it would arrive on his desk to be censored. He would open it and place his intelligence report in the envelope and stamp it 'Passed by Censor' for posting on to his German masters in Holland.

Silber passed much valuable information to his contacts in Holland but undoubtedly the most important of his coups was his discovery of the navy's use of Q ships. A young woman living in the naval base of Devonport sent a 'chatty' to her friend in Holland in which she wrote:

We are happy to have my brother Phillip at home. We were always worried for his safety while he was at sea but he now he has a shore job in Devonport and is likely to remain here for some months. It is something to do with refitting old ships but he does not tell us much, but as you know he is a gunnery officer.

This snippet of gossip was just the kind of lead to secret information that Silber was seeking, so he took a day off to visit the young woman with the credentials of a senior official in the British Censorship Department. He produced the letter she had written and spoke sternly to her about her careless talk, so that she became apprehensive about herself and the effect it might have on her brother, who had told her about it. She described all she knew as Silber softened and coaxed her into giving as much detail as she could, and this clarified the roll of Q ships in the war against U-boats. He left, saying that he really should report her for her lapse of security to a foreign national but he would overlook it this time and telling her not to disclose their talk to anyone, including her brother.

The German security services received Silber's report and from then on U-boats were ordered not to surface and give the Q ship a chance to uncover her guns. In future independent merchantmen were to be sunk on sight in unrestricted U-boat warfare. Silber was cautious in his activities and able to obtain much useful intelligence to send to Holland, so his activities were never detected. He returned to Germany after the war when the British Censorship Department was closed down and in 1932 wrote a book about his experiences, entitled *Invisible Weapons*.

The episode was an embarrassment for the British government, but it had its successes as well, and one of those emanated from the vigilance of another British postal censor who found a newspaper going through the mail to a suspect address in Holland. The paper was sent on to the counter-espionage department of MI5 to be tested and it was found to have a note in chemical ink. The writing would have been invisible without the test and simply read, 'C has gone north. Am sending from 201.'

The message was urgently investigated by the inspector in charge, who had only had one clue, the postmark on the paper was 'Deptford'. Further enquiries found that there was only one house in the town numbered 201 and that was a baker and confectioner in the High Street. The proprietor was found to be a Peter Hahn, of German birth but nationalised as a British subject, who denied any connection to the message even though a bottle of chemical ink and a special pen were found in a search of his shop. Hahn still denied everything but the neighbours gave Special Branch detectives a description of a man of distinguished bearing named Muller, who they thought was Russian. A search traced him to a boarding house in London, but he had recently left to go north to Newcastle where he was arrested and found to be a German agent of considerable experience.

Muller had been briefed by German intelligence to obtain naval design secrets and had produced some high-grade intelligence that he had sent to his German masters by an ingenious method. The information was placed in advertisements in English provincial newspapers for articles for sale, rooms to let and articles wanted, according to a prearranged code. He then mailed the newspapers to a 'letterbox' in Holland. MI5 continued to send papers containing valueless information after Muller's arrest and was paid several hundred pounds by the Germans for its troubles, but the information was soon found to be of little use to them. Hahn was sent to prison for seven years and Muller (if that was his name) was sent to the Tower of London and shot by firing squad in the moat, where many other German spies who were active in Britain would meet their end.

The Admiralty code breakers still had a substantial advantage over their German intelligence opponents as the German High Command did not question the security of its codes and the cipher books containing secret coding keys. The conviction that its codes were unbreakable and still unbroken was due to the unquestioning confidence in the codes' own security, and that was the cardinal sin of the German intelligence in both of the wars. Typically, the officer commanding the German cruiser squadron of which the *Magdeburg* was a part is known to have voiced fears about the safety of the SKM code book to the *Admiralstab* but he was ignored.

No substantial change in German code and cipher systems occurred until late in 1917, and even then the way that the codes and code books were changed was so casual that the new codes were easily penetrated by Room 40. German intelligence procedures in both wars exhibited a trust in their coding systems that proved far from justified. The dependence on the security of the Enigma and other coding machines in the Second World War was as fatal to signals confidentiality as losing the three *Admiralstab* code books was in the First World War.

These were not the only gaps in the German security shield, however, the directional service was able to locate the source of many transmissions mainly because the captains of both German U-boats and Zeppelins 'talked' too much on air. That enabled the British 'Y' service to gather much useful intelligence on their procedures and the locations of their vessels and bases but they were also able to get a 'fix' on the conversations between the German aircraft base controllers.

German wireless transmissions from Nauen were easy to pick up as the signal was so powerful, they could easily reach the Mediterranean, their colonies in Africa and even America. Signal strengths could be picked up quite easily across the North Sea on England's east coast, but the U-boats' responses as they began to voyage further into the Atlantic were growing fainter. To cope with the increasing number of fainter interceptions coming from the far Atlantic more listening stations were built on the west coast of Ireland, which was at that time still part of the British Empire.

The signals intelligence achievements of the Admiralty's Room 40 had lessons for Britain's intelligence community in both wars, the main one being the way intelligence evaluations were managed. The way that the convoy system was managed, or rather mismanaged, by the hidebound senior officers of the British Admiralty was an important case in point. Merchant shipping losses were at crisis levels in 1915 with the loss of forty-nine ships in the month of August, but senior officers at the Admiralty refused to accept the obvious solution of gathering the vessels into convoys under naval protection. British shipping was still operating on a peacetime basis – unarmed, uncontrolled and unescorted – while the Royal Navy was engaged in aggressive but unrewarding patrols along the German and Belgian seaboards.

Finally, Prime Minister Lloyd George lost patience and ordered the admirals to assemble the merchant ships into convoys as sinkings reached unsupportable proportions. As soon as the convoy system was instituted the number of ships lost dropped dramatically, but still many in the Admiralty refused to accept the intelligence figures that proved its effectiveness.

Karl Doenitz was a young U-boat captain in 1918 and was taken prisoner when his boat *U68* was sunk in the Mediterranean. When he was interrogated by the British he was recorded as saying:

> The introduction of the convoy system in 1917 robbed the U-boat of its opportunity to become a decisive factor in the war. The oceans at once became bare and empty; for long periods of time the U-boats, operating individually, would see nothing at all; then suddenly up would loom a huge concourse of ships ... surrounded by a strong escort of warships of all types ... the lone U-boat might well sink one or two of the ships, or even several; but it was a poor percentage of the whole. The convoy would steam on. In most cases no other German U-boat would catch sight of it and it would reach Britain bringing a rich cargo of food stuffs and raw materials safely to port.

Doenitz, who became grand admiral of the Nazi U-boat fleet, came to the conclusion that U-boats had to concentrate in sufficient numbers to be able to overwhelm the convoy escorts. The 'wolf pack' strategy that his U-boats subsequently used to such good effect in the Atlantic in the Second World War evolved from the experiences he had had in the First World War, until stronger escorts, more efficient radar and information from Bletchley Park finally defeated the U-boat.

Ships using information transmitted to them from Room 40 in the Admiralty were routed away from the area in which a U-boat was operating and this proved increasingly effective. By 1916 the Admiralty knew the position of nearly every U-boat at sea, as well as the position and course of every British convoy, and this data was plotted in the Admiralty War Room. But there was an incredible omission. They did not plot these two invaluable pieces of intelligence together for almost a year. Arranging the routes of the convoys to evade the U-boats was not introduced until late in 1917, and when they finally did the countermeasure saved many ships from destruction. Before the convoy system was arranged, warning many of the smaller merchant ships in the proximity of U-boats or mines would have been impossible as many of them had no wireless transceivers on board.

Such a warning would have fallen on literally deaf ears, but the convoy system arrangement appointed a convoy commodore with his own special transceiver installed in his ship. He would act on information from Admiralty transmissions and maintain order among the ships under his command, and warnings or advice would be given about the route they intended to take and the dangers that lurked there. Advice or orders would be passed on to his 'flock' by signalling lamp. Getting a message to the commodore of any of the many convoys at sea to skirt a minefield or avoid a marauding U-boat was the ultimate reason for Room 40's efforts.

Unfortunately, some reactionary senior naval officers in Whitehall never accepted the concept of the convoy, or just stuck to the idea that the convoy was a protective measure. It proved not to be so, as the bait of a fleet of merchantmen all clustered together drew U-boats to try and attack the assembly of rich targets, only to be attacked in turn by the convoy's escorts. The number of enemy submarines sunk increased sharply as the convoy system came into being in 1917 and the losses of merchant ships decreased.

Ships continued to be attacked and sunk, but they were mainly lone vessels that were not escorted for some reason, so the convoy system and Room 40's intelligence had saved the day in the first Battle of the Atlantic. Losses that had become critical dropped dramatically and the system became accepted by almost everyone by the end of the First World War. So much so that the convoy system was immediately instituted as war began in 1939 and became a major part of British naval strategy in the Second Battle of the Atlantic.

My father served on an escort vessel on the first convoy leaving Nova Scotia, within days of war being declared in 1939, and spent more than a year shepherding convoys through the U-boat-infested Western Approaches. He never saw a gun fired in action as the convoys his ship was escorting were directed away from waiting U-boats by Ultra intelligence reports of mines and torpedoes from Bletchley Park.

Room 40's intelligence war involved recording even the smallest detail into a huge database of facts about enemy practices that enabled the listeners and code breakers to extract useful nuances of information for its intelligence evaluations. The database even contained such details as the Christian names of many of the U-boat captains. The huge mass of details was often recorded in order to be cross-related with other data in complex ways. All records had to be handwritten with pens with a steel nib that were dipped into an inkwell; computers or even biros had not been invented at that time and would not be available for more than half a century.

Keepers of the vast information registry recorded every detail of the slightest interest; the massive task produced a sea of index cards tended by more than 100 dedicated men and women. Intercept service personnel had to be dedicated, with a range of skills that enabled them to send or receive Morse characters at a rate of 120 a minute as well as being familiar with enemy wireless style and procedures. They had to send or record transmissions, sometimes only faintly heard, without strain, as well as watching for any quirks or errors in their opponent's transmission. It was most often the mistakes made by the enemy operator that proved to be the key to breaking a code, but they could only be identified by listening closely for long hours to coded enemy transmissions.

The work made demands on the patience and sometimes health of the operators as they sent or received long and meaningless coded strings of letters and numbers that meant nothing to them. It needed intense concentration over long periods, as any wrongly read letter might render the whole coded message unbreakable. Accuracy in taking down the sometimes almost illegible signals at the rate of one letter or figure a second was essential. Operators often became so skilled in their task that they were sometimes able to tell the identity of the individual German signaller sending the message. The subtle differences in speed and technique could be heard in the 'fist' of the enemy signaller as he transmitted a message on the Morse key and could only be detected by the trained ear.

Reading the signals was one thing, but locating where they came from was another and this was done by the directional service mentioned earlier. Direction finding (DF) experiments were first instituted by the British Army in trying to identify the location of transmitters behind the German lines in France. In this, the army showed a rare 'first' over the navy in intelligence matters – but it was an important one.

Admiral Hall, of Room 40, first heard about the technology by a roundabout route as relations between the Admiralty and the War Office, just across the road in Whitehall, were strained. They had agreed to co-operate in the early days of the war but that soon deteriorated as the two intelligence bureaus began to compete. The navy showed itself to be the better of the two – and flaunted it – so relations were at breaking point. The admiral had heard about the army's efforts through the Marconi Company, which was helping both of the services in their scientific efforts to fight an increasingly technological war.

The navy quickly adopted the innovation to set up DF stations in Aberdeen, Birchington, Flamborough Head, Lowestoft, Lerwick and York to monitor the transmissions from enemy shipping and submarines. As operators gradually mastered the effects of magnetic deviations and other variables their service became remarkably accurate and effective. At the end of 1914 Admiral Oliver was able to report to the First Lord of the Admiralty that they had managed to track the course of a specific U-boat as it had left port and sailed across the North Sea and into the Atlantic. That was the first step in Room 40 being able to plot and track the positions and movements of nearly all the U-boat fleet at sea as the aerials strung out across the coasts of Britain picked up the conversations of U-boat captains.

Interception and tracking was only possible when enemy vessels began to transmit – unlike in the Second World War when short-wave radar was able to identify the low profiles of a submarine far out in the Atlantic. The real difficulty of U-boat hunters in the First World War was that once the U-boat submerged there was little they could do to track it as listening and underwater detection devices did not yet exist. Nor was there much in the form of anti-submarine weapons such as depth charges – they did not come into use until 1916 and were so primitive that they only sank two U-boats in that year.

Before the war the Admiralty had thought of the submarine only as a defensive weapon to protect its bases, but the thinking changed one calm

September morning, eight weeks after the war had begun. Three British battle cruisers, the *Aboukir*, the *Cressy* and the *Hogue*, were patrolling in line off the Belgian coast when the *Aboukir* was suddenly torpedoed and began to sink. The *Cressy* came to her aid and began to pick up survivors when she too was torpedoed. Then the *Hogue* closed with the two sinking ships to rescue survivors and was torpedoed in her turn. The author's great uncle was fond of relating how he survived the sinking of the *Aboukir* to be picked up by the *Hogue* only to be sunk again and finally rescued by a Dutch fishing boat as they watched the *Cressy* sink.

Capitan Weddigen of *U29* sank all three ships with only three torpedoes, causing the loss of more than 1,500 men, more than all those who died at Trafalgar. Weddigen went on to be a U-boat ace in the war, helping to slaughter much of the British maritime fleet.

Room 40's monumental task of tracking the plague of U-boats was difficult, but occasionally Admiral Hall used a trick of his own, as happened in Irish waters at the mouth of Waterford Harbour. It was a busy port, so specially designed minelaying U-boats regularly laid mines in the approaches to the harbour and, just as regularly, British minesweepers swept the channel clear of them. Room 40's interception team was able to establish that the German listening service was intercepting and decoding the British wireless signal that reported when the channel to the port had been swept clear of mines and was safe to use again.

Hall arranged that the harbour be closed for a week and the port's minesweepers should not to attempt to sweep the mines that the U-boat had laid. He then sent a wireless signal in the code that the Germans had been using, reporting that the harbour channel had been swept. The message was intercepted by the Imperial German Navy. It immediately dispatched minelaying *U44* to lay more mines in the channel entrance. It struck one of its own unswept mines and sank; the U-boat commander was rescued, but he was outraged and complained bitterly about the inefficiency of British minesweepers.

The U-boat was not the only threat to Britain, however. The German battle fleet was awaiting its chance in the base at Kiel although it knew it was no match for the British Grand Fleet that was waiting in Scapa Flow to pounce. The Royal Navy had a powerful fleet and if it came to a confrontation the German Admiral Friedrich von Ingenohl knew that he would face a formidable enemy, so he opted for a hit-and-run tactic. He would try to lure a single squadron of the British fleet into battle. He left port to shell the English seaside town of Yarmouth as bait. Room 40 had decoded the order for the German fleet to leave harbour, although its intentions and destination were unclear.

The German squadron shelled the town heavily and then got away without loss, so its admiral was much encouraged and he decided to have a repeat performance. The German fleet bombarded the Yorkshire towns of Scarborough and Hartlepool and got away with it for the second time. Churchill's account of the event explains why:

On the morning of 16 December at the Admiralty at about half past eight I was in my bath, when the door opened and an officer came hurrying in from the War Room with a naval signal that I grasped with dripping hand 'German battle cruisers bombarding Hartlepool'. I jumped out of the bath with exclamations. Sympathy for Hartlepool mingled with what Mr. George Windham once called 'the anodyne of retaliation'. Pulling on my clothes over a damp body I ran downstairs to the War Room. The First Lord had just arrived from his house next door. Oliver [the admiral] who invariably slept in the War Room and hardly ever left it by day was marking the position on the map. Telegrams from all the stations along the coast affected by the attack and intercepts from ships in the vicinity speaking to each other, came pouring in two or three a minute. The Admiralty also spread the tidings and kept the fleets and the flotillas continuously informed of all we knew.

The bombardment of open towns was new to us at the time. But after all what did that matter now? The war map showed the German battle cruisers identified one by one within gunshot off the Yorkshire coast. While 150 miles to the Eastward between them and Germany cutting mathematically their line of retreat, steamed in the exact position intended, four battle cruisers and six of the most powerful battleships in the world … only one thing could enable the Germans to escape annulation at the hands of a superior force … while the great shells crashed into the little houses of Hartlepool and Scarborough, carrying their cruel message of pain and destruction to unsuspecting English homes, only one anxiety dominated the thoughts of the Admiralty War Room. The word 'visibility' assumed a sinister significance …

The German battle cruisers had disappeared into the fog.

The next battlefield was in the centre of the North Sea when Ingenohl ordered his subordinate, Admiral Franz von Hipper, to take his squadron of battle cruisers to carry out a reconnaissance of the Dogger Bank for stray British vessels. The transmission was again intercepted by Room 40 and decoded for Admiral Oliver, who immediately took the transcription to Churchill. He ordered Admiral John Jellicoe, with the British fleet, to rendezvous at position 55 13N 3 12E at seven o'clock the next morning near the Dogger Bank. The trap had been laid and the British naval forces were mobilised to catch von Hipper's force at first light.

When the first sightings were reported, an account of the scene at the Admiralty is recounted in Churchill's vivid prose:

> There can be few purely mental experiences more charged with cold excitement than to follow, almost minute by minute the phases of a great naval action from the silent rooms of the Admiralty. Out on the blue water in the fighting ships amid the stunning detonations of the cannonade, fractions of the event unfold themselves to the corporeal eye. There is the sense of action at its highest; there is the wrath of battle: there is the intense, self-effacing physical or mental toil. But in Whitehall only the clock ticks and quiet men enter with quick steps laying slips of pencilled paper before other men equally silent who draw lines and scribble calculations and point with the finger or make subdued comments. Telegram succeeds telegram at a few minutes interval as they are picked up and decoded often in the wrong sequence, frequently of dubious import and out of these a picture always flickering and changing arises in the mind, and imagination strikes out around at every stage flashes of hope or fear.

The trap on von Hipper's battle cruisers was closing, but not fast enough as the German warships ran from the British Admiral Beatty's battleships that pursued them at the best speed they could with guns blazing. But once again the fog of war intervened. U-boats were said to be sighted by Beatty, although Room 40 had plotted the nearest one as being many miles away. This caused the British ships to hesitate and finally a flag signal was misread, allowing von Hipper's squadron to slip away into the mist – all except one.

The heavy cruiser *Blücher* was the last and slowest in the line of German warships and Beatty's lumbering heavies caught up with the laggard to reduce her to a blazing wreck. The victory was only partial and not what the British public expected of its navy with the tradition of Nelson to live up to, but

Room 40 had done its duty. Not that the navy could tell the world what Hall and his code breakers had done in intercepting the critical messages, even though they had been misread in the heat of battle by the fleet commanders.

The result of this near victory for the Royal Navy was that the German fleet found bombarding British seaside towns a very unrewarding operation. Churchill's description above of the scene in the Admiralty's War Room would have been re-enacted several times in his life, first as First Lord of the Admiralty and then three decades later as prime minister. The tension, so vividly described, must also have been present as he waited for initial reports of the pursuit of the *Bismarck*, D-Day and many other high dramas in both wars. One of the most dramatic of these would have been the battle that the Imperial German Navy named the Battle of the Skagerrak but is better known to the British public as Jutland.

THE *LUSITANIA*

But first, an account of the torpedoing of a single ship that had a serious political effect on the war that the destruction of so many other vessels in the Atlantic had failed to achieve. Germany's most critical theatre of war was not the constant battle in the trenches in northern France, still less the badly managed diversion of Gallipoli. It was the strangling of Britain's supply routes, as well as that of her army in northern France, by decimating her fleet of merchantmen bringing food and the provisions of war across the Atlantic.

British ships had always been a legitimate target for the U-boats but the neutral status of ships that were also carriers of food and supplies to sustain Britain's war effort were more debatable targets. It was a dilemma for the Germans, whose policy swung between unrestricted U-boat warfare and that of leaving American and other neutral ships to sail unmolested, and back again to sinking any ship the periscopes could see. American objections, in particular, were that their nationals were in danger while travelling on British ships. So it was with the *Lusitania*.

The great vessel was carrying many American passengers in spite of the German embassy in America warning them that they were going into danger by sailing in a British vessel. On 5 May 1915 the great liner crossed the Atlantic and made landfall off the southern coast of Ireland after an uneventful voyage, only to be informed by the Admiralty that a U-boat was operating in her area. To prove it, there were reports of *U20* having already sunk four other ships off the coast of Ireland by torpedo or gunfire – the *Earl of Lathom*, the *Cayo Romano*, the *Centurion* and the *Candidate*.

Captain Turner, commanding the *Lusitania*, was therefore aware that a U-boat was operating in the area so he plotted his ship's course to minimise the risk of an attack – or so he thought. Kapitänleutnant Walther Schwieger of the *U20* had recently received orders to sink all ships sighted, and he made a record of the three and a half hours during the attack and sinking of the *Lusitania* in his ship's log:

1.45 p.m.   Excellent visibility, very fine weather. Therefore surface and continue passage; waiting off the Queenstown Banks seemed unrewarding.

2.20 p.m.   Sight dead ahead four funnels and two masts of a steamer steering straight for us (coming from the SSW towards Galley Head). Ship identified as a large passenger steamer.

2.25 p.m.   Dive to periscope depth and proceed at high speed on an intercepting course in the hope that the steamer would alter to starboard along the Irish coast. Steamer alters to starboard and sets course for Queenstown so permitting an approach for a shot. Proceed at high speed until 3 p.m. in order to gain bearing.

3.10 p.m.   Clear bow shot from 700 metres (G. Torpedo set for 3m depth, inclination 90 degrees, estimated speed 22 knots). Torpedo hits starboard side close abaft the bridge, followed by a very unusually large explosion with a violent emission of smoke (far above the foremost funnel). In addition to the explosion of the torpedo there must have been a second one (boiler of coal or powder). The superstructure above the point of impact and the bridge are torn apart, fire breaks out, a thick cloud of smoke envelopes the upper bridge. The ship stops at once and very quickly takes on a heavy list to starboard, at the same time starting to sink by the bow. She looks as if she will quickly capsize. Much confusion on board; boats are cleared away and some of them lowered into the water. Apparently considerable panic; several boats fully laden, are hurriedly lowered, bow or stern first and at once filled with water. Owing to the list fewer boats can be cleared away on the portside than the starboard side. The ship blows off steam; forward the name Lusitania in gold letter is visible. Funnels painted black, no flag on the poop. Her speed was 20 knots.

3.25 p.m.   As it appears the steamer can only remain afloat for a short time longer, dive to 24 metres and proceed out to sea. Also, I could not fire a second torpedo into the mass of people saving themselves.

4.15 p.m.   Come up to periscope depth and take a look around. In the distance a number of lifeboats; of the Lusitania nothing more can be seen. From the wreck the Old Head of Kinsale bears 358 degrees 14 miles. Wreck lies in 90 metres of water (distance from Queenstown 27 miles.) Position 51 degrees 22' 6N 8 degrees 31'W. The land and lighthouse very clearly visible.

The liner sank in about twenty minutes, taking 1,195 passengers – men, women and ninety-four children – down with her, of which 140 were American nationals.

There was outrage as the implication of total war on civilians, and particularly children, in an unrestricted U-boat campaign began to be realised. The people of America were incandescently angry about their countrymen's deaths, and this took them another step towards joining the Allies in the war.

Churchill was accused of deliberately orchestrating the sinking of the liner to bring the United States into the war, but it is difficult to see how he could have influenced steering the ship into danger without actually being on the liner's bridge. Room 40 had given the warning of the presence of *U20*, but U-boats were not their only concern. The German *Hochseeflotte* was getting restive, and the listening stations could tell this from the increasing radio traffic activity being intercepted from Kiel. Admiral Scheer, who had been promoted to command the German fleet, ordered its readiness and on the following day a secret communication was intercepted at the Admiralty indicating that the fleet was leaving harbour. Admiral Jellicoe was putting to sea with the Grand Fleet even before the ships of the German fleet had left harbour, and expectancy rose to fever pitch in the Admiralty War Room.

The two great fleets began to close for battle; the British had the advantage in numbers although their ships were generally older than their German counterparts, which became evident as they closed for battle. Von Scheer's fleet was outnumbered by twenty-eight Dreadnought battleships in the British fleet to sixteen in the German fleet, as well as nine British battlecruisers to five German. The Germans were outgunned by 270 heavy guns to 200, and in spite of the age of the British fleet it had the edge on the Germans in the speed of its ships.

The Grand Fleet was crossing the North Sea to give the enemy a surprise, but an error in the intelligence system between Room 40 and the Admiralty War Room made the fleet think that it had more time than it really had. It caused it to steam slowly to its rendezvous in order to save fuel and so the two fleets made first contact at 2.20 in the afternoon and not the early morning as Admiral Jellicoe had hoped. The heavy guns began to thunder as the daylight hours shortened and the German fleet ran for home in a fierce running battle. The British fleet engaged the rear of the retreating German one, helped by intercepted wireless transmissions from the German admiral who was directing his fleet on which course to steer to return home. Admiral Scheer's messages were decoded by Room 40 and their content relayed to Jellicoe, who chose to disregard them.

Earlier errors made by the Admiralty, including one that placed the German cruiser *Regensburg* close to Jellicoe's own ship, shook the admiral's faith in the accuracy of the intelligence reports. Jellicoe placed no reliance in further decrypts and summaries of the German fleet's movements. He so distrusted the reports he was getting that he took no further notice of Room 40's signals, which clearly indicated the course the German fleet was taking. Jellicoe chose to disengage from the *Hochseeflotte* as darkness drew in because he knew that the Germen seamen had the advantage in a night action in both training and equipment. The German ships finally passed through their own channel of protective minefields into harbour to lick their wounds and repair the damage they had sustained.

Jellicoe's contact late in the day with his German opponents and the consequent lack of daylight had robbed him of the crushing victory that was expected of him and the failure to use Room 40's intelligence robbed the British people of their expected maritime triumph. The Kaiser claimed a victory and not without reason – he had fewer losses than Jellicoe's fleet, which had lost fourteen ships to Germany's eleven and the British had lost twice as many men as the Germans.

It was a tactical victory for the Germans, but they had not broken the economic blockade imposed by the British Navy on Germany's increasingly hungry populace. As an American journalist in London put it, 'The German fleet has assaulted its jailor and is now back in jail.'

The blockade of Germany's ports, which was a major part of the British strategy in both wars, had begun to bite into the German economy. At the end of the First World War, when the German people were virtually starving, the cordon around her seaboard by the British Navy was made all the more effective by Room 40 operators. They located blockade runners trying to sail for a home port with Y listening stations and the related DF service that was pinpointing U-boats out in the Atlantic. The British Navy managed its blockade with the minimum number of warships by focusing the British Naval Unit's effectiveness in the war at sea by listening for the enemy.

This also made a difference in the air war. Zeppelins that bombed London were mainly based in Belgium within range of the Y stations, who were able to locate them as they took off because of the constant requests by their commanders for location checks using the HVB code book. The Zeppelins made many raids, scattering bombs over London and the south-east of England, but as bombers they had their shortcomings. They were able to cruise at 10,000ft and were difficult to catch, but the British Y stations tracked them as they passed over the North Sea. They would cruise at a very high altitude for aircraft of that time and the B.E.2 biplane fighters that defended London were not able to climb to that height easily.

It took almost an hour for a pilot to reach the Zeppelins cruising at that altitude, but Room 40 was able to give fighter planes the time to scramble and take off in good time to intercept the enemy bombers. Ordinary ammunition was found to be of little use on the huge airships but a newly developed incendiary bullet was designed, not only to puncture the gas bags of the dirigible but set them alight as well. Shooting down a Zeppelin provided a spectacular display for Londoners as they lit up the night sky crashing down in flames.

The *Luftstreitkräfte* (Imperial German Air Service) soon decided against using airships. It began using the Gotha heavy bomber instead, so that bombing raids became more effective. More than 200,000lb of bombs were dropped on southern England during the war. The scars of some of those bombs are still to be seen today in Lincoln's Inn Fields and Farringdon Street in London, but the Gotha air raids over south-east England proved more costly to the Germans than the Zeppelin ones as they lost more than sixty aircraft. Finally it was decided to no longer attack England but concentrate air power over the battlefields of northern France, where it mattered.

In northern France military intelligence was mainly focused on the less wide ranging and more static war of the trenches directed by the War Office in Whitehall, just across the road from the Admiralty. Co-operation with Britain's allies was better than that practised between the British Army and Navy. Inter-service squabbles were frequent between the various intelligence services, as already described.

The French Army and Navy spoke and co-operated with each other very little, as did the Italians; indeed they both seemed to speak to Room 40 more than they did to each other. There was a continuous and friendly flow of information between London and Moscow, probably based on the Russian generosity in sending the SKM code book rescued from the German cruiser, *Magdeburg* to Room 40. Staff were exchanged as well; at least one of the Russian cryptographic staff, Ernst Fetterlein, joined Room 40 and stayed until he found a place among the staff at Bletchley Park in 1939. Co-operation with Moscow ceased dramatically with the Communist Revolution in 1917 although Admiral Hall was relieved to discover that there was no leak of British intelligence secrets when Lenin made peace with Germany.

The most flagrant lack of communication between intelligence services was to be found between American army intelligence and the navy's intelligence in the Second World War, which was all a part of the conflict between the two American services as a whole. The pointless squabbles would have reached high levels of comedy if the cost had not been so high and the results not so important.

Britain's prime example of inter-departmental squabbling at that time was the spat between MI6 and SOE, although MI6 still managed to generate enough opportunities to row with MI5, as I can attest – but more of that later.

As the war progressed, Room 40 began to evolve from the decoding of enemy wireless signals to a more broad-based intelligence bureau that produced a number of clandestine operations. Several espionage activities were revealed by Hall's code-breaking team, particularly through the newly set up diplomatic department's code-breaking that reaped rich rewards in frustrating German espionage endeavours.

One was an early germ warfare operation by a German spy ring in Spain, among whom was Wilhelm Canaris, who was destined to become the head of Hitler's *Abwehr* intelligence agency in the next war. The plan was to infect Spanish cattle and mules earmarked to be exported to Britain and to carry ampoules of anthrax hidden in sugar beet, as well as cholera bacilli to contaminate rivers, but the plot was disclosed to the Spanish authorities. An operation to smuggle the steel-hardening additive Wolfram, which German industry needed badly, was also narrowly frustrated by a team of British agents. An Irish insurrection, with Sir Roger Casement at its head, was also being hatched with arms being brought by U-boat into Ireland. It was discovered by a Room 40 radio interception, leading to a police tip-off. These were just a few of the many German-directed espionage actions that Room 40 frustrated during the war, mainly based in Spain or Portugal.

The main focus of British strategy during both wars was to bring America into the fray as her ally and in this the Germans seemed to work against their own interest in many ways, including that of the sinking of the *Lusitania*. The most disastrous mistake that Germany made was about to be revealed by the diplomatic section of Room 40 and would finally give America little option but to declare war on Germany ...

THE ZIMMERMANN TELEGRAM

The story began in Brussels at the start of the war in August 1914, when the Germans entered Brussels and took over a powerful signals station for their own use. The station was regularly used by the German Diplomatic Service, who used the *Schlüsselbuch* code book of the German Foreign Office, whose code keys were extremely complex. It needed exceptional cryptographic skills to decrypt messages and the signals intelligence station was under pressure with an increasing flow of military and diplomatic traffic.

The German staff at the station lacked skilled men and Alexander Czek, who was a gifted radio engineer, came to their notice by offering a German signals officer an innovatively designed radio set. He later repaired the station's heavy duty transmitter at a critical moment and the bureau's staff found him to be not only technically competent but also a good linguist. Gradually he became trusted in the signals office and sometimes filled in when German staff cryptographers were off sick, and his skills in all aspects of signals intelligence turned out to be widespread.

He gradually became a trusted member of the German signals bureau, so much so that he came to the notice of British intelligence. They reminded him that the Germans had attacked Belgium and of all the atrocities that they had committed there, but it took the British agents a little time to convince Czek to co-operate. Finally he was persuaded to provide the British with the German codes, although he told them it would not be easy. He did not have custody of the code book, but he finally devised a way of providing a 'crib' for them as he took down the coded message in rough, then copied the encoded message afresh, pocketing the rough copies, which he passed on to the waiting British spy. The Germans finally became suspicious of him, not because of Czek's work for them but because he was seen in the company of members of the Belgian Resistance Movement. British intelligence could not afford to lose such a valuable contact so he was spirited away across the border into neutral Holland and from there made his way to London and Room 40 at the Admiralty. From the information that he gave to Hall's code breakers they were able to decipher all German Foreign Office transmissions right up to the end of the war.

By 1918 the people of Britain and France were war weary, sick of the slaughter, fearful of the rising U-boat menace and could see no trace of Germany's will and ability to fight beginning to weaken. There was one possible light at the end of the tunnel for the *entente cordiale* and that was for America to join in the fight to lend new vigour to the offensive against the German trenches. The American people were drifting slowly towards the declaration of war with episodes great and small, only one of which was the sinking of the *Lusitania*. Unfortunately for the hopes of the *entente* there was one great obstacle – America's President Woodrow Wilson had just been elected into the White House on a 'no war' ticket, although the American ambassador and his staff in London were fortunately pro-British. They would later help future events along, even though they could not gainsay their president's anti-war position.

Even Germany's declaration that they would shortly inflict unrestricted submarine warfare on neutral ships could not shake Wilson's resolve to stay out of the war. A fleet consisting of more than 100 U-boats threatened to become operational in the Atlantic, rather than just the dozens that had been active up to that time. Their orders would be to sink any ship sailing in British waters and that would inevitably mean the sinking of many American ships, but America's deciding factor for joining the Allies in the war arrived at 9 o'clock in the morning on Wednesday, 17 January 1917 in Room 40.

Admiral Hall's account of the event began with a routine day at the Admiralty as he sorted through his usual batch of dockets, intercepts and accompanying papers that had landed on his desk overnight. The door burst open and one of his senior code breakers handed him a message pad containing probably the most important intercepted message in the history of secret intelligence. It was only partially decoded, but the transmission read:

```
Berlin to Washington W. 158 16 January 1917

Most Secret for your Excellency's personal information
and to be handed on to the Imperial Minister in Mexico
by a safe route.

We propose to begin on 1 February unrestricted
submarine warfare. In doing so, however, we shall
endeavour to keep America neutral. If we should not
succeed in doing so we propose to Mexico an alliance on
the following basis.

(joint) conduct of war
(joint) conclusion of peace

Your Excellency should for the present inform the
President of Mexico secretly that we expect war with
the USA and possibly Japan ... and at the same time
to negotiate between us and Japan ... that ... our
submarines  ... will compel England to peace within a
few months.

Acknowledge receipt
Zimmermann.
```

The message was a clear proposal for Germany to offer co-operation to a neutral neighbour of America to jointly declare war on the United States. This was an undoubted act of war – the question was, how to use the message to Britain's advantage? Hall locked the message and subsequent ones in the drawer of his desk and sat down to work out the best way to use the information. He faced the age-old problem of the intelligencer – how to make use of the information he had got without disclosing the source of the information on which he needed to act. Hall felt the reaction of the American president and his people was unpredictable, particularly those in the mid-west and west coast, many of whom were of German extraction. They would all need to be convinced that a partially decoded telegram really proposed that Germany wanted to enter into an alliance with Mexico to go to war with America and Japan and that it was not somehow a conspiracy.

Hall's problem was twofold: how to disguise the fact that the source was Room 40, and how to present the information to the president and his electorate that would convince them the telegram was not a fiction dreamed up by the devious British. This was particularly so because Hall confidently expected the Germans to deny everything and turn the tables on the British for suggesting that the Imperial German Foreign Office should ever stoop so low.

Hall decided to wait until 1 February when unrestricted U-boat warfare would be declared and wait for the American president's reaction – if it was war then the telegram would not be needed. The German ambassador to the United States of America, Count Johann von Bernstorff, was firmly against the unrestricted use of the U-boat weapon attacking any and all shipping in the Atlantic and told his government so. In spite of this, the German government was convinced that submarine warfare would end the war in its favour so von Bernstorff had to tell the American president of his government's decision. In answer to the threat, President Wilson decided to break off diplomatic relations with Germany but he still fell short of declaring war, although he continued to favour the Allies in all sorts of ways. Hall saw that it was time to use the telegram – but how to do so?

The American ambassador in London was Walter Page, a convinced anglophile who was as disappointed as his friend Hall at his president's decision. He and his staff's collaboration would be essential in the way the telegram would be treated, collaboration that could not be guaranteed from the British Foreign Office. Hall talked to senior Foreign Office officials about the intercept but they put up ludicrous objections of all kinds, from 'use of private telegrams was ungentlemanly' to 'we do not wish to influence a neutral state in Britain's favour'.

American diplomats were more understanding so Hall invited Edward Bell of the embassy to meet him in Room 40 to show him the full text of the now completely decoded Zimmermann Telegram. Bell was astounded and assured Hall that the telegram would take his country to war, but Hall asked that he and the ambassador should keep the matter quiet until a decision was made by Prime Minister Arthur Balfour. Ambassador Page was an old friend of the president and it was suggested by Bell that Hall hand the telegram to Page for onward transmission to Washington. Hall was concerned about his bureau's security and wanted the telegram from the German Foreign Office to appear to be intercepted by the Americans to provide a cover to safeguarde Room 40.

The German Foreign, Minister Arthur Zimmermann, had sent the telegram to Germany's Ambassador Bernstorff in Washington using the new and unbroken code recently delivered by U-boat. Ambassador Heinrich Eckhardt, the German ambassador in Mexico, had not had a visit from a U-boat and so did not have the new code book and he had to use the old one, which Room 40 had broken. German transmissions were sent to Bernstorff in America by high-powered transmitters at Nauen but it had to go through the US government wireless station in Long Island. Bernstorff then arranged for the American wireless station to transmit the message in the old code to Mexico without the Americans asking questions about what was in the coded message.

Room 40 was able to read the Zimmermann Telegram sent to Eckhardt once it had passed through the American wireless station. Hall suggested that the American security agencies should seize copies of the Zimmermann–Bernstorff–Eckhardt transmission, which the Americans did. They decoded the message (with the help of British code breakers) at their embassy in London and were able to send the clear text to Washington. The United States ambassador, Walter Page, was able to assure the American public that the Zimmermann Telegram had been intercepted and decoded on US territory (the embassy *was* American territory). Room 40 was off the hook and the United States had a cable secured from the Western Union office so the Zimmermann Telegram text was released to the press. At that, America's isolationism vanished almost overnight. Any arguments about the voracity of the telegram were quickly silenced as Zimmermann confirmed to an astonished world that he was the author of the document. He had offered Mexico an alliance if she were to attack her neighbour the United States – America had had enough.

On 6 April 1917 Congress in Washington voted unanimously to declare war on Germany; it did not mean the end of the war but it marked the beginning of the end. America was not yet ready to partake in the conflict but her declaration was enough to give a boost to the flagging morale of the British people, who rejoiced at what seemed like a glimmer of light in the darkest days of the war.

The unrestricted U-boat campaign that Bernstorff had informed President Wilson about was unleashed and the effect was felt immediately. Room 40 still maintained clear information on the locations of U-boats and even sometimes the intentions of the enemy vessels. Messages like that received by the Gibraltar wireless station on 1 January 1918 – 'Enemy submarines may be expected to pass through the straits going east during the nights of 1 to 6 January' – were being sent daily and sometimes even hourly to virtually all shore stations and ships. There were often indications of potential attacks by U-boats, but the possibility of a counter-attack by warships was still limited by ineffective weapons.

Hydrophones and depth charges were still in the very early stage of development and the most deadly weapon was still the mine, but when used in conjunction with Room 40's information this could be made very effective. Convoys were slow in getting properly organised even up to the end of the war but that was not surprising as nobody had experienced the working of the convoy system until the Admiralty was forced to accept it. The Russian Revolution in 1917 and the consequent release of German troops from that front to reinforce the last great German offensive needed the American troops to counter it, but they were incredibly slow in coming. Their troopships needed safe passage across the Atlantic but when they did arrive their new fresh soldiers scored a bloody victory at Belleau Wood. Their presence in Europe was America's first step on the path to being a global superpower, but they would not have been there if the Zimmermann Telegram had not been intercepted and decoded.

America's unpreparedness extended not only to its armed forces but also to its intelligence services, so an undetected espionage campaign was being directed and financed by Franz von Papen at the German Embassy in Washington even before the United States declared war. German agents were sabotaging much of the American war effort, for which industry was beginning to build up a supply of munitions.

The American Cryptographic Bureau was first formed in 1918 and began to counter von Papen's efforts. It was able to catch and execute at least one German spy in its midst before the end of the war. A key interest of von Papen and his masters was how the Zimmermann Telegram had been betrayed, but because of the precautions of Room 40 the Germans were only looking for the culprit in America. A prime suspect was Ambassador Eckhardt and his secretary in Mexico, but for the rest of the war almost everyone in the diplomatic and espionage network came under suspicion.

Intelligence reports from Room 40 were beginning to detect signs of unease and suspicion between Germany and her ally, Austria–Hungary. The 86-year-old Emperor Franz-Joseph died in 1916 and was succeeded to the throne by his young nephew, Karl. The new emperor was a lot less keen on the war than his predecessor; he had made secret approaches to the French but they had broken down.

The weakness in Germany's alliance was clear. President Wilson issued 'Fourteen Points for Peace' in 1918 and Karl immediately seized on it and sent a telegram to the king of Spain asking for a secret meeting to discuss possible peace terms. The details of the terms reached Room 40, who intercepted the messages between the emperor and the Spanish king. Both the British prime minister and the American president knew the terms of the proposal before the Spanish ambassador came to present them: the president cabled Balfour, the British prime minister, saying that he found difficulty composing his face to look surprised at the ambassador's presentation.

In October 1918 Room 40 was beginning to intercept signals from the *Hochseeflotte* in Kiel, indicating that it was preparing to put to sea with Admiral von Hipper in command. Then intercepted signals began to carry more confused messages for the operators as the listening stations heard about increasing references to court martials and deserters. Finally mutiny broke out in von Hipper's fleet. Signals went out to his officers to secure their wireless transmitters and their codes and it became obvious that the insurrection was spreading. Revolution was spreading across Germany with councils of soldiers and sailors taking charge of their units and ships, followed by the abdication of the Kaiser.

An Armistice was signed on 11 November 1918 with economic terms so severe that they would cause bitterness and resentment among the German people until it became a major cause of the next war. Some of the terms of the Armistice were, in brief:

All occupied territories in France and Belgium to be evacuated immediately.

The immediate repatriation of all prisoners of war.

The west bank of the River Rhine to be vacated.

A bridgehead into all German territories.

Payment of the costs of the Allied Army of occupation.

Restoration of all damaged property.

The handing over of 5,000 railway locomotives, 15,000 wagons and 5,000 trucks.

The surrender of all Germany's guns, aircraft and submarines and the entire *Hochseeflotte*.

The German soldiers climbed out of their trenches and marched home with all their weapons in good order to be treated as heroes. The war at sea enacted a strange anti-climax as the *Hochseeflotte*, consisting of nine battleships, five battle cruisers, seven light cruisers and forty-nine destroyers and all the U-boats that could make it across the North Sea, were escorted into Rosyth by the Royal Navy before being interned at Scapa Flow. The surrender terms were harsh but the worst of them was the condition that the economic blockade would remain in place. The British wanted to re-establish their export markets before a starving German populace had the time to start trading their wares in exchange for the food they so badly needed. The tranquillity of a ceasefire settled on the trenches in northern France and the waters of the North Sea but the German people had to wait for its blessings of peace and plenty, which took some time to arrive.

In the trenches there was little celebration as message pads containing the news were announced by the officers to their men in the front line. The curt message read:

```
Official radio announcement from Paris - 6:01 am
November 11 1918

Marshal Foch to the Commander in Chief.

Hostilities will be stopped on the entire front
beginning at 11 o'clock November 11 (French Hour).

The Allied troops will not go beyond the line reached
at that hour on that date until further orders.

[Signed Marshal Foch.]
```

THE INTERWAR
YEARS

Many soldiers believed that the Armistice was only a temporary ceasefire and the fighting would begin again soon. Watches were constantly checked as eleven o'clock approached and then as night came there was an unearthly quiet as men gathered what wood there was to light log fires in the trenches for the first time in four years. Men were still uncertain that enemy batteries might not be spying on them and they spoke in nervous low tones, their minds numbed to the shock of the sudden peace. What would come next? Gradually the thought of going home began to emerge and the reality dawned as showers of Very lights lit up the shell-pocked landscape and the celebrations began.

In London the joyous atmosphere went on for weeks, but soon the return to peacetime standards began. Room 40 or ID (Intelligence Division) 25, as it had been renamed, was restructured and its staff began reorienting themselves to the new objectives they had been given. The extraordinary crew of ID25 would begin to return to their old callings, ranging from the Stock Exchange and academia to the law and authorship (Neville Shute, whose full name was Neville Shute Norway, was one of these).

First, however, there had to be a celebration of deeds done and remembered in a riotous party, and on Wednesday, 11 December 1918 a farewell concert was held in the ballroom of St Ermin's Hotel with song, dance and verse.

Not all the team would depart, however. A core of that extraordinary group was 'hooked' on the intelligence game – Clarke, Dilly Knox and a few others soldiered on through the interwar years, led by Alistair Denniston.

The end of the war was as unexpected by the British public as it was in the trenches. The crumbling of the German nation's will to resist came not so much from its army but the starving civilians and a fleet that rarely put to sea to face the British. The government, drained and exhausted, decided to ask the Allies for a ceasefire in the form of an Armistice. They were presented with demands amounting to surrender and were sorely perplexed. The head of the Armistice delegation, Matthias Erzberger, sent a telegram to Berlin asking for instructions on how to proceed and was told, 'Get the best terms you can but sign', which left it with no alternative.

Negotiations were not made any easier for the delegation because the wireless message they had sent asking for guidance had been intercepted, along with its reply. Marshal Foch knew that the unfortunate German delegation had no cards to play. Foch made sure that the Germans met on French soil, and in a railway carriage parked near to the front line in Compiegne Forest the disconsolate Germans sat down to sign the document that ended the war. Erzberger slowly realised that the terms with which he was presented were not a ceasefire but a capitulation, but under instruction from Berlin he signed anyway. In doing so, the stage was set for the next war.

In London the news broke in the early morning and its effect was slow to register. An account of how the glad tidings were received and the jubilation that followed appeared in the *Daily Herald* newspaper:

The news was spreading hand to hand, the morning newspapers became common property and all over the city the flags began to break out and float idly over the streets, for it was still early morning and the colours drooped. About eleven o'clock as the war ended the crowds watched with momentary stillness as the clocks ticked away towards the dawn of peace; its hour unsullied by the noise and gesticulation. It all broke out later but it was impossible to notice how many people were taking the news solemnly and how one saw eyes that were not without the suspicion of tears. But the dawn did not last long for the day of jubilation was at hand. Girls in blue linen overalls had broken loose from their factory bonds and by one o'clock the throng had formalised themselves into jubilant processions. They gathered numbers as a snowball gathers bulk and those first thoughts that lay so near to tears were swept away in a rush of tramping feet and choruses of song. As the afternoon wore on the crowds in the streets thickened. But it was a crowd that had its discipline – four years of war had not gone for nothing. Orderly platoons and battalions led by anyone with a big enough flag could lead a shouting army; one such was headed by a small man solemnly holding a flag had the triumphant air of a conqueror. The noise and shouting of the processions went on into the night but as the high spirits wearied themselves they were gradually dampened by rain and exhaustion.

The war finished and within weeks the great military machine slowed and began the process of dismantlement, so that Britain could return to normality – or as near normal as the crosses, row on row in northern France and elsewhere, and a national debt bigger than our country's gross national product would allow. Room 40, or ID25 as it had been renamed, would change out of all recognition as it left its rooms in the Old Admiralty Building and went to new and unremembered offices. Rear Admiral Sir Reginald Hall, who became the most outstanding spymaster that British intelligence had ever produced, went into well-earned retirement and many of his team began to fade away to their old callings.

The mood of Britain, meanwhile, took on a frenetic air, particularly in London in the early years of the peace as cultural and fashion changes, particularly among the young, celebrated their release from the tension of war. The flappers and bright young things danced the Charleston while drinking newly devised exotic cocktails to excess, and the scene was regarded with distaste by the press and older generation. London's night clubs and hotel bars overflowed with affluent young men in dinner jackets, or sometimes 'tails', celebrating their release from duty in the mud and death of the trenches.

The country had suffered a surfeit of war and turned its back on all things military. After all, the war had been fought to end all wars and another was unimaginable. The nation's attitude was reinforced during the next decade, with the 1929 Wall Street Crash causing an axing of the country's public services and particularly the armed services. The navy got off relatively lightly in the austerity as its purpose was to protect the trade routes to empire, but the army and air force were drastically reduced. The value of intelligence and code-breaking was a lesson well learned, however, and although British intelligence capability was vastly diminished its core was fortunately not extinguished.

THE NEW INTELLIGENCE SERVICE

The cutback and reorganisation of the British fighting forces began in 1919 and, as a part of it, the government's Secret Service Committee recommended a complete reconstruction of intelligence facilities in a scheme that created a unified code-breaking service. The amalgamation of the two intelligence and cryptanalyst organisations was proposed in which the newly named ID25 acted largely as the country's strategic agency and the army's MI1b Intelligence Section as the tactical arm. Both bodies were incorporated into a new agency named the Government Code and Cipher School (GC&CS) with a very much reduced staff of fewer than fifty cipher and administrative officers and staff.

Commander Alistair Denniston RN was appointed the head of the new agency with little military intelligence work but still the function of decrypting the dispatches of foreign diplomats in London. The new agency was also moved from its Admiralty home into offices in London's Strand and, as a result of its changing function, was placed in the tender care of the Foreign Office. Captain (and later Admiral) Mansfield Cumming RN, who had been appointed head of the Secret Intelligence Service (which had flourished under his eccentric leadership) in 1909, was appointed as head of the new agency, later to be known as MI6.

Quite suddenly, in 1923, Cumming died and another naval officer, Admiral Hugh 'Quex' Sinclair, was appointed. He had earned his strange nickname by reason of a pronounced nasal speech enunciation. The selection of Admiral Sinclair at the head of MI6 established the continuance of naval influence in intelligence affairs for another twenty-five years until well after the Second World War.

In the early interwar period the nature of intelligence began to change as secret messages, which were now mainly of a diplomatic nature, were once again sent by a restored cable network rather than by radio telegraphy. Cable messages (intercepted with the co-operation of cable companies) were now the stuff of the GC&CS small team's decryption and evaluation work.

In 1925 the GC&CS decryption service moved into the third floor of SIS Headquarters at 54 Broadway as one of many government economy measures. The staff were housed in No. 54, which was described as a dingy building with an ancient lift (shades of 28 Victoria Street as described in the preface) that served a warren of offices made up with wooden partitions. Builders moved in to construct a narrow passageway connecting 54 Broadway with 21 Queen Anne's Gate, a quiet adjacent back street full of beautiful Queen Anne and Regency buildings, making a perfectly discreet back entrance for a secret organisation. MI6, which would soon be renamed the Secret Intelligence Service (SIS), needed to keep the comings and goings from prying eyes and so St Ermin's Hotel had become established as the more public but unofficial adjunct of the staff of Broadway Buildings. The triumphs and disasters of the Secret Intelligence Service would be celebrated in the Caxton Bar for decades to come.

By the 1930s the three organs of the British intelligence community were fairly well established, but they would suffer much painful change as the next war approached. MI5 was, and still is, the service responsible for the internal security of this country in close co-operation with Special Branch of the police. The more glamorous service is the SIS, which people still refer to as MI6 although it gave up that title some years ago, and is the true secret service, as its name implies. The two organisations divide the intelligence community functions neatly into home and away, providing our nation's security and safety. The people in MI6 call the organisation 'the Office', but outsiders such as their co-operators (sometimes) in MI5 tend to call it 'the Firm'.

The mysterious people who worked in Broadway called themselves 'friends', but the general public generally call anyone who associated with any of the foregoing organisations a 'spy' or a 'spook'. Nothing makes an intelligence operative wince as much as the use of the term, as it is almost invariably wrongly applied by the public or, even worse, the media. A spy is usually a foreigner deeply imbedded in his own country's military or intelligence network, who is willing to hand over vital secrets to the intelligence agency of another state. The spy can betray his country either for money, which often makes him suspect and unreliable, or for political convictions usually without monetary considerations, which usually makes for the most reliable kind of intelligence source.

The spies and go-betweens are usually known as 'assets' and could often be someone recruited from outside the service to do a small job such as collect or deliver a package or message. The controller who handles the asset or spy with whom they are communicating will certainly be a 'friend'. These are just a few of the code words for characters or functions in the language of the intelligence community. The term 'spy' is therefore *just* acceptable to an intelligence officer as it is looked on as a necessary but unpleasant evil, whereas that of 'spook' is disapproved of and can only be used in a jocular way. It can describe a friend or operative in the service in a light-hearted way, but as it is a term of which the media is fond it is generally one of mild derision.

The third organ of the intelligence community was (and still is) the Government Code and Cipher School (GC&CS), which is probably a term descended from a cover for Bletchley Park in its early days. It was based in Broadway until it moved to the 'Park' and from there into the 'Donut', as GCHQ now calls its hugely impressive building in the Gloucestershire countryside.

Secrecy has always been the watchword of the security service and was maintained by a system termed 'need to know', whose principles were fairly rigorously applied so that most operatives knew little of any major operation until it was over and sometimes not even then. Even people quite near the top did not know much about matters outside their ken that did not concern them, so it was possible for them to be cocooned in their own section without knowing how their work fitted into the greater scheme of things. In all of its operations the service often carried secrecy to extremes, the identity and image of the head of the service was always a deep secret (that only the press knew about) until fairly recently, as was the location of its offices.

The move into Broadway Buildings in 1925 was intended to be shrouded in mystery, so the new head of the agency, Quex Sinclair, decided to put up a notice in the entrance proclaiming that it was the offices of 'Minimax Fire Extinguishers'. London taxi cab drivers (who were always valuable intelligence informants) knew exactly what was going on; they were always dropping off individuals who had been engaged in clandestine matters and their equipment. As a result, the Minimax notice at the entrance was modified one morning by a chalked message on the pavement outside the building, 'This way to the British Secret Service offices'. After a short fit of apoplexy Sinclair ordered the chalked direction to be washed off the pavement and the Minimax sign to be taken down, although the location of the British Secret Service offices was still protected by everybody who had signed the Official Secrets Act.

Many legends attached themselves to the building over the years, such as the rumour that a blind matchstick seller whose pitch was outside the underground station opposite the Broadway Buildings in the 1930s was known to be a German (or Russian) spy, but to my knowledge that piece of intelligence was never confirmed.

Most of the interwar years were taken up by both MI5 and MI6 investigating and surveying the Communist Party, both at home and abroad, which rather caused them to take their eyes off the ball as to what was happening in Germany and Italy. The rise of Bolshevism in Russia in 1917 had alarmed the intelligence services from its beginning, and as a result even 'Blinker' Hall had warned against the emerging threat:

> Hard and bitter as the battle [against Germany] has been, we now face a far, far more ruthless foe. A foe that is Hydra-headed and whose evil power will spread over the whole of the world ... That foe is Soviet Russia.

I think that was the generally held view by the public in Britain at the time. The development of the British Communist Party as a revolutionary movement in Britain in 1920 alarmed the British Establishment and press. An increasing amount of the time and resources of both MI5 and MI6 was spent in monitoring and trying to counter its growing influence, with the surveillance of anyone affiliated to the Communist Party of Great Britain or its many front organisations. That task was carried out by the Special Branch Intelligence Unit based in the old building at Scotland Yard, but interception and decoding of wireless messages from Moscow was done from Broadway.

In 1927 it was revealed that the British communists were being financed with Russian funds from the Kremlin and this began a rift in Anglo–Russian relations. Prime Minister Stanley Baldwin wanted to distance himself from Soviet Russia and her intrigues, so he told Neville Chamberlain, who was then his foreign secretary, to read out the contents of several GC&CS intercepts to an attentive and crowded House of Commons. The fact that the diplomatic codes of the Russian Embassy were compromised and being read by GC&CS showed to any foreign diplomat reading Hansard that their diplomatic codes had been broken and their secret messages were being read by the British government.

Sinclair, at Broadway House, was appalled by the action but it was Denniston and his code-breaking section who were most affected and he complained most bitterly that 'his own government had betrayed his organisation's work beyond question' – strong words for a civil servant (members of the intelligence service were civil servants and were expected to comply with the rules of discretion of government employees).The Soviets at their embassy realised, as a result of the disclosure, that their coding system had been broken so they began the use of an almost unbreakable cipher system called a 'one-time pad', which GC&CS was unable to decode.The incident illustrated a fundamental tenant of intelligence – 'if you discover a secret, keep it secret that you know or it will slip away from you'.

The interwar period was a time of decline for Britain's security services, due to both lack of funds and Sinclair's lack of leadership. This led to a drastic lowering of standards in the agency and its operatives.They were paid little and were mainly recruited from the ranks of retired military men, generally of a certain age, who were expected to donate their services and be dependant financially on their own pensions. Morale among agents was low and performance even lower.

For years, the normal disguise of agents who operated in embassies abroad was that of a passport control officer.That cover for 'legal' intelligence agents based in British embassies was well known to most foreign security services, who could immediately recognise someone from the passport control department in an embassy as a poorly disguised intelligence man.

The Passport Office in Petty France, just round the corner from St Ermin's, became a natural control centre for the superannuated agents being run in European countries and elsewhere. Claude Dansey was a senior intelligence officer whose office was on the first floor of the Passport Office and he was able to witness the ineffectiveness of the service.The Foreign Office was not blind to its shortcomings, nor the fact that the service was an important part of its organisation, and was very disturbed.The foreign secretary consequently made an extraordinary proposal to Dansey, who was requested to create a secondary intelligence network that operated separately from that based in Broadway.

The new operation was to be based at the Passport Control Office and would be quite a separate operation from Sinclair's but still under Foreign Office control with Dansey in charge. He immediately began to use his considerable international contacts to recruit major figures in business and banking as 'illegal' intelligence agents who did not have diplomatic protection but could undertake covert projects denied to official diplomatic agents. Anyone with a legitimate reason for international travel such as seamen, business people and other travellers (but particularly journalists), who could be persuaded to give the new organisation worthwhile intelligence information was approached.

Dansey called his new bureau 'Z' and called himself 'Colonel Z'. He no longer recruited establishment figures as agents on the basis of the 'old school tie' qualification, as they were generally well-known members of the best London clubs. The Z organisation began looking for potential agents who knew what kind of intelligence information would be of value and how to obtain it. Dansey gave himself the label of Z1 and numbered each of his recruits Z2, Z3, Z4, etc. as he slowly gathered the members of his network together. However, progress was slow until Hitler came to power. As he became chancellor of Germany in 1933 he began to make threatening noises, which was the impetus for the Z organisation to really begin to grow and take shape into an effective force. The truly remarkable thing was that Sinclair at MI6 knew little or nothing of Z being run from the Passport Office less than a mile from his own office at Broadway House, but he was suffering from cancer and acting most strangely.

By 1937 the headquarters of Z had moved to Bush House in London's Aldwych and Dansey began to recruit agents and informants from the media so that he was building up an effective network of agents mainly in Europe. The journalistic profession was a good friend to the intelligence community (just as they are today) so the Kemsley Newspaper Group regularly provided 'foreign correspondent' covers for MI6 agents, along with the *Daily Herald* (now a defunct publication). Cover for agents as journalists was provided by the *Times*, the *Daily Telegraph* and the *Observer*, among other publications, and Dansey even financed a highly successful film production company called London Films. Its chief executive was Alexander Korder, who sent MI6 men around many sites in Europe on the pretence of looking for locations for shooting films that he may, or may not, have decided to make.

Another entertainment figure was Bertram Mills, whose circus travelled, partly on behalf of the service, all over Europe. Mills became a senior MI6 officer with an involvement in the Fortitude Operation before D-Day and he remained an 'asset' long after the war.

Dansey's network was building nicely until just before war began, when the network was set at nought by a crass lack of security and awareness in Holland. A secret communication, said to come from a group of disaffected German Army generals, was received by SIS that said they wanted to talk about overthrowing Hitler. This would have been exciting stuff if it were true, but it was not. The disaffected generals were in fact the German *Abwehr* intelligence in disguise, but the local MI6 intelligence network in Holland was taken in by it.

Even worse was the fact that Major Richard Stevens, the head of the MI6 station in Holland, and Captain Sigismund Payne-Best, heading the quite separate Z Section, had amalgamated their two organisations in contravention of all security practice. The two British heads of networks met their German contacts at Venlo in Holland right on the German border and they were hijacked into a waiting car and driven into Germany at high speed. Both men were interrogated by the Gestapo and as a result the Nazis were able to roll up both of the intelligence networks in Holland, Belgium and other parts of Europe. The inquest after the disaster caused Z to be absorbed into the main body of MI6, although some of the intelligence networks survived in neutral countries for some time.

The Z organisation had rung the alarm bells about Hitler in 1938 and it became evident that he was the real enemy so both Z and MI6 oriented themselves to face the new threat. The reorganisation of the services began with the creation of a new section of more than 100 operatives dedicated to sabotage, subversion and destruction that would later be amalgamated into the Special Operations Executive (SOE). That part of the service was intended to operate within enemy territory and that enemy was clearly now Nazi Germany, although the security services still had members of the Communist Party in its sights.

The reorganisation also expanded its Section 5, dedicated to counter-espionage, to which the Foreign Office added the Radio Security Service, taken from a resentful MI5 who were beginning to have some success intercepting German signals traffic. As war loomed Admiral Sinclair began looking for a home for both MI6 and GC&CS outside London and away from the threatened bombing of Britain that the Luftwaffe had already shown it was so devastatingly capable of in Spain.

Bletchley Park was identified as being an ideal situation for Denniston's legendary code-breaking team but it could not be installed due to a complicated squabble between the Foreign Office and the War Office about who should pay for it. Finally Sinclair ran out of patience and bought the place with £7,500 of his own money (the equivalent today of well over £¼ million). The purchase allowed the first of the GC&CS code breakers to enter the country house, which was to become their famous home on 15 August 1939, a couple of weeks before war was declared.

Sinclair had purchased and set up the future base for the nation's intelligence services but died of cancer soon afterwards, to be succeeded by his deputy, Sir Stewart Menzies, who only maintained a very loose administrative hold on the 'Park'. Menzies allowed the code breakers a good deal of leeway within the organisation, which allowed Alistair Denniston to spend the autumn of 1939 in the 'phoney war', preparing and expanding the code-breaking team. He organised them into the system that would work so well during Britain's travails in 1940 and the years beyond using the methods that had worked in Room 40.

The interwar years were also a formative time for cryptography. Europe's military learned the secrets of Room 40 from an indiscrete talk by Professor Ewing, reported in the *Times*, that revealed the Admiralty's Room 40's role in shaping the war's progress. It let the cat out of the bag and left the British intelligence community incandescently angry as it became obvious to the international intelligence community how important a part coding and code-breaking had played in Britain's successful war effort. The message was clear to the General Staff of Europe's armies that the interception and decoding of enemy transmissions was vitally important, although most of them had achieved some progress in the field themselves.

Morse code transmissions were still the principal method of communication for ships, aeroplanes and troops as the Second World War approached – just as it had been in the first. The difference was the huge increase in volume of wireless traffic that was occurring as the armies of Europe were learning to move with motorised speed rather than that of the horse, which had been the chief mode of transport in the First World War. The complexity and speed at which the war machines of nations were developing meant that the nature of communications needed to evolve to keep up with it. Lessons about security, or lack of it, had been learned the hard way (particularly by the Germans) so the use of code books – particularly if those books were to be available to ships or troops in contact with the enemy – had to be limited. Ciphering had to take a different form that did not depend on code books or cipher keys easily obtained by any enemy seeking to read the encoded messages. The military men of Europe began to embark on the mechanisation of ciphering their communications with such enthusiasm that the production of coding machines became almost a small industry.

CODING MACHINES

Room 40 is said to have been working on a mechanical enciphering machine at the end of the First World War and there is a prototype of a device of that kind in the First World War exhibition in the Imperial War Museum. It probably was not adopted as a practical proposition, but its existence certainly confirms that the possibility of machine encipherment was being considered by the cryptanalysts at that time. It is probable that if Room 40's machine had reached any formative stage it would have been largely mechanical in operation; certainly the one on show in the museum works on a purely mechanical principle.

The development of electro-mechanical technology after the war allowed several sophisticated ideas for mechanical enciphering machines to emerge in both Europe and America. One early device was invented by a Dutchman, Hugo Koch, who produced a machine whose purpose was seen by him as a secure way of protecting business and commercial secrets, although he had overlooked the important military market. Koch did not make a commercial success of his machine so he sold his rights to a German manufacturer, Arthur Scherbius, who began to produce the Enigma machine and market it to the military as well as the private sector.

The concept of this early device, at least when compared with what it would eventually become, was simple, but it established the basic concept of turning wheels inside a wired electro-mechanical machine. The method created millions of possible substitutions for any letter in the text of a message with many electrical paths, so that the machine could encipher a message with such a huge number of possibilities of coded substitutions that it appeared impregnable.

The German *Wehrmacht* believed the machine's security to be absolute, and so decided to make the device the centre of its wireless command network. The *Wehrmacht*'s Enigma project produced not a single machine but a whole family of them. They served as an integral part of the German High Command's communications network, and it ordered more than 100,000 machines during its lifetime. They were used by the German *Heer* (Army), the *Kriegsmarine*, the Luftwaffe, the SS, the German railways and even the waterways, each with their own variations in their coding mechanism.

One of Bletchley Park's principal code breakers, Gordon Welchman, explained how the Germans safeguarded their security within their own system, which, of course, added to the problems of decoding facing Allied code breakers:

> The Germans had adopted the principle that their communications must not rest on the machine itself but rather on the 'key' that would determine how the machine was set up for a particular purpose. Moreover they were concerned with both external and internal security. The wanted to prevent their enemies from reading their messages and also prevent their own units from reading messages that were not intended for them. For example, three of the many different types of Enigma traffic were messages between operational units of the regular army and air force, messages between Hitler's private army, the SS or *Schutzstaffel*; and messages involved in the training exercises of new signals battalions. All three kinds of messages were enciphered on identical Enigma machines, but the regular army and air force units were not to be allowed to read the text of SS messages. Nor were trainees to be permitted to read the texts of the other two types of traffic. Consequently different keys were issued for different types of traffic. This however, did not quite solve the problem because messages of different types were often transmitted on the same radio net. It was therefore necessary to provide means by which a receiving unit operator would know what type of clear text was hidden behind the enciphered text and whether he had the necessary key to read it. The Germans chose to solve this problem by using a three letter 'discriminant' transmitted in the unenciphered message preamble. This discriminant was not a part of the key; its purpose was simply to indicate which of the many keys was being used. A cipher clerk would examine the discriminate of each incoming message to determine whether he had been issued with the key used for its text encipherment. If he did have the key he would set up his Enigma machine and decode the message but if not he could not.

Enigma had more than 200 variants in its key system for the many communications purposes used by Nazi Germany, before and during the war. I was offered Enigma machines several times on the black market in Berlin immediately after the war when everything was for sale for a few cigarettes. I refused the offer of what looked like a funny-looking typewriter, whose purpose and value did not become obvious until Bletchley Park's secrets were disclosed almost thirty years later.

As war loomed the future belligerents created many coding machine designs of their own using the advantages offered by the emerging technology of electrically activated encoders in conjunction with rotors and levers. The new electro-mechanism promised greater ease, flexibility and, most of all, security for their messages, both commercial and the military. The public sector, such as banks, international traders and cable telegram providers, still depended on code books, mainly for brevity and also for security, but there was little flexibility in code book-based messages. They began to see advantages in the coding machines because of more detailed confidential messages that could be sent and received more quickly using fewer encryption staff, thereby reducing the possibility of information leaks.

As the market for coding machines increased so the science of cryptography, codes and ciphering methods became more sophisticated and cryptographic methodology even more arcane. All the big defence contractors of the time developed their own line of encoding machines with varying levels of sophistication for business, but the market for coding machines was still being led by the military. The German High Command realised how much information its enemy had gleaned from its cryptographic system in the First World War and was determined not to allow the same enemy to gain such an advantage again.

Enigma allowed the German panzers to co-ordinate their blitzkrieg actions, for which they could become famous, with a sense of absolute security in their communications. The German Army that overwhelmed Europe between 1938 and 1942 had the best-equipped wireless and cryptographic system in the world at the time. But there were flaws in their procedures. The first of them was spotted by Gordon Welchman, even before Bletchley Park had begun to decode the Enigma messages on any scale, using the technique he called 'traffic analysis', but he was not the only practitioner.

Harry Hinsley was working on naval codes at Bletchley Park early in the war during the disastrous Norway campaign, when British forces there were completely out-generalled by the Germans. The Royal Navy's aircraft carrier HMS *Glorious*, with two escorting destroyers, was about to return across the North Sea after providing air support for the beleaguered British Army. He noticed an increasing volume of wireless transmissions on the *Kriegsmarine* frequencies. He took it to mean that German warships would be on the move from their base in Kiel and sent a warning to the Naval Operational Intelligence Centre in the Citadel – that mysterious, ivy clad granite fortress built next to the Admiralty Building. He warned them that German warships were putting to sea, but the naval planners took no notice of a young civilian in a still untried intelligence organisation that had no naval experience or knowledge. The German battleship *Scharnhorst* intercepted the *Glorious* and her escort and all the British ships were sunk with all hands after a brief engagement. More than 800 men died and a valuable aircraft carrier was lost. The Admiralty learned a hard lesson and any communication received from Bletchley Park was given priority from that time forward.

The navy was not the only service to benefit from traffic analysis. Gordon Welchman at Bletchley Park began to track the movements of the German Army as it swept across France and began to close the trap on the British Expeditionary Force at Dunkirk. The explanation of the way that the German units were tracked was given by Welchman himself:

The Germans, in their concept of a blitzkrieg, felt that many groups of fast-moving fighting, command support and staff elements would need effective communication among themselves where ever they might be and furthermore that the activities of those groups would have to be tied into the High Command system. The elements of each co-operating group were to be served by signals detachments operating a 'radio net' on an assigned radio frequency. Under ideal conditions any message transmitted by any radio station operating on the net on the assigned frequency would be heard by all the other stations. One station of the net would act as control to ensure that no two stations would cause interference by transmitting at the same time. There were many such nets, so that messages originating at any point could be relayed to any other point. The call signs were simply a means of identifying the individual elements that were participating in this overall radio communications system. When passages were passing between elements within a single radio net the preamble would contain the call signs of the originator and intended recipient(s) of each message. When a message was forwarded to other elements their identifying call signs would be included in the message preamble. Thus by studying all the call signs we had an opportunity to learn something about the structure of the enemy's forces. As the call signs were changed every day however the detective work had to begin anew every twenty-four hours.

Our intercept operators listened to the Enigma messages and their preambles, writing them out by hand on standard forms. The main part of the form was used for the succession of five-letter groups or 'words' which constituted the indicator and text of a message enciphered on an Enigma machine. At the top of the form was a space in which the intercept operator entered the preamble that the German operator had transmitted ahead of the message. Indeed the form used by our intercept operators must have been very similar to the form used by the German cipher clerks. Our intercept operator, however also entered the radio frequency on which he was listening and the time of the intercept.

By means of tracking who was talking to who without even decoding the message Welchman was able to create a picture of the German Army's structure and its movements. This enabled him to warn the British general, Lord Gort, of the danger the panzers posed as they manoeuvred round his defensive perimeter. That would have been of substantial assistance to Gort as he ordered his defence and planned the skilful withdrawal of his army to the Dunkirk beaches for evacuation.

The Enigma machine network had been put into service by the *Wehrmacht* in its early form in the 1920s but an anti-Nazi German, a French intelligence officer and a small team of brilliant Polish mathematicians caused its eventual downfall. In 1931 Hans-Thilo Schmidt, who hated Hitler and the rising Nazi Party, gave the Enigma instruction manual to Captain Bertrand of the French military cryptographic bureau. Bertrand offered the information to his own people as well as the British and the Poles, but only Marian Rejewski, who was one of three bright young Polish mathematicians, accepted it. From the manual he and his team worked out the theory of the machines, and by the late 1930s they were reading the German Army coded messages.

The Poles shared the knowledge with their British friends before the war started, giving Denniston a simulated Enigma machine. Deep in a wood in Poland the exchange was made, whereupon Denniston's group put the machine in a suitcase and carried it back home through Germany under the noses of the Nazis. Poland was invaded a few months later and the mathematicians fled, taking their brilliant crypto analytical work with them, and after many adventures they passed all their knowledge on to British intelligence.

The mathematical algorithms that the Polish mathematicians created provided the foundation of what Denniston and his team were able to do in Bletchley Park, enabling the first decryption of an Enigma transmission on 31 May 1940 when they broke the Luftwaffe key just as British troops gathered on the beaches of Dunkirk for evacuation.

The signals intelligence that Enigma provided during the Battle of Britain enabled RAF Fighter Command to keep track of what actual losses the German Luftwaffe was suffering, their estimates of future aircraft numbers engaged and how they viewed the progress of the battle. It was one of the first of many Ultra intelligence evaluations that guided British and American commanders in many land, sea and air operations throughout the war. The British government always acknowledged the crucial help of the Polish cryptographers to Britain, so after the war the head of MI6, Sir Stewart Menzies, presented the original Enigma machine back to the Polish government in a ceremony held at 54 Broadway.

The principal innovation that Koch had incorporated into his machine was the *walze* (rotor) that was being incorporated into many other machines developed at the time, although with many electro-mechanical complexities. Enigma was a difficult machine to operate as it needed a team of two or even three people to code and transmit a message and another three at the other end to receive and record it. To operate Enigma the message had to be written down and then enciphered. As the string of characters had to be transmitted in Morse, it was a tedious and often inaccurate machine to operate. The difficulties helped the code breakers in Bletchley Park to break Enigma's code as it was usually the mistakes that a machine operator made that would allow the cryptanalyst to break into the code.

The Enigma machine was not only almost universal in use throughout the German armed forces down to the lowest levels of command, it was also used by the Italian Navy. In addition, the Japanese used a version for communication with the Nazi government.

A much more important machine, in terms of high-level intelligence, was the Lorenz SZ40, of which only about thirty were made to relay Hitler's thoughts to his highest *Wehrmacht* commanders. For that reason it has been dubbed 'Hitler's Blackberry'. Bletchley Park broke the Lorenz code with the help of the world's first computer, called Colossus, which analysed the machine's code to reveal that the workings were partly based on the mechanism of a teleprinter. The Lorenz code had a fatal flaw, which was a repeat pattern in every forty-second letter of its output, providing a 'crib' for the code breakers that enabled the Park to read the most valuable strategic information of all.

Another machine was the *Geheimschriber* (or Secret Writer) encoder, one of which is on display at the Imperial War Museum. It was mainly used over land lines and for that reason was more secure than the Lorenz and far more efficient than the Enigma.

Lastly, the *Schusselfernsschreibmaschine*, which was known to Bletchley Park as 'Sagefish', was one of the Germans' principal encoding machines and was often used in conjunction with Enigma. Its code remained unbroken during the war and to obtain a machine was one of the objectives of TICOM (the Target Intelligence Committee), whose task was to examine (and confiscate) any German coding technology of interest to the Allies before the Russians did. I served for a while in a TICOM operation in Berlin after the war and have to regretfully report that the Russians often got there first and used much of the cryptographic know-how to their advantage in the Cold War.

The British encoding machine was called Typex and was an adaptation of the principle of the Enigma machine, but with an increased number of rotors that gave it exceptional security. One of the machines was seized by the Germans at Dunkirk in 1940, but without its rotors, and another was taken in a very bad state of repair when Rommel captured Tobruk. German B-Dienst cryptanalysts tried to crack the settings of the machine but gave up because they assumed that if their Enigma machine was impregnable using four encoding rotors what chance did they stand with a machine that had more?

Typex was the main coding machine used by the British and Commonwealth forces and used the principle of encoding rotors, with a variance on the commercial version of the German Enigma machine. It came into service in 1937 and there were probably about 12,000 manufactured with a number of name variations, although 'Typex' was the accepted one. The machine was a considerable improvement on the standard Enigma machine because it was totally secure and had a number of enhancements for the operative built into it. It was driven by between five and seven rotors, compared with the three or four fitted to Enigma (the *Kriegsmarine* increased the number of rotors during the height of the Battle of the Atlantic, to the dismay of Bletchley Park). The Typex machine's security depended on its settings rather than its mechanism and would have needed a considerable cryptographic effort to 'crack' it.

There were many advantages over Enigma in the field: a principal one was that the machine only needed one operator. The mechanism of the device encoded and decoded automatically and the text of the message was recorded on to paper tape and, because of the structure, Typex was totally secure. This was confirmed when I served with TICOM, who investigated the whole range of German intelligence files and confirmed that the Typex codes had never been broken.

German *Abwehr* intelligence lost the signals intelligence war to its competitor at Bletchley Park largely because it did not try hard enough to break the British codes for a number of pressing reasons. In addition, it did not have the great good fortune of having the equivalent of the Polish cryptanalysts' team on its side to show it that an encoding machine was breakable if it really tried.

Britain and Germany were not the only countries involved in designing and manufacturing encoding machines. The Dutch company Crypto AG designed the Hamelin range of machines and launched a wide range of crypto machines that were compatible with NATO (North Atlantic Treaty Organisation) standards for use during the Cold War. The Americans also produced a wide range of machines, the most successful of which the US Army called 'Sigayan', but because of the vicious squabbles between the two services the US Navy called its same machine the 'ECM'.

Russia's successful cryptographic history dated from the German invasion in 1941 and was so successful that the German *Abwehr* encryption bureau gave up trying to decrypt any interceptions it made of Russian wireless traffic. Over the years the Soviet Union is said to have produced a number of cipher machines, of which little is known (at least by me).

Some smaller countries have made their own machines but suffered from a lack of a home market to give the necessary sales base to make their product a success; nevertheless they still tried. One of the most prolific designers of cryptographic machines was Sweden, followed by Switzerland – but that was rather a sad story. Before the war the Swiss licensed one of the German Enigma K-series machines for their tiny army, but after a bit they found that both the Allies and the Germans were reading their radio traffic. They then developed their own NEMA (*Neue Maschine*) encoder but its design was not very sophisticated and its code was immediately broken by the British, who continued to read much of their coded transmissions for some years.

While Britain retained the skills of its First World War security organisations and continued to develop them in the interwar years, no matter how amateurishly, nearly all the other countries in Europe, with the possible exception of Russia, were neglecting theirs. When the war began the United Kingdom was able to field the foremost cryptanalyst teams in the world while virtually all others had to start from scratch.

The Nazis, coming to power in 1933, found within weeks that their National Socialist objective of a one-party state meant that it needed to control its people. It had to maintain surveillance of all electronic messaging facilities. All of Nazi Germany's electronic means of communication were controlled and the extensive tapping of telephones and wireless transmissions was routine. The *Forschungsamt des Reichsluftfahrtministerium* (FA), who carried out the universal monitoring of all from the highest to the lowest, became known and feared as a dangerous organisation to upset.

Goering set up his own intelligence system that monitored all newspapers, magazines and published items of interest, and intercepted letters and conversations (which were often listened to by means of secret microphones). All government employees above a certain level had their telephone conversations intercepted along with party workers, particularly those in high places. The FA, in co-operation with Goering, played a crucial role in the downfall of the Brownshirts and particularly Ernst Röhm, who was murdered for his political sins that were monitored assiduously.

The FA also had an international role and played a major part in the German *Anschluss* (or takeover) of Austria by penetrating that country's communications system to identify individuals who were dissenters to the movement. They were quickly dealt with by the Austrian Nazi Party. The FA was a principal weapon in creating the authoritarian state that Germany was to become, using an internal intelligence bureau as an instrument of repression.

Bletchley Park thought it had identified all the Nazi intelligence and security systems that were active in Hitler's Germany during the war, but when TICOM came to examine Germany's intelligence records it found, to its astonishment, that it knew nothing of the existence of the FA system. I visited the headquarters of the FA after the war in the '*Haus am Knie*' in Berlin's Charlottenburg District and was impressed by the sophisticated electronic communications equipment still there, even though it had suffered heavily in the fighting as the Russians took the city.

The Imperial War Museum has exhibits in its Secret War Gallery from the interwar years, mainly of relics from MI5 surveillance operations – an intercepted postcard sent personally from Hitler to the Union of Fascists in

London sending his best wishes is an interesting one. The most outstanding item, however, is an Enigma machine of the kind developed in the interwar period, complete with rotors that are shown separately.

The German signals intelligence network proved the effectiveness of Enigma, as it was to be first used in anger in the invasion of Poland, the build-up to which began in June 1939. The Nazis complained that there were too many customs officials controlling the borders of the Free Port of Danzig, to which the Poles replied in a caustic manner. The response was a barrage of propaganda aimed at Poland from government circles in Berlin. The British government had been pursuing a policy of appeasement with Hitler for two years but now realised that the policy was not working against a dictator who was intent on war. Britain and France agreed to offer mutual military assistance should any of them be attacked, as rumours of an impending coup in France similar to that which took place in Czechoslovakia swept through Europe.

The world held its breath in July as Britain, France and Russia agreed to offer each other mutual support if any of them was attacked, but then Europe's statesmen were amazed as Germany and Russia entered into a non-aggression pact. It was signed by the foreign ministers Molotov and Ribbentrop, but what the world could not understand was that these two nations had always been sworn enemies. It was not known that there was a secret protocol to the pact – they had agreed to attack Poland jointly and share out the territory that was captured between the signatories.

On 25 August Hitler ordered the assault on Poland for the next day. He revoked the order when Mussolini informed him that Italy was not prepared for war, which left Hitler 'considerably shaken', but nevertheless he recovered to give the order on 31 August. German armed forces attacked Poland at 4.40 a.m. the following day and the panzer divisions rolled forward into action against Polish cavalry.

The German attack ended all hope of peace with Britain, but France was still clutching on to the hope of avoiding war. All through the next couple of days France was trying to convene a four-power conference to resolve the crisis. Meanwhile, the Stukas were bombing Warsaw while Prime Minister Neville Chamberlain was trying to bring France into line and enter the inevitable war together. The country and British Parliament, who now saw how pointless appeasement had been, were at boiling point and unaware of the confidential negotiations in which Chamberlain was immersed.

On the afternoon of 2 September the division bells of the House were ringing in St Ermin's Hotel, as well as every other venue that Members of Parliament frequented, to summon them to the House. Neville Chamberlain was dining in the House of Commons with his foreign secretary and others when, at 10.30 p.m. on that historic evening, its members, who were afraid that another Munich was in preparation, arrived *en masse* in the restaurant to demand action. Chamberlain had no option but to tell the assembled delegation that he would send a telegram to the British ambassador in Berlin, Sir Neville Henderson, asking him to send an ultimatum to Hitler the following morning. It demanded that if German troops did not cease all aggressive action against Poland and begin to withdraw from Polish property by 11 a.m. that day, 3 September 1939, then Britain and Germany would be at war.

At 9 a.m. on 3 September, Henderson arrived at the German Foreign Ministry but Ribbentrop refused to see him and he was received instead by the Foreign Ministry interpreter, Dr Schmidt, who was handed the ultimatum. Schmidt hurried to Hitler's headquarters in the Reich Chancellery where he translated the document to his Führer, who 'sat like someone turned to stone'. Finally he turned to Ribbentrop with an angry, 'What now?' as Schmidt left the room to break the news to the crowd of ministers and high-ranking Nazis that thronged the anti-chamber. Goering then turned to him and said, 'If we lose this war may heaven be merciful to us' (it was not, Goering stood among other Nazi war criminals in the dock at Nuremberg in 1945 to be condemned of war crimes before he committed suicide).

Two hours later, as the church bells rang in Britain for the morning service, the British ultimatum expired and Britain and Germany were at war.

THREE

THE WAR'S BEGINNING

SOE'S FORMATION

The epic tale of SOE in the resistance movement in Europe began in July 1940 when the German panzers had swept across Holland, Belgium and France, causing the British Expeditionary Force to be rescued by the little boats from the beaches of Dunkirk.

British soldiers had met a new kind of warfare, developed ironically by a small group of English military thinkers led by Captain B.H. Liddell-Hart who envisaged this new kind of mobile lightning strike war. The First World War was based on attrition of the enemy, which had cost three British lives for every two German ones, so the German High Command had translated the new military theories into a blitzkrieg technique. Its very effective strategy was to use mobility to attack an opposing army by cutting off its supplies and communications rather than by use of the expensive frontal attack that battered the enemy into submission.

Mobility and new weapons such as the use of Stuka dive bombers was the key to blitzkrieg and it worked very well against the Polish Army of 3 million strong. The Poles had only had one motorised division against a smaller German Army composed of six armoured and four motorised divisions, so the Germans, with their superb communications based on the Enigma machine, were able to literally run rings around the more conventional Polish Army.

A new mechanised and unorthodox form of warfare enabled the new German Army to manoeuvre around the Poles in such a way that their army was brought to its knees in eighteen savage and devastating days.

The new blitzkrieg was a simple technique that stunned its opponents, concentrating overwhelming armour and men behind smokescreens on a limited sector of enemy defensive lines while using dive bombers to act as long-range artillery. An armoured spearhead and shock troops would attack with the intention of creating a gap in the enemy defences in order for motorised infantry and artillery to pass through the breach. That spearhead of shock troops would pass through the gap and fan out into the enemy's rear, bypassing their strong points to attack soft targets such as road and rail junctions, therefore paralysing supply, reserve and command units and causing chaos in the enemy's rear echelons. Every effort would be made to encircle or capture defenders rather than drive them back.

Finally the spearheads would move towards key towns or cities while motorised infantry would collect prisoners, reduce strong points and contain defended pockets. Marching infantry of more conventional troops would then move up to protect the spearhead formation's gains and carry out supply and administrative tasks for the forward units.

The Polish campaign was the first demonstration of the blitzkrieg technique using armour and motorised infantry in such a concerted, agile and speedy style of manoeuvre on the battlefield. Blitzkrieg, as a new form of warfare, obviously worked far better than the broad frontal attacks that had cost so many lives in the First World War and it created a fearsome reputation for the German Army. The new methods of attack worked so well that it not only surprised the Polish Army but also the German High Command, who were taken aback at being able to defeat a Polish Army of 3 million men with only 10,000 casualties of their own.

On 10 May 1940 the German Army attacked neutral Holland and then, using the same blitzkrieg form of attack on the British and French armies, breached its defences at Sedan. A whirlwind advance of the panzers through the countryside of northern France caused the French to surrender as the Germans entered Paris and the British Expeditionary Force was left with its back to the sea.

The British Army's evacuation at Dunkirk meant that it left every bit of its equipment on the French beaches and had its back to the wall with very little left with which to fight back. I remember the aftermath and emotion of that time well. We all watched in dismay as the soldiers returned to Pembroke Barracks in Portsmouth, from where they had left to go to France with such high spirits less than a year before.

However, just because the army had suffered a disastrous defeat from which its men had been rescued by a miracle, it did not feel the need to deviate from its customary routine. On a sunny Sunday morning following their return from Dunkirk the troops mustered as usual for church parade and the spectators, who were used to smartly turned out soldiers, watched aghast at the sight of those men. Most of them did not have a complete uniform as they marched, or rather walked, to church like exhausted and beaten men. Regulations demanded that every soldier had to carry his gas mask, but there were not enough containers for them. Some had cut up cardboard boxes in which to put their respirators and others had even wrapped their masks in newspaper. They looked like the remains of a defeated army. As they filed out of the garrison church after the service a crowd gathered to watch the shabby troop of men form up to march off. Slowly some in the crowd began to applaud and then the applause increased in volume until all the crowd were clapping emotionally, some with tears in their eyes. The soldiers looked startled at first, but then their stance and attitude began to change and as they marched back through the crowd and into the barracks gates they no longer looked like beaten men.

While British troops were being ferried from the beaches on 31 May 1940 there was a small but significant victory at Bletchley Park as the Luftwaffe cipher key to its coded Enigma transmission was broken. Enemy aircraft began to approach the seaways into Portsmouth Naval Base to lay mines in the Solent, mainly at night.

Then began the expected major air attacks on the mainland, and it targeted Portsmouth, where I lived; the first of thirty attacks throughout the lovely summer weather of the Battle of Britain. The aerial battle fought in a clear blue sky over our heads was seen as a preliminary to the invasion. Hitler's air force was trying to destroy the British fleet in its harbour in preparation for landing his panzer divisions on the beaches of Kent and Sussex in south-east England.

Those events were the backdrop to the formation of SOE, created by Westminster politicians as a secret and independent fighting force, originally as a defensive measure dedicated to the subversion and sabotage of invading enemy forces. It was planned as a fourth armed force whose place was unique among Britain's fighting forces, designed to damage an invading enemy's lines of communication and operational effectiveness with almost suicidal soldiers left behind as the enemy advanced over their hiding places. Its formation was also a deep secret, so secret that most of the members of the other three armed forces it was going to support knew little about its operations until later in the war.

The collapse of France and the predicament of Britain in 1940 precipitated a revolution in strategic thinking by senior military and political figures (chief among them being Churchill), who created this new form of warfare. In that desperate summer, with the expectation of a German invasion at any time, decisions about such matters as the formation of an entirely new irregular fighting force acting outside organised military action that would normally have taken years to agree now came to fruition in weeks.

As Fighter Command of the Royal Air Force fought the Luftwaffe to a standstill in the skies over southern England, the possibility of invasion faded and a new concept and spirit took over in SOE and turned its thinking from defence to offence. The concept of a resistance movement in Europe began to take shape based on the will of the people in Europe to resist the Nazis. One of the first to voice resistance to the German invaders was General Charles de Gaulle when he broadcast a rallying call to his countrymen on the BBC telling them there was still hope. However, he did not then know that it would be based on SOE.

The seeds of such an irregular fighting force already existed in departmental units within the Foreign Office, the War Office and other ministries, so Churchill ordered them to be brought together to form its basis. One of the principal architects in this amalgamation of departments of government was the Minister for Economic Warfare, Hugh Dalton, who wrote to Lord Halifax, the foreign secretary, saying:

> We have got to organise resistance movements in enemy-occupied territory compatible to the Sinn Fein movement in Ireland, the Chinese Guerrillas now operating against Japan, the Spanish Irregulars who played a notable part in Wellington's campaign or – we might as well admit it – to the organisations which the Nazis themselves have developed so remarkably in almost every country in the world. This organisation must use many different methods including industrial and military sabotage, labour agitation and strikes,

continuous propaganda, terrorist acts against traitors and German leaders, boycotts and riots.

It is quite clear to me that that an organisation on this scale and of this character is not something which can be handled by the ordinary departmental machinery of either the British Civil Service or the British military machine. What is needed is a new organisation to co-ordinate, inspire, control and assist the nationals of the oppressed countries who must themselves be direct participants. We need absolute secrecy, a certain fanatical enthusiasm, willingness to work with people of different nationalities and complete political reliability. Some of these qualities are certainly to be found in military officers and if such men are available they should undoubtedly be used. But the organisation should be, in my view be entirely independent of the War Office machine.

Halifax went with Dalton's paper to the prime minister, who then got Cabinet approval for the project and agreement that it should go ahead. On 16 July 1940 Churchill invited Hugh Dalton to create the Special Operations Executive, known to all as SOE. It was born with Churchill's instruction to Dalton that he was to simply 'set Europe ablaze' – although the fire would take some time to take hold.

Sir Frank Nelson was the first Head of Operations of SOE and known to insiders by the code name 'CD'. Nelson bore the brunt of the workload to create the blueprint that SOE would follow for the rest of the war. Nelson wore himself out with the intense pressure of work and had to resign from his post in May 1942, to be succeeded by his second in command, Sir Charles Hambros, who had been a distinguished merchant banker. Hambros was given an expanded directive by his friend, Winston Churchill. It was to be a secret organisation with two tasks – to foster the spirit of resistance in Nazi-occupied countries and create a nucleus of trained men (and women) to act as a 'fifth column' to help in any country that Britain intended to liberate. (The term 'fifth column' was coined during the Spanish civil war when General Franco was attacking a well-defended city with four columns of troops. When asked how he would assault the city he said it would be easy as he had a fifth column within the city walls, and so the term took hold.)

Churchill decided that SOE's task would be to make assaulting any German-occupied country using conventional forces a lot easier by creating all sorts of disruption and acts of sabotage in the rear of the enemy with the help of anti-Nazi patriots. His concept would be on a far bigger scale than Franco, of course, with the target for SOE being whole countries and not just a city. 'Churchill's Private Army', as some called it, gave birth to a new and expanded concept of warfare. It would also create a heroic legend of daring, adventure and suffering for a band of men (and women) that would make an important contribution to winning the Second World War.

Neville Chamberlain, who had been Churchill's predecessor in the office of prime minister, was asked to draft detailed instructions of the formation of SOE for Dalton's guidance, and in his last political act Chamberlain wrote a 'most secret' paper dated 19 July 1940 for the new prime minister. A few days later he went into hospital with cancer and never came out again, but the document that he authored was treasured by SOE as its founding charter.

Meanwhile, the Battle of France and the Dunkirk evacuation was seen as a triumph for Hitler and was celebrated as a victory throughout Germany, seen by its people as the end of the war. Bells rang out and flags fluttered as the German people celebrated what they thought was the end of the fighting and the *Wehrmacht* began to demobilise some of its 'heroes'. Hitler was convinced that Britain would have to surrender, but the conviction began to fade as Churchill's intransigent speeches were broadcast to the world.

The Führer was disappointed – 'Did the British not realise when they were beaten?' he trumpeted. He issued Directive 16, ordering his generals to submit plans for the invasion of England's southern coast. Britain's strategic situation appeared so desperate that the few senior politicians and military men who knew of the formation of the new force pinned their hopes on the rather sketchy plans of SOE. Sabotage and subversion in the midst of the enemy forces seemed to them to be one of the few weapons, along with a sea blockade and air strikes, left to Britain with which to attack the enemy.

The progress of SOE in becoming an effective fighting force was going to be very slow in coming to fruition as it needed to build up its skills and resources to join the fight. Resources of any kind were scarce and also desperately needed elsewhere as the defence of Britain's beaches and airfields was being prepared against the threat of Hitler's Directive 16. There was much discussion about the directive that led to Operation Sea Lion, but it achieved no cohesive invasion plan. In fact, it created three plans – one for the German Army; one for the *Kriegsmarine* and one for the Luftwaffe – each of which had little in common with the others. The only common denominator between the three of them was that any invasion attempt would be impossible until the Luftwaffe had destroyed the Royal Air Force and dominated the skies over Britain.

SOE IN ACTION

Germany's military *Abwehr* intelligence service estimated that the British Army could muster eleven infantry divisions, several of them woefully understrength, plus one armoured division (most of whose tanks had been left in France). The movement of British troops to a battle area on the coast would have to be by train as most of their transport had also been left on the beaches and any trains would be harassed by the Luftwaffe.

General Jodl, commander of the army operation, planned landings on 30 miles of English coastline with more than thirty of his divisions stretching from Portsmouth on the south coast to Ramsgate at the Thames Estuary. The huge list of materiel that he submitted as being necessary for his army's landing included almost 3,000 bicycles and the feed for thousands of horses. Horses were the army's principal method of transport, as its wagons were still largely horse drawn; its reputation for a high degree of mechanisation was mainly with the panzer divisions, although they could perhaps depend on the British vehicles captured at Dunkirk.

The German High Command was planning its major seaborne assault as though it was a river crossing, and probably not a very wide river at that. The *Kriegsmarine* knew better, and said so; it knew that only a much narrower bridgehead than that envisioned by the army's planners would be possible. To support the army, the force it thought it would need required more than 400 ships and attendant vessels such as tugs etc., and the German Navy had nowhere near that number available.

Very few purpose-built landing craft were available to land troops in the shallow waters of the English coast (the Allied invasion of Normandy suffered the same shortage in 1944). The initial assault landing would consist of a single wave of boats of all sizes, shapes and speeds in shallow waters, requiring many of the troops involved to use paddles or rafts to get them ashore. The evacuation of the wounded would be impossible in the first week as the vessels would not be available; further, a convoy of the size contemplated for the invasion fleet could not travel at more than 3 knots (1 knot is about 1.1 land miles per hour).

The shortest crossing between Calais and Dover would take eight hours, so the timing and place of the landings would be no surprise for the British defenders. The first wave of assault troops would have to hold out for at least six hours before the boats were loaded up and returned again, and always under air and sea attack. The speed and return of the invasion fleet with reinforcements for the initial wave of troops would also have to depend on the uncertain tides and weather of the Channel and men and supplies would have to be landed on to open beaches.

The *Kriegsmarine* planned a much narrower bridgehead on which only three divisions would land between Folkestone and Beachy Head. The High Command said this was unsustainable (and it probably was). While the discussion was going on the opening phase was taking place, and the Luftwaffe had been tasked to destroy the Royal Navy in harbour at Portsmouth and RAF Fighter Command aircraft in the air or on the ground. When that was done the operations could commence and progress without hindrance.

The world looked on, assuming that Britain would fall to the German assault, including America's ambassador in London, Joseph Kennedy, who reported back to President Roosevelt that the Luftwaffe's overwhelming might would crush a small, inexperienced and fledgling Royal Air Force. Both Kennedy and the German Luftwaffe underestimated the power of radar to guide the British fighter planes in their attacks on the German bombers during that 'Spitfire Summer'. The white vapour trails criss-crossing each other high in the blue skies of August, while the occasional tak-a-tak-a-tak of machine gun fire from aircraft in aerial combat became an indelible memory for those of us who witnessed it.

By the autumn the Messerschmitt fighters and Dornier bombers had taken too much punishment. They gradually ceased coming to Britain during the day and switched their target to London at night. Their incendiary bombs started the worst fire raids in the capital since the Great Fire of London in 1666. On Sunday, 29 December the bombers came by night and most of Victoria Street went up in flames. The Blitz went on unremittingly every night, from that time and on through the winter into 1941. Bombs were scattered over Westminster, as the records of the council attest, and its Air

Raid Precautions reports, held in the archives, give terse accounts of many incidents that occurred.

One single report, of many, records how an oil bomb exploded at the junction of Caxton Street and Broadway, only yards from St Ermin's where an Auxiliary Fire Service fire crew was fighting a fire. Christ's Church, which stood on the green just to the south of the hotel, was blazing fiercely as an oil bomb sprayed the area with burning oil and injured and burned eight firefighters there. In the same incident two women working with a heavy rescue unit engaged in digging people out of bomb ruins were both killed. The bomb was one of many that dropped on Westminster that night and it was not an unusual nightly experience for many people in the borough during the months of the Luftwaffe's incessant Blitz on London.

Staff of the various intelligence agencies who occupied the hotel and Caxton Hall would have been working night shifts to maintain SOE's preparation to send its agents into the field, but they would undoubtedly have dived under their desks as the bombs fell around the hotel. Work was going on in the hotel as SOE evolved its plans to create its unorthodox and ungentlemanly war, which called for unique responses to the request to keep Europe ablaze. That posed a problem for SOE, which had to prove that enough of the population of occupied Europe would be with it to create a worthwhile resistance movement to justify its existence. The lack of response to de Gaulle's call to action to his countrymen was disturbing, but a reaction to the brutality of the German occupation was beginning to emerge as it began to directly affect the people of the occupied countries.

The plan was to drop SOE agents into regions where promising resistance movements were beginning to emerge; agents would then be expected to create and maintain active resistance groups. When the effectiveness of a group was proven they would be supplied with arms, ammunition and other resources needed to attack the Nazi occupying forces. SOE had to find the right candidates to train as agents capable of developing and operating resistance groups in the occupied countries and communicating their activities and needs in ciphered wireless signals back to their control in London. The groups had to be directed to their best effect in the underground war, so there was a great deal to do – but where would they start and how could they set about the task?

Among the intelligence officers working in Caxton Street was Kim Philby (of whom we will hear more later), who had been a *Times* correspondent and was recruited at an early stage in the war to work for MI6. He was working in the personnel section responsible for training when he recalled walking into his office in Caxton Street one morning to be surprised to meet an old friend, Guy Burgess, from his days at Trinity College in Cambridge. Burgess had been recruited in 1939 from the BBC Talks Department and told Philby that he had proposed to Lawrence Grand that he would be responsible for establishing a school for training agents in espionage techniques. He asked Philby to help him, and as a result Philby wrote in his book, *My Silent War: The Autobiography of a Spy*:

> It was an astonishing proposal, not because it was made but because it had not been made before. No such school existed. Guy argued the case for its necessity, obvious now but new then. He outlined the subjects of the syllabus. At the end he suggested that such a college should be named 'Guy Fawkes College' to commemorate an unsuccessful conspirator who had been foiled by the vigilance of the Elizabethan SIS. It was a neat touch but he could hardly have suggested the Guy Burgess College.
>
> At last I had got my teeth into something. I broke the subject up into its component parts, syllabus, selection of trainees, security, accommodation and so on and produced a memorandum on each subject. I have forgotten most of what I wrote.

The title, when it was chosen, was less obvious and the school was eventually called the 'Inter-Service Experimental Department'. But to those who were in the know it was called the 'D School'. Burgess' syllabus for the new school included propaganda, organisation of subversive cells, the art of spreading rumour and propaganda, the use of arms and explosives, wireless telegraphy and so on.

The curriculum for the training schools had been established, but by mid-1941 the first SOE agents were just finishing their training and available to place into Europe. It had to meet the practical problems of agent placements, which were complex, but a strong and growing indication of anti-Nazi feelings among the indigenous population in the occupied countries was beginning to be obvious. The problem was to see how to harness the growing feeling for resistance to the needs of the Allied war effort.

Objectives for SOE's future aggressive cloak-and-dagger operations were being considered, drafted and prepared even while actions to combat the invasion threat in south-east England were still informing the immediate thinking of SOE. As the invasion threat faded, the organisation that had been formed from the merger of the three existing clandestine departments in the Foreign Office, the War Office but the SIS was becoming more belligerent. about it.

The Foreign Office had created a propaganda organisation designated 'EH' after Electra House (its headquarters) to spread information and misinformation wherever it disturbed the enemy. SIS had formed a Section D (which some say stood for 'destruction') to investigate irregular means of weakening the enemy's infrastructure, mainly by sabotage. The War Office expanded its Military Intelligence (Research) Section (MIR), looking into the possibilities of guerrilla warfare undertaken by regular uniformed troops who later became the elite forces such as the Commandos and the SAS (Special Air Service).

The air of daring and adventure in SOE was still in the process of being created with the help, and sometimes even disapproval, of various government departments, particularly the more hidebound civil servants among them. The objectives of SOE were out of line with the principles of MI6, which felt it needed to lure the enemy into a tranquil state of mind while it probed its secrets – on the other hand, SOE simply wanted to blow things up.

The military did not approve of 'amateurs' attacking the enemy in what they saw as such a haphazard way, particularly as the 'upstarts' would not wear uniform and, even worse, would be independent of their control. Worse still, the new organisation was being formed from an amalgamation of parts of the sections already formed within the War Office as well as MI6. Section D, within Military Intelligence, and MI6 both had vaguely similar objectives so developing methods of irregular warfare was not an entirely strange idea to them, although the army still disapproved of an undisciplined rabble.

The propaganda arm of SOE never fitted into its structure easily and was separated from the organisation later in the war, but the other two military sections were ordered to co-operate. They came to a working agreement on their division of activities: the MIR participated in irregular operations that could be undertaken by regular uniformed troops such as the Commandos or SAS, while Section D dealt with truly undercover work that was, in Churchill's words, 'unavowable'.

Section D was initially housed in the basement of SIS Headquarters at 54 Broadway but soon outgrew its accommodation there, both physically as well as probably not being made welcome by its MI6 hosts. The new organisation chose rooms in a most unlikely venue for a secret organisation – St Ermin's Hotel, which had already been in use as an informal meeting place for the secret intelligence community for some years. Ever since MI6 moved in at Broadway around the corner the SIS officers had made a habit of lunching, dining and generally entertaining their guests there so the hotel was well known to the staff of Section D. Sometimes extra rooms were taken for interviewing (or interrogating?) potential recruits or other contributors to its body of intelligence knowledge.

The amalgamation of Section D and MIR into SOE began its new life in a few rooms in the hotel, but within a few weeks it began to overflow just around the corner on to the sixth floor of Caxton House and soon the fifth floor as well. The continuing expansion of SOE meant that the team had to search for larger premises to house its rapidly expanding staff.

In the meantime, Admiral Quex Sinclair, the director of MI6, had appointed Major Lawrence Grand of the Royal Engineers to head Section D. Grand's appointment was made on the basis of his unusual methods in dealing with the Pathans while fighting them on the Indian frontier, where they were constantly stealing British ammunition. He replaced ordinary cordite with high explosive in the bullet cases of every tenth round, which effectively discouraged the practice, but while some disapproved of the ungentlemanly practice it certainly appealed to Sinclair. It seemed to him just the attitude needed for waging irregular warfare in what became unofficially known as the 'sabotage service' of Churchill's ungentlemanly warfare.

The task of implementing ideas and methods for subversive operations in Nazi-occupied Europe was described by Grand as like having to move the pyramids with a pin, but he was gradually making some progress. He was portrayed by one of his colleagues as being a striking personality – tall, handsome and well-tailored with a heavy dark moustache. He constantly wore a red carnation, smoked cigarettes almost without cease through an elegant black holder and had an equally elegant wit. He was brim-full of ideas and energy and had the rare gift of giving full trust to those under him and backing them up without question against outsiders. Unhappily he also had a gift for rubbing staid men up the wrong way, so instead of setting Europe ablaze it could be said that SOE set Whitehall on fire. It was rather an unfortunate trait in an organisation that needed to exist in an environment of secrecy, and it was not always possible to explain its reasons to staid civil servants (although when it was needed the authority of the prime minister could be played as a trump card).

Grand and his merry men moved into St Ermin's, where one of his officers described how the first agent was recruited. He was George Hill and had worked in Russia in 1917 during its Revolution in the First World War. He was with SIS even before it became MI6 and practised sabotage activities of various forms in aid of the White Russians against the communists in both Russia and the Ukraine. He had become an expert in explosives and, in the process, specialised in the use of guncotton, which was the army's standard explosive for the demolition of buildings (although it needed a large amount of the stuff to get a satisfactory explosion). Guncotton was made of the same chemical as nail varnish or ping-pong balls, all of which were highly flammable and could even be explosive in large quantities, but unfortunately its bulk made it unsuitable for covert sabotage operations.

On his return to Britain in 1920 he was awarded a medal and wrote about his experiences. Major Grand had read the account and so invited George to lunch on the 4th Floor of St Ermin's, where he invited him to join D Section over the dessert. George accepted the invitation (and the dessert) with alacrity and was given the whole of northern Europe to look after as his 'patch'. He began to collect intelligence about the numerous countries he was to cover. He was sent on a course to bring him up to date with the advances that had been made in explosives and other devices since his sabotage experiences in Russia and all that had occurred in the 'phoney war' before the German panzers attacked first the French and then the British armies in the Battle for France.

George went to Paris to liaise with French intelligence organisations, who were already co-operating with Section D before SOE was formed (although with a rather amused distain, as the idea of irregular warfare was still at a very formative stage). The concept of an organisation that waged war by sabotage was new to them, as it was to nearly everybody else at the time, but they were at least polite to George. Nevertheless, he made some good contacts in French military intelligence that would stand SOE in good stead later on in the war.

He began by discussing sabotage with the French and the Belgians, who were coming round to SOE's way of thinking. They wanted to form their own resistance groups so he supplied them with explosives (which George called 'sweets' and 'toys'). When the Germans broke through at Sedan, George was nearby and, as the panzers raced through northern France, he commandeered a Rolls-Royce and drove back to Dunkirk to catch one of the last boats lifting troops from the beaches in the evacuation.

On his return to England he re-joined Major Grand, who posted him to a newly formed SOE industrial sabotage school at Brickendonbury Manor in Hertfordshire. The manor specialised in explosive trials as demonstrations for its students as a part of the SOE agents' course on what they could do in sabotage. The manor was one of SOE's network of almost twenty experimental establishments, developing many new and innovative weapons to create mischief in Europe. It was part of an even greater number of SOE training schools, generally established in grand country houses, where agents were taught the basic skills needed to survive in enemy territory. As a result of their preference for big houses SOE came to be known to some as 'Stately 'Omes of England', even though many of the more spartan ones were to be found in the Highlands of Scotland.

The training schools were tough and demanding in order to make agents resilient, as you might imagine, to make the agents fit and self-reliant and explain to them in detail what, where and how to attack anything (or anyone) that was of benefit to the enemy.

One of the principal objectives was industrial plant, so the principles of industrial production were taught and how to put a stop to it with the use of incendiarism which, it was explained, was preferable to explosives in bringing a factory to a halt. The use of water to quench the ensuing flames could be even more damaging to a factory's production line than the fire itself. Setting light to a factory or its store of materials would expose delicate machinery to the weather, but water could also destroy plans, drawings and paperwork as much as the conflagration. A fire could also make it difficult for the investigators to determine its cause, rather than the use of explosives that would undoubtedly alert the enemy to the saboteur's presence. It also uses up the stock of explosive materials that could be used for other, and maybe better, purposes. Arson was therefore seen as the better and more destructive option.

More physical means could also bring the enemy's war production to a halt. For instance, breaking the iron casting mountings of a machine with a heavy hammer – if you could not find a good excuse to carry a heavy hammer into a factory you should not be in SOE, you were told. Fractured castings in the body of a heavy lathe or other machinery were more difficult to repair than steel components and trainees were told that if they attacked machinery, they should preferably make it a main bearing or main casting while the machine was in motion as the machine could help in its own destruction. Non-standard or complicated machines should be a prime target in a production line, particularly if they were at a bottleneck in the factory layout. If there was an opportunity to attack a line of similar machines they should not all be damaged in the same place as the enemy could cannibalise parts of some machines to repair damage on some of the other ones. Blackmailing factory owners became an effective form of sabotage, and persuading the owner to destroy aspects of their own factory's output and damaging their own source of income was an option. The other was to call in the RAF to flatten the factory, which often proved to be an effective means of persuasion.

When other more devious methods of damaging enemy resources failed, agents were taught to use explosives of various kinds. The most popular one in the early days was dynamite, or 'jelly', of which there were several types. The early types would sometimes sweat, which could make explosive material unstable – as I found when I was engaged in bomb disposal in Berlin at the end of the war. Sweating was a common condition with several kinds of explosive, particularly when a piece of ordnance had been buried in bomb ruins, damp and undisturbed for some time and then suddenly unearthed to be exposed to the warmth of the sun. As it warmed up the explosive contents of the shell, bomb or grenade could ooze out and become very unstable. The only safe way of dealing with such a device was to keep it wet by hosing the device down.

Dynamite in its stable military form or TNT (they are not the same kind of material) were both suitable for SOE operations and could be used to suit different kinds of demolition problem. By far the most favoured explosive for an agent was plastic explosive (PE), which was an incredibly versatile material that would stand all sorts of mistreatment. It had a similar feel to Plasticine, with a reddish-brown colour, and it left the smell of marzipan on your hands when you handled it – that was a dead giveaway to the Gestapo when they were interrogating a suspect after a bomb incident. The material was incredibly good tempered and could be dropped or hit (our instructor hit it with a hammer as we dived for the door and he even put a lighted match to a piece with no result).

It could be cut up into different sized lumps and carried around in your pocket, where the warmth would make it easier to mould into different shapes. A small lump could be used for literally melting the steel of a short section of a railway line by tamping it into the T-section of the rail, or the base of an electricity transformer, or crevices of machinery. It was not suitable, however, for trip wires or booby traps because it needed a primer (like a timer) the size and shape of a pencil and detonator cord to set it off. The whole kit could be carried in a small pouch or handbag but could do a great deal of damage, as a small amount of PE could derail a train or severely damage an aircraft (if you could get near one).

Placing and setting a small charge could easily be handled very simply by one man or woman – but if the PE was safe, the detonator needed to set it off was a lot less so because it contained fulminate of mercury, which was a highly volatile material. The device could be set off by the warmth of the body and could blow the hand off an unwary handler. The detonator could be attached to a time pencil, operated by acid eating away at a copper wire in a specific amount of time. It gave the agent time to be elsewhere when the device went off and with a small charge PE could cut a few inches out of a rail, which was quite enough to derail a train. It was one of the most effective pieces of equipment that SOE used against railways, pumping stations, conveyors, pylons and other targets in occupied Europe. Sabotaging the rails was such a danger to trains in parts of occupied Europe that the Germans used to tie some of their hostages to the front of trains to discourage SOE sabotage.

Agents in the security services were controlled by senior executives or 'friends' based in Caxton Street (and later in Baker Street), who generally came from 'good' schools and were often well connected socially. Their work was generally to direct operations but their terms and conditions of employment were somewhat sparse, as described by Lieutenant Commander Arthur Langley, an ex-SIS officer:

> One was not officially employed by anybody and was paid in cash; there was no security, no pension, or any kind of health cover for us or income tax return. Officially we did not exist when we went on an assignment so when an operation was given to us it was usually outside the law; if we were caught by the police then you were on your own. If you were caught by the counter-

intelligence organisation in another country any connection with your service would be officially disowned.

The situation with regard to money seems not to have changed much by the 1960s as it is said that ex-MI6 officer Peter Wright, the author of the bestseller book *Spycatcher*, wrote it because he did not have the pension he had expected for his years of service as an agent. Another who felt short-changed in his pension was Commander Denniston, who had been an important figure in the forming of Britain's intelligence community. The security services were never generous with their emoluments, although that now seems to have changed if you view the terms and conditions of employment offered to potential agents advertised in the national newspapers.

The other operational level was the field officer who was dropped by one means or another into 'the field', as they all euphemistically called occupied Europe, with no danger money. They were drawn from all levels of society and were paid according to their rank, on a monthly basis in advance, into their bank account in the usual way.

Recruitment into the service in the 1960s was to some extent who you knew, or more likely who knew you, but that all changed with the advent of the Cold War and Philby, Burgess and Maclean's defection to the Soviets. Public perception of these men is that they were traitors to their country – and so they were during the Cold War – but in SOE's early days during the war they served their country well. Both Burgess and Philby helped with the creation of SOE experimental stations and training schools that were at the centre of the preparation of agents who were to be launched into Europe.

The experimental stations' purpose was to provide working tools (generally of a lethal kind) for the saboteurs and demolition experts who were to be dropped, often literally, into Europe. Other options were to land agents from submersibles on to deserted beaches, so there was a training station on Staines Reservoir with a seagoing branch in Fishguard Bay. Wireless research, production and packing for dispatch – often by parachute – was centred on Wembley, and a camouflage section was housed in London's Natural History Museum. One station, based in Roydon in Essex, was where papers and passes of all kinds were forged in the 'dodgy documents' section, which was taken over by SIS after the war. It moved into Artillery Mansions in Victoria Street, where I got to know it, just across the road from St Ermin's Hotel.

Almost all the experimental stations produced bizarre explosive devices of one kind or another, such as a bicycle pump that blew up more than tyres (they were exchanged quietly for the real ones on German-owned bicycles to wait for a flat tyre). The most popular device was the 'clam', which the cloak-and-dagger boys and girls could put in their pocket and quietly plant on a motor vehicle or even an aeroplane if they had a chance. It had a few ounces of very high explosive and could blow a hole in most things, but its most important attribute was that it could be timed so the agent could disappear before the device went off. They cost 5 shillings to make and the Russians took almost a million of them (and even then they were always asking for more).

Weapons of all kinds were created in the experimental stations, including one that I experienced to my cost called the PIAT (Projectile Anti-Tank). It was an absolute pig to use as it was difficult to cock and when you pulled the trigger it had a kick like a mule that could knock the operator back a couple of feet – although the explosion it could cause up to a 100 yards away could be very satisfying!

Some of the senior instructors in the training schools became legendary figures and one such was Major George Rheam, the commanding officer of one of the most effective training schools in the network, who some described as the founder of modern industrial sabotage. Rheam had a great deal of practical experience in working with heavy electrical switchgear, transformers and railway traction equipment before the war and knew about the design and construction of such heavy equipment. Little was known about how explosives could disable or destroy heavy machinery as the war began, so Rheam's experience gave a unique background to the subject he was teaching. He demonstrated the effects of explosives on machinery by turning his training school grounds into a demolition derby with suitable machinery and plant scrounged from scrapyards for miles around. He was able to show his potential agents where to put the least amount of explosive for the largest amount of damage. He somehow acquired a German Junkers 88 bomber (used), a Great Western Railways locomotive and a Churchill tank to show his pupils their weak points and where to put the explosive charge. Rheam had the knack of being able to look over a factory and within a few minutes locate its bottlenecks and show the way they could be destroyed, sometimes in very inventive ways.

The syllabus of a training school would vary a lot with each intake of agents and the country or region in Europe from where they came and generally were going back to, although each course had some aspects in common in its tuition. In an SOE pamphlet entitled *Training Lectures and Statistics*, probably meant for instructors, a few points are worth mentioning, although most of it was stating obvious and common sense. The average SOE operative (if there was such an animal) had such a diverse range of tasks to perform, in so many countries and cultures, that writing a guidebook would have been difficult, but there were a few common rules of conduct.

A target was defined as anything that was helpful to the enemy, but concern was expressed in the manual for the local population because the enemy's favourite reply to subversive attacks was often to penalise the locals. If possible, an attack was to be made to look like an accident or an act of God and if the locals were inclined to tolerate the enemy it suggested delaying action until public opinion had swung away from the Nazis. New organisers of resistance groups were urged to concentrate on small or easy targets with only one or two collaborators, as a successful attack, however small, would build self-confidence in the team, and could inspire others to come forward. When planning an attack, operatives were advised to consider the possibility of using bad weather or time of year, the state of the moon or national holidays to present an opportunity to press it home.

When surveying a factory that was heavily guarded by the Germans, operatives were to consider the possibility of attacking small workshops that supplied the factory with sub-assemblies, as they would provide a softer target than the protected one. Electrical supplies that fed the enemy's factories sometimes used transformers that were out of town and unguarded, also hydroelectric plant, pipelines and telephone lines, so saboteurs were to consider the weakest points of communications and energy transmissions. If the target was too difficult to penetrate, then overhead cables or poles were to be destroyed and operatives were urged to remember that every attacker who got away from a successful attack was worth a lot more to the leader than a newcomer.

If any of the group was caught it could endanger the future of the organisation, so operatives were to never leave any wounded – a stark warning. They were also warned to never appear jubilant following an attack as it may draw attention to them and make others suspicious. Instead, they were told to go about their work after a success without celebrating because their time would surely come ...

The main effort of SOE's Resistance Army in its European battlefield had to be concentrated on the all-important Atlantic coast, where the assault on Hitler's fortress would be, when and wherever it might come. In no previous war and in no other theatre of war were resistance forces so closely linked to the main military effort.

The geopolitical direction of the organisation came from London, since most of the senior Allied military staff that would plan and direct the D-Day assault on Normandy were there, but it was the southern flank of Hitler's fortress in the Mediterranean that was assaulted first. Churchill had described it as the 'soft underbelly of the Axis' (although it proved not to be as soft as he suggested), so the SOE station in Cairo had an important function in making ready the sites of future landings.

SOE had divided its organisation up into individual sections for each country and sometimes it had several subdivisions in a country, to deal with the various quasi-political interests of the diverse resistance groups. There were, for instance, five subdivisions in France; an important group here was the communist one, which was almost always one of the most effective fighting groups – if perhaps not always as effective as it made out.

Polish resistance to the Nazis had been fierce and unremitting from the beginning and pre-dated SOE's operational activity by many months. The Polish reaction to Hitler's assault on their country in September 1939 was immediate and almost universal; in addition to the escape of the brilliant team of Polish cryptographers, a whole exodus of young men and women began to travel to Britain to bolster the Allies' war effort. When Britain stood alone after Dunkirk her only allies were the Polish people who had escaped from the Nazis in their droves – enough trained Polish pilots escaped to form two squadrons in the RAF and accounted for more than 200 German aircraft shot down in the Battle of Britain.

The Polish Army fought with great courage (and venom) against the Germans – the author witnessed the results when he went to visit the graves of the men of his own regiment, the Queen's Royal Regiment, who fell at the Battle of Monte Cassino in Italy. Viewed from the heights of Monte Cassino Monastery an adjacent hill appeared to be covered in snow even though it was the height of summer, we were told that it was an array of tombstones of the Polish soldiers who had fallen in the battle. They had all escaped from Germany's advancing panzer divisions, most of them with the help of a resistance movement that spontaneously sprang into life to meet the need to escape as it arose.

The soldiers of Monte Cassino were not the only ones. Strong contingents of Polish escapees came to Britain and joined SOE; so many in fact that they were allocated several training schools of their own. One was an extraordinary Polish woman, Krystyna Skarbek, who was the first of her sex to join SOE. Her incredible adventures in the resistance have been the subject of several books. When Krystyna began she was given a British cover story and papers under the name of Christine Granville, which she adopted as her true name after the war.

Krystyna (later Christine) ran an escape route over the high Tatra Mountains into neutral Hungary in some of the worst snowstorms in living memory, acting as a guide for Polish and RAF escapees into Hungary (which had not yet joined the war). Sir Owen O'Malley, who was the head of the British Legation in its capital, Budapest, helped Christine with resources and money; he telexed his Foreign Office masters in London to ask if he could have a budget to help the escaping men. He was astonished by London's reply as the Foreign Office was not known for its generosity – he was given an unlimited budget for the purpose.

Christine's adventures became the stuff of legend. She rescued many people, including sixteen British airmen who spoke no Polish at all. They were housed in a Warsaw asylum for the deaf and dumb until they joined the escape route to freedom. Christine carried out many feats of espionage, she also smuggled rolls of film recording the German Army massing on the Russian border in 1941 before it attacked the Soviet Union. Her many exploits were rewarded with the George Medal, the OBE and the *Croix de Guerre*, and she survived the war only to be murdered in 1952 by an obsessive colleague with whom she worked at the Reform Club in Pall Mall.

Christine was one of many Polish nationals who were trained by the SOE to join its underground network and who provided London with a great deal of valuable intelligence. A joint SOE operation with the Polish Home Army provided vital data about the V2 rocket and also described the scale of the Holocaust, as well as details about the German troop movements through Poland on their way to the Russian front.

The Polish Home Army staged an uprising against its German occupiers as the Red Army advanced towards Warsaw, but the Russians held back on military assistance and the Poles suffered more than 200,000 casualties, many from Nazi executions. The Special Duties Flights of the RAF that were supporting the uprising by dropping supplies of arms were refused landing rights at Soviet-held airfields, even if they had suffered battle damage. They were even attacked by Soviet Air Force fighters despite the Russians being our allies. The Russians were not the friends of the Polish people. The British nation owes much to those Poles who escaped to fight for Britain – more than we can ever repay.

Much of the strength of the German Army was sucked away in events in eastern Europe as the Nazis invaded one country after another in preparation for the assault on Soviet Russia, all of which proved fertile ground for SOE to create mayhem among the Nazi occupying forces. They sent many missions into Czechoslovakia. An outstanding one was Operation Anthropoid, which was the assassination of the Protector of Bohemia, Moravia and Slovakia, SS-Obergruppenführer Reinhard Heydrich. He was better known as the 'Butcher of Czechoslovakia' for his executions and murders of so many Czechoslovakian people.

A team was trained to carry out an attack on Heydrich. The agents taking part in the operation were Czechoslovakians Josef Gahcik and Jan Rubis, who each were SOE operatives trained at Brickendonbury Manor in Hertfordshire. Joseph and Jan boarded a Halifax bomber at Tangmere Airfield – after signing their wills – to be parachuted into Czechoslovakia near Prague; they planned to attack Heydrich in his car as it slowed down on a sharp bend on his usual daily route from work. The Sten gun of an SOE man jammed at a critical moment and a running fight ensued in which Heydrich was badly wounded and subsequently died. The Nazi retribution on the Czechoslovakian population was swift and terrible. The village of Lidice where the Germans thought the SOE men had used a safe house was obliterated; the population were all shot or sent to a concentration camp and the village buildings were demolished – not a trace of Lidice remains today.

The SOE operatives became fugitives and took refuge in the church of St Cyril and Methodius in Prague while the Gestapo rounded up more than 6,000 Czech civilians, of whom only half survived their imprisonment. The SOE men were betrayed to the SS, who surrounded the church where they were hidden and after a long gun battle the survivors turned their guns on themselves rather than be captured. The operation met its objective but the price was so high that Czechoslovakian resistance in Prague was damaged to the extent that it was not able to resume its activities again until the end of the war. (The author visited St Cyril's during one of his trips to Prague a few years ago and was surprised and impressed to see that flowers had been laid at the church for the SOE men who gave their lives more than sixty years ago in that desperate venture.)

Hungary tried hard to maintain its neutrality but was placed under German military occupation, giving SOE little time to contact and develop potential resistance leaders, and there was a similar situation in Albania. A team lead by Julian Amery parachuted into the region, only to find that the communists were fighting the republicans rather than the Germans in an internecine war between themselves. Albania and Hungry were therefore never major factors in the resistance struggle against the Germans, but Yugoslavia was another matter. As with most eastern European countries and some in the west, there was more than one resistance horse to back in the rugged terrain of the Kingdom of Yugoslavia. The main ones were the Chetniks under Draža Mihailović and the communists under Josip Broz Tito.

The Chetniks contacted SOE first and as a result immediately received a supply of arms and supplies under the supervision of an advance party led by Major 'Marko' Hudson. He later encountered Tito's communists and came to the conclusion that he led a much more effective campaign against the German occupying forces than the Chetniks, who he subsequently discovered were actually co-operating with the Germans. SOE support was immediately redirected to the communists, who made very good use of all that they were given and became a painful thorn in the side of the German Army, engaging it in some major battles.

The royalist government in London favoured the Chetniks, who were pro-royalists, so the rearrangement of support was not well received and made relations between the government and SOE very difficult. However, Tito's resistance movement proved to be so effective that it was obviously the only movement to back. Tito's group soon grew into an army and became a major force in defeating its country's occupiers. His army actually outfought the occupation forces, who had to retreat out of Yugoslavia. Tito's campaign against the Germans was outstanding, his performance in Yugoslavia made the communist group the most effective resistance movement in Europe.

It was now the turn of Greece to be invaded by the Italians, who met a desperate defence from the Greek Army for some months, but when the Germans came to the aid of the Italians the Greeks were eventually overwhelmed. British troops had been sent to support their ally but had to retire – some to Crete and some to Egypt – as the Greek Army surrendered. British policy discouraged any form of resistance or sabotage by SOE in Greece as it was felt that it might have serious effects on relations with her neighbour, Turkey. That was a prime consideration in any action in the Mediterranean region, but Cyprus was a different matter. It had been captured by German paratroopers and the island was now under the command of General Major Heinrich Kreipe.

A small SOE group consisting of Major Patrick Leigh Fermour, Captain William Moss and two Cretan agents, Georgios Tyrakis and Emmanouil Paterakis, decided to kidnap the general from under the noses of his own troops and take him to Egypt. They landed in Crete, some by parachute and some by sea, and were sustained by the population as they made their plans to ambush their quarry on his way to his quarters in the evening. The small party did that in a most audacious way and hiked to the coast with their prisoner to rendezvous with a British motor launch to take them to Egypt. It was a very neat SOE operation that left many senior German officers serving in the more remote posts of Nazi-occupied Europe feeling uncertain about their security.

Meanwhile, the priorities in Greece had changed. The railway through Greece had been identified as a main supply route for Rommel's Afrika Corps fighting the 8th Army in the desert, where things were not going well for the British. They needed all the help they could get, so the disruption of the railway supply route took priority over possible Turkish concerns. An SOE party commanded by Colonel Edie Myers parachuted into Greece to destroy the rail link and found several different guerrilla groups active in the mountains (as ever). One of them was the republican EDES and another was inevitably the communist ELAS group, who co-operated with Colonel Myers in blowing up a central span of the railway viaduct at Gorgopotamos. The rail link was cut for some months, but the Italians who had been guarding the viaduct eventually repaired it, so another six-man Commando party returned to destroy another of the rail viaducts at Asopos. That cut the rail connection from Thessaloniki through to Athens and Piraeus for the second time and more permanently.

Intelligence was as important as sabotage in the operations, and SOE teams regularly reported on the strengths and movements of the Luftwaffe to their headquarters in Cairo. The repair and servicing of German aircraft on the two main airfields near Athens was an important indication of the *Wehrmacht's* plans and capabilities in the region.

SOE's increasing activity in the Balkans irritated Stalin, who regarded it as *his* sphere of influence, so when the preparation for Operation Husky (the invasion of Sicily) began he was reassured that the target was not the Balkans. Co-operation between SOE and the Russian security services then increased notably and as a result covert SOE flights into northern Norway were given clearance (which had been denied before) to divert to Murmansk in an emergency. The clandestine exchanges increased even more, and the first NKVD (Russian Internal Affairs) agent was parachuted into Germany in late 1943 from a British Halifax bomber.

Aircraft usage by SOE was at a premium in the early days as senior RAF officers took the view that their bombers had a great deal to do in attacking the enemy and resented their diversion for any other purposes. They were overruled and SOE was donated the services of 138 and 161 Squadrons, based at Tempsford Airfield, by a grudging RAF. The squadrons were equipped with light Lysander aircraft. These workhorses for SOE could carry three passengers and two panniers loaded with weapons over a range of about 700 miles. For longer hauls with greater loads there were a few Hudson light bombers, which had a range of 2,000 miles carrying a dozen passengers, but they required a landing strip more than twice as long as that needed by the Lysander. The aircraft could land on a rough dirt strip 400 yards long, and during the war transported almost 150 agents to and from occupied Europe under the noses of the Nazis and often at great risk.

One Lysander, piloted by Guy Lockhart, took off from Tempsford with a 'Joe', as they called their mysterious passengers, for a pick-up at Arbigny in occupied France, but the French reception committee had spent too much time in the local bistro. They had not chosen a good landing site and had laid out a flare path across a ditch. Guy's aircraft came to a dramatic halt in the ditch, making his aircraft totally unserviceable. He and his passenger set fire to the plane and made a rapid escape before a German patrol came to investigate the bonfire. Guy and his party made their way south towards the coast. The French resistance found them a friendly boat, which took them to Gibraltar, where Squadron Leader Lockhart learned that he had been awarded a medal for his exploits.

Not all agents were men, more than 3,000 women agents joined SOE to be sent into Nazi-occupied Europe to join the resistance and cause the German forces much trouble and distress. The ladies were entering enemy territory, but a British Armed Forces Regulation banned them from carrying weapons so it took special authorisation by Winston Churchill to permit them to carry and use arms. Two of the first women agents to be parachuted into France were Andrée Borrel and Lise de Baissac, both fluent French speakers who specialised in locating drop zones for agents while posing as archaeologists. They and French resistance members risked their lives frequently – if they were out after curfew in suspicious circumstances it could mean that they would be sentenced to death.

Other women served in different ways, such as Patricia Martin who was an agent in the diplomatic community and serving in the Rome post as France fell to the German panzers but before Italy entered the war. She was asked by spymaster Wing Commander Winterbotham to find out Italy's intentions using her diplomatic connections to attend frequent functions where she came into contact with high-ranking Italian officers. Mussolini's son, Carolino, was among her confidantes so she was able to confirm MI6 and the government's fear that Italy intended to enter the war in alliance with Hitler.

Most women agents were young so Mary Lindell, the Comtesse de Milleville, was one of the oldest at 47 years old when she was flown from Tangmere in Sussex to Thalamy in France in the October Moon period. She was an MI9 agent helping downed RAF flyers and other escapees to flee from the Nazis using escape routes into Spain over the Pyrenees and on to Gibraltar.

Women made a huge contribution to the resistance movement and were particularly good at being wireless operators, or 'pianists' as they were called, and they could sometimes go unsuspected into places or past a checkpoint where a man could not. One pianist was carrying her wireless in a suitcase while walking in a Paris street when an official Gestapo car pulled up beside her. A senior Gestapo official leaned out of the window and asked what she had in the case. With a coquettish look she said, 'I have a radio transmitter here and I will be telling London all about you this evening.' Disarmed by the reply, the Gestapo man told her that she was far too pretty to be involved in that kind of nonsense and drove on. A man could not have handled a situation like that, so SOE had to be a truly equal opportunities employer.

In western Europe, the Germans had a very firm grip on the population and there were both winners and losers in the conflict with the resistance in some occupied countries. One of the disastrous losers was the resistance movement in Holland. Major Herman Giskes was the newly appointed head of German *Abwehr* counter-intelligence in Holland where he was able to devastate the Dutch government's secret service (or *Inlichtingendienst*) resistance operations in its own country.

Giskes was told by an informer that two SOE agents with a transmitter had been parachuted into Holland to set up a resistance network of agents. He responded to the informer, '*Gehen sie zum Nordpol mit ihren gesschichten* [go to the North Pole with your tales]'. He soon changed his mind when his *Abwehr* listening station intercepted an SOE transmitter in The Hague, reporting the safe arrival of the two agents who had begun their operations. Giskes' 'Operation *Englandspiel*', which he recounts in his book *London Calling*, started with the capture of the two agents followed by many other arrests, but what was crucial was the seizing of their radios and documents. It enabled Giskes to receive and send messages to London Central pretending to be an SOE agent. In addition, German listening services had also tuned into Tempsford's air traffic control frequencies to monitor the flights of aircraft carrying agents. Every 'drop' into Holland was intercepted and captured without London realising it and almost one in five of the planes delivering supplies and agents were shot down because the Luftwaffe knew they were coming. Then, two Dutch agents, Dourlein and Ubbink, who were code-named 'Cabbage' and 'Chive', were dropped into Holland and captured by Giskes but managed to escape. Making their way to Switzerland they told staff at the British Embassy that SOE networks in Holland had been penetrated and they were completely controlled by the Germans.

The two agents were sent back to Britain, only to be thrown into jail because Major Giskes had used an SOE transmitter to report that the two escapees were Gestapo agents. The total penetration of the Dutch resistance movement by German *Abwehr* intelligence could not last, and when he had squeezed all he could from his captives Giskes sent a wireless message to SOE in London:

```
Gentlemen
Recently you have been trying to do business without our
assistance STOP We think this rather unfair in view of
```

```
our long and successful co-operation as your sole agents
STOP But never mind, whenever you come to pay a visit
to the continent you may be assured that you will be
received with the same care and result as all those you
sent us before STOP So long STOP
```

Thus, *Englandspiel* came to an end and more than fifty agents that Giskes was holding were sent to a concentration camp, of whom only two survived the war. An inquest into the operational failure of SOE by both the British and Dutch governments was carried out after the war. They found that security checks built into the transmissions of agents in Holland were ignored and the standard practice of dropping an agent unannounced into Holland to make sure the operation was going well never took place. The Dutch Commission of Enquiry visited London after the war only to be told that the thousands of transcripts of radio messages that had passed between Dutch agents and London had been destroyed.

Even Herman Giskes (now a civilian), who gave evidence at the enquiry into the matter in London was puzzled by the disastrous lack of security control throughout the operation. The whole thing seemed like a cover-up for SOE's Dutch Section in London, but the debate as to the rights and wrongs of the 'North Pole Operation', as Giskes named it, still goes on. The defeat of the SOE operation in Holland had far-reaching effects on Allied plans. General Alanbrook, who was a chief military advisor to the British prime minister, wrote in his *War Diaries* that the assault on Europe should have been made in Holland. That option had to be discarded as it was felt that in preparation for a successful landing the destruction of communications and transport facilities of the defenders needed to be carried out by an effective resistance force.

The preparation for the D-Day landings was now centred on the coast of Normandy, but the activities of SOE had to include the strengthening of its actions throughout France. The mounting pressure on German forces and their supporting infrastructure by the resistance took many forms, but their efforts had to be carefully orchestrated. A concentration of resistance efforts in the Normandy region could have led the Germans to believe that the D-Day landings would take place there, so not only did resistance attacks take on many activities but they also had to be diffused all over Belgium, and particularly in France.

One important action took place in the French town of Creil where the SOE agent Jean Savy discovered a huge ammunition dump containing more than 2,000 V-1 Flying Bomb components and their launch sites adjacent to it. It was an indication of the flexibility of the RAF's 'special duties'-based air taxi service that Savy was able to immediately hitch an unscheduled lift on a Lysander to bring a detailed description of the dump back to London. Further careful air and covert ground reconnaissance enabled the RAF to pinpoint and destroy the huge store of Flying Bombs and their warheads in raids on a stone quarry at Saint-Leu-d'Esserent, where the warheads were stored. It would be difficult to estimate the number of lives saved in southern England by this action. The 'buzz bombs', as the V-1 was known to us, wrought havoc among the people there, as I know to my family's cost.

Another SOE attack that blunted the Luftwaffe's capability was an attack on a factory at Figeac, in France, that manufactured 300 variable pitch propellers a week for its bombers. With the direction of the friendly works foreman, who told them where to place small explosive charges in a few essential machine tools, they brought the production of this important facility to a juddering halt.

Factories were not the only aspect of the German war effort attacked by SOE operatives. They blocked the railway line between Toulon and Marseilles with a derailment in a tunnel (always the most difficult place to cope with a derailment) near Cassis. Having caused the first problem they complicated its repair by destroying the breakdown train that came to clear the wreck, and this kept the important rail link blocked for weeks. The same group put thirty railway engines out of commission in one week and damaged thirty more, before most of its members were arrested after being denounced by a Frenchman – he was tracked down and executed after the war.

Denunciation and arrest were not the only dangers for resistance groups working with SOE. One group was on a dropping ground in France one dark night when a parachuted container full of grenades hit the ground too hard. The container went off with a bang loud enough to wake up a nearby German SS unit, who pursued the group that had arranged the reception. One of them climbed a tree where he had to stay for a day and a night, still managing to note the strength and methods of the SS search party for future use.

Special Duties squadrons of the RAF were able to supply the resisters, but there were never enough supplies or arms for the groups. SOE was able to get some medical aid to them that was often badly needed in the remote hideouts in the forests or mountains of Europe. One medical officer accompanying a group who had slept overnight in a French chateau was surprised by a unit of German counter-intelligence troops that burst in upon them. The group reacted vigorously to the threat. It counter-attacked across the gardens of the chateau, led by the medical aid officer, revolver in hand and wearing nothing but a monocle. The event was remembered with relish by the communards of the region long after the war was over.

SOE activities on the coast were sometimes in support of regular troops, and particularly centred on sabotaging the ports on the French coast such as Bordeaux and Saint-Nazaire, and included the assault on Dieppe and the raid on Bruneval. Proposals were made to slip agents ashore under cover of Commando raids but no agent really wanted to begin his work in a fully alerted area during or after a raid. They were able to help in other ways, however. Commandos planned a successful raid on shipping in Bordeaux Docks with a small team armed with limpet mines designed by the research stations of SOE, which also gave training in how to use them. The Saint-Nazaire Raid (Operation Chariot) was designed to destroy the only dry dock on the French coast offering a potential refuge for Germany's biggest battleship *Tirpitz*. The great warship posed a constant threat to the Royal Navy and British shipping in the Atlantic, so in preparation SOE agents had carried out a technical survey of the installations in the dock and harbour. Training was given to demolition parties on how to place explosive charges to best effect on a mock-up of the dock gate mechanism erected at Brickendonbury Experimental Explosives Station. They also made up an explosive charge of one and a half tons of TNT to place in the bows of HMS *Campbeltown*, which rammed and later blew up the dock gates to destroy any possibility of the *Tirpitz* using Saint-Nazaire as a haven.

The Dieppe Raid was the subject of much scouting and advice by SOE, for what turned out to be a most unsuccessful operation whose secret was revealed only recently by academic research into contemporary documents. The main objective was to capture one of the Enigma machines* being

---

* The Kriegsmarine Enigma had added another rotor six months before the raid, making Bletchley Park unable to read U-Boat transmissions. The objective of the raid was only disclosed recently by research of contemporary documents by a Canadian University.

used by the *Kriegsmarine* in its harbour headquarters but it was unsuccessful as the port entrance was too heavily defended. However, it did gain some lessons for the coming landings in Normandy, the main one being to avoid 'bumping' into an offshore German convoy as the gunfire alerted the German garrison.

The Bruneval Raid was a small scale but important operation to capture, dismantle and spirit away a German *Würzburg* radar device to determine how the thing worked. SOE's provision of a German speaker to shout confusing orders in the dark did not help much as nearly all the garrison was asleep and the only sentry could not find the telephone to sound the alarm. The operation was completed in a couple of hours, enabling the raiding party to give the scientists a working radar device that helped them understand its mechanism. The technical knowledge gained from the examination enabled British scientists to devise a method of blinding German radar using strips of aluminium foil cut to a specific width to coincide with the German radar frequency signal. The 'window', as the strips were called, was scattered from British bombers and created confusing ghost images on German radar screens.

Commando and SOE activities along the French coast and mainland continued with small actions by aggressive teams of agents and elite military forces. Their hit-and-run tactics infuriated Hitler and as a result he issued an order that all sabotage units, in uniform or out, who fell into German hands were to be slaughtered to the last man. This murderous order did not affect the attitude of the personnel of SOE and the resistance very much as they were invariably in civilian clothes and as such were outside the Geneva Convention. They knew very well what to expect if they were caught, particularly by the Gestapo or SS troops.

The battle between British intelligence and German counter-intelligence intensified as the D-Day assault was seen by all as inevitable. The uncertainty for the defenders was where and when the Allies would strike. MI6 developed a string of operations designed to keep Hitler guessing as to where the blow would fall. The people in Broadway gave him several options, would it be Norway, Belgium, Pas-de-Calais or Bordeaux? The deception operation known as 'Bodyguard' (because Churchill decided that the true secret should be hidden in a 'bodyguard of lies') leaked every possible landing place to Berlin by the devious use of double agents and signals intelligence.

A part of the Bodyguard plan was Operation Fortitude, which was the creation of a virtual army seen from the air as row upon row of tented camps – but there were no troops in them. Plywood aeroplanes and blow-up tanks with one of the Allies' best generals, George Patton, in command created a virtual invasion force to deceive the *Abwehr*. Hitler fell for it, and he made his best guess as Pas-de-Calais for the expected landings; this was confirmed when Bletchley Park decoded a wireless signal to Tokyo from the Japanese Embassy in Berlin after a personal briefing from the Führer. Pas-de-Calais was closest to their English base and the most likely place for an assault, Hitler told the ambassador. He had decided to keep much of his military strength there and he would fortify it strongly.

Even more convincing was the fact that General Patton was visited regularly in well-publicised meetings by General Bernard Montgomery, who was known to be directing the preparations for D-Day. That was another deception, because the visitor was not Montgomery but Clifton James, his lookalike, dressed up as the general to take photographs with Patton for the press as a part of the well-planned long-term cover story.

The disinformation programme was created by both MI5 and MI6 in conjunction with the use of German agents, who had been captured as they landed in Britain and 'turned' by the security services, to give highly imaginative reports of what the Allies were *not* doing in preparation for the landings that were never going to take place. One stream of fictitious reports sent by a double agent code-named 'Garbo' were so convincing to the Germans that they sent extra funding to pay imaginary agents who Garbo had invented with the aid of his controllers. A senior American general, Bedell Smith, gave it as his opinion that the Bodyguard operation, and in particular the Fortitude part of it, was the biggest single hoax to mislead Hitler achieved by the Allies during the war.

Meanwhile, the drumbeat of military preparations in southern England sounded faster and faster as the build-up for the great assault grew. SOE activities increased massively as the time approached and resistance groups proliferated all over Europe, but particularly in France, as did their attacks despite squabbles between rival groups. The secret army was growing fast, as were the number of tasks being requested of them by SHAEF (Supreme Allied Expeditionary Forces) to disrupt the enemy's rail and road communications and other tasks ahead of the D-Day landings.

The success of the resistance actions and deception programmes was going to be especially important to the Allies as they planned to land only thirty-seven divisions in France compared with the almost sixty German divisions occupying France. The diversion of at least some of the enemy forces from the battlefield by any means that SOE and the Resistance could devise was going to be essential to the success of the Allied landings. Disruption of the German Army's transport system to stop it moving its troops to reinforce the defenders of the beaches would also prove of critical importance to the outcome of the battle.

SOE COMMUNICATIONS

Preparation for the D-Day assault included visits by SOE personnel to army units to explain what they could do to help on the day and the days following, much to the surprise of the regular soldiers. However, when they got over their surprise there were many requests for the targeting of specific objectives. Some of the acts were not sabotage but sometimes the reverse.

'Counter-scorching' was the preservation of structures and objects that the Germans might want to destroy. The preservation of bridges was a popular activity among French resisters, partly because any German explosive charges they dismantled could be used elsewhere. The contribution of the Resistance Army that SOE had created meant that no German in an occupied country felt safe, particularly in France where the threat they posed kept eight divisions busy and away from the firing line at a critical time.

The numbers of Frenchmen joining the resistance increased enormously as it became evident that D-Day was drawing near – some wanted to redeem their reputation so they would not be accused of collaboration. More than 4,000 tons of arms and supplies had been dropped to the resistance groups since SOE had begun to nurture the movement; now there were more resistance fighters than weapons for them to use. The attacks on the Germans doubled and redoubled as the day of liberation began to dawn, and the beaches of Normandy were not the only battlefields in France. The cost was high, however. Hundreds of resisters, as well as many innocent bystanders, were rounded up and put into concentration camps, many never to come out again. More than 200,000 French men and women were killed or died in the camps and almost half of them were resistance fighters. Nevertheless, the secret army continued to grow.

Many of those who were caught were doing the most dangerous job in the resistance in occupied Europe – that of the wireless operator. The transmitter they generally used was a short-wave Morse transceiver, or transmitter and receiver combined, called the B Mark II, one of which is on show in the Secret War Galleries of the Imperial War Museum. The device weighed 30lb and fitted into a small suitcase. Its frequency range was quite wide – 3.5 to 16 megacycles a second – but with a maximum output of 20 watts its output was quite weak. To compensate for that it required a well-spread 70ft aerial that would have been difficult to conceal from prying eyes.

To determine the exact frequency within which the set would transmit required at least two crystals; one for daytime transmissions and another to transmit at night. They were delicate and could shatter if they were mishandled or dropped, and they were of a size that could fit into the palm of the hand so they would be fairly easy to wrap up into clothing in a suitcase or some other well-cushioned place. The transceiver itself was difficult to disguise if an operator was stopped for a search, although occasionally an agent would be able to bluff him or herself out of a dangerous situation – women (generally young ones) were better at doing that than men.

The devices the operators had to carry around made them vulnerable, but not as vulnerable as when they were actually transmitting to their London-based controller. The *Abwehr* intelligence service had many direction finding teams and they were always listening to try and get a 'fix' on a transmission and could do so in a matter of minutes. A long transmission could bring the Gestapo to an operator's door within half an hour, but they had a trick that enabled them to do so more quickly. They systematically cut off the electricity supply substation by substation as the operator began to transmit. By listening for an interruption in transmission it enabled the Gestapo to pinpoint an area for its counter-espionage team and cut down the time it needed to get to the location of the operator to arrest him or her. This was not always simple as the operator was usually armed, and just as usually, had at least one bodyguard, so gun battles often transpired. The German counter-intelligence service lost a number of its most experienced men that way and the others became less than enthusiastic about breaking in on wireless operators in the process of transmission.

In spite of this, a number of transceivers were captured so SOE devised security tricks for its operators such as introducing specific spelling mistakes or other deliberate variations in a message to indicate that the operator was under duress. Agents who were caught often did co-operate, sometimes with a gun to their head, and so would begin a deadly game between the Gestapo and the operator in London with the captured agent in the middle.

The variations in a message could not necessarily be depended upon as mistakes could be accidental, either in coding (which was very complex and often made under emotional pressure), transmission or even in interception. 'Fingerprinting', which identified the 'fist' of the agent, was another method of detecting the identity of an operator. Each operator had his or her own style of sending Morse on the key; it could be as distinctive as handwriting. Agents were therefore asked to make a recording of a typical transmission before they left to go into the field so that any doubt as to the pattern of transmission could be compared. The German wireless telegraphy teams soon became aware of that trick, though, and made a practice of recording any SOE transmissions so that they could copy the style of an agent they captured and start many 'radio games' with the British controllers.

Another form of messaging began in the summer of 1941 when the BBC began to broadcast messages quite openly that had a prearranged secret meaning of their own. These would provide a major communications service for SOE. It helped to direct the activities of the Resistance Army with little risk. SOE controllers might want to warn or inform an individual, a group or the whole network of agents of an impending event such as an aircraft landing or drop, confirm the bona fides of a newly arrived agent or announce the beginning of a military assault (such as D-Day).

Strange and meaningless messages, such as 'Alphonse has tight trousers' or 'Marie's shoes are black', were broadcast nightly after the evening news following the announcement, 'here are a few messages for our friends in Europe'. We could hear them broadcast and would wonder what they meant – the author remembers the mystery of it all as his family sat around the radio in a sitting room in warmth and safety listening to the messages to the resistance. The meaningless words and phrases that were a call to action against the Nazis clearly spelt danger to our anonymous friends and it brought home to us the drama and danger of the SOE agents and the secret Resistance Army.

The messages continued night after night for almost two years, reminding us how men and women of the resistance were out after the curfew (dangerous in itself) to sabotage the German war machine in hostile occupied Europe. The increasing number of messages that were broadcast began to take its toll on the announcers, who protested that they could only read nonsense messages accurately for about fifteen minutes. Brendan Braken, the Minister of Information, had to step in to limit the number of messages that announcers would be asked to read but as D-Day approached he gave authority to increase the number again.

The BBC surpassed itself in its broadcasts of news and coded messages as the invasion fleet assembled. Among them was a message quoting the lines of a particular poem. The German *Abwehr* knew that the poem was significant, but not its purpose, and so they imagined that it was a call for railway workers to cause a major disruption of French railways. The full meaning of the message seemed to be confirmed when almost 1,000 interruptions of various kinds occurred in the French rail network.

The BBC had broadcast to 'our friends in Europe' the first lines of the poem *Chanson d'Automne*, or *The Autumn Song*, on 1 June 1944. Its opening lines later became famous; it alerted the French resistance leaders to the fact that Operation Overlord would be launched within two weeks. The words have taken their place as one of the best-known poems in the French language. Its first line read out that evening was, 'The long sobs of autumn violins'.

French resistance leaders who were in on the secret began their preparations for supporting the assault on the beaches. The people of France anticipated with mixed hope and anguish as they knew that the battle would rage across French soil. In London, General de Gaulle knew nothing of the D-Day plans because his Free French organisation was not thought to be secure following a leakage of information about Operation Menace in Dakar. The British government and intelligence community was very nervous about the security of its secrets and there was no greater secret than the time and place of the D-Day landings.

De Gaulle was summoned to see Churchill on the evening of 4 June as the invasion fleet was proceeding to its assembly points south of the Isle of Wight for its momentous voyage to the shores of Normandy. Churchill broke the news to the French leader at the last moment and then asked him if he minded French troops being used in the operation (the question had already been answered, as the fleet was already at sea with French soldiers aboard). De Gaulle immediately agreed to his countrymen spearheading the invasion force in the liberation of France, but to say that he was not happy about the cavalier way that he had been treated was an understatement.

The following morning French troops were some of the first ashore as dawn broke, followed closely by many others commanded by a French general. Meanwhile, French resistance leaders who had been made aware of the coming assault some four days before their leader were beginning on a huge programme of destruction of the roads, rail and communications that supported the German occupation forces.

The nightly broadcasts of the BBC had been listened to with high expectation waiting for the next lines of the poem to be broadcast – they did not have long to wait. On 5 June, the BBC in London broadcast the next lines of the poem *Autumn Song* after the late night news at 11.15 p.m. – 'Wound my heart with a monotonous languor'.

Allied forces were about to land in France within the next few hours so the long-planned sabotage campaign of the French resistance to paralyse the French railway system and telephone communications gathered to an even faster pace. Its actions were designed to damage and reduce the German Army's ability to react to the Allied assault, which was coming via an Allied Armada of 5,000 ships at dawn the following day. It would unleash an invading host on to the beaches of Normandy. At the German 15th Army headquarters near the Belgian border they had been listening for the poem for weeks. A highly stylised version of the event was given in the screenplay of the film *The Longest Day*:

Lieutenant Colonel Hellmuth Meyer was the 15th Army's Intelligence Officer; he also headed the only counter-intelligence team on the invasion front. At the heart of the set-up was a thirty man radio interception crew who worked in shifts around the clock in a concrete bunker crammed full of the most delicate radio equipment. Their job was to listen, nothing more but each man was an expert who spoke three languages fluently and there was hardly a word, hardly a stutter of Morse code whispering through the either from Allied sources that they did not hear. Meyer's men were so experienced and their equipment so sensitive that they were able to pick up calls from radio transmitters in military police jeeps in England over a hundred miles away. That had been a great help to Meyer. American and British MPs, chatting with one another by radio as they directed troop convoys, had helped him no end in compiling a list of the various divisions stationed in England. For some time now however, Meyer's operators had not been able to pick up any more of those calls which was significant. A strict radio silence had been imposed which was yet another clue to the many he already had that the invasion was close at hand.

In January, six months before Admiral Wilhelm Canaris, then Chief of German Military Intelligence had given Meyer the details of a fantastic two-part signal broadcast from the BBC which he said the Allies would use to alert the underground prior to the invasion. Canaris had warned that the Allies would broadcast hundreds of messages to the underground in the months preceding the assault but only a few would actually relate to D-Day. The remainder would be fake and deliberately designed to mislead and confuse but all the messages would have to be monitored in order not to miss the all-important ones. At first Meyer had been sceptical as it seemed madness to him to depend on one message and he knew from past experience that Berlin was often wrong. The Allies seemed to have fed every German agent from Stockholm to Ankara with the 'exact' place and date of the invasion and no two reports agreed but this time Meyer knew that Berlin was right. On the night of June 1 Meyer's men, after months of monitoring had intercepted the first part of the Allied message just as Canaris described it. It was not unlike the hundreds of other coded messages that Meyer's men had picked up during the previous months. Daily, after the regular BBC news broadcasts coded instructions in French, Dutch, Danish and Norwegian were read out to the underground (Poland was too far for the BBC transmitters to be reliably received so instructions went out to them by wireless). Most of the messages were meaningless to Meyer and it was exasperating to be unable to decode phrases as 'The Trojan War will not be held' or 'John has a long moustache'.

The message that followed the BBC news on the night of June 1 was announced in French 'Kindly listen to a few personal messages' which was the queue for Sergeant Walter Reichling to switch on his tape recorder. There was a pause and then '*Les sanglots longs des violins de l'automne*' made Reichling suddenly clap his hands over his earphones, then he tore them off and rushed out of the bunker and into Meyers quarters. 'Sir, the first part of the message – it's here', gasped the sergeant, so together they returned to the bunker to hear the recorded message. On either the first or the fifteenth of a month that Canaris had warned them to expect. Now they had to listen for the second line '*Blessent mon Coeur d'une langueur monotone*' [wounds my heart with monotonous languor], but what did it mean?

On the morning of 6 June 1944 the meaning became clear to all. I can distinctly remember the cultured voice of the BBC announcer, Alvar Liddell, proudly announcing 'D-Day has come' – so had the ultimate test of SOE and the secret Resistance Army that it had created in Europe.

FOUR

D-DAY

Plans for the D-Day landings plans had been first formulated in 1943 and were overseen by General Eisenhower's staff at their headquarters in Norfolk House in St James' Square, not a mile from St Ermin's Hotel. The Allied armies' assault on Hitler's '*Festung Europa*' (Fortress Europe) had to be planned meticulously by teams of military planners, some of whom felt the intensity of strain and responsibility of their work so much that they suffered nervous breakdowns. The burden of their decisions, as they planned how an armada of 1 million men and all their equipment would cross the Channel to attack Normandy's strong shore defences, weighed heavily.

Much of the planners' work was to solve the huge logistical problem of maintaining an unfailing supply to meet the needs of a multitude of fighting men while under attack by the defenders of the coast. The German garrisons had been in occupation there for several years and so had time to fortify defensive positions and build gun emplacements as well as cover the beaches with lethal obstacles and mines. The initial assault would not be easy, but once the Allied assault established a foothold it would need supplies to exploit the initial landings in the days and weeks following D-Day. The invaders would need enough 'stuff' to take on the best of the German panzers aggressively if they were going to succeed in their crusade to liberate Europe.

The French resistance could assist in initially delaying German troop movements and hampering communications that would enable the Anglo-

American host of soldiers to get ashore, but then they would have to win the battle. Failure was inconceivable for the Allied armies, as they would have been pushed back into the sea from where no retreat would be possible, Hitler's generals would never allow another mistake to take place like that of the successful British evacuation at Dunkirk.

Every conceivable item that the Allied army needed had to be landed and brought over the beaches, probably under enemy fire or air attack and in all kinds of weather. To make sure the initial wave of assault troops had everything that they needed to win the battle and survive was a huge logistical problem – but it was about to increase manyfold.

The original plans for the invasion consisted of an assault by three divisions supported by airborne troops and commandos over a 50-mile stretch of coastline, until General Bernard Montgomery was appointed to command the Allied land forces for the operation. He studied the plans and immediately increased the strength of the initial landings to five divisions with twenty more divisions to reinforce the beachhead within days. Supplying a force of this size and kind would require many thousands of tons of guns, ammunition and supplies that would have to be landed over open beaches; it was a massive challenge that could only be made more uncertain by the weather.

THE HARBOUR

The disastrous raid on Dieppe had shown clearly that the Germans were determined to deny the use of any European port on the Atlantic coast to Allied forces for as long as possible. The first day of the landings would require more than 10,000 tons of arms and ammunition to be unloaded on to small barges and run ashore through the ocean surf, which would only be possible if the weather was kind. The solution planners devised was to create not just one but two artificial harbours in what became the most ambitious and demanding military engineering project the world had seen at that time.

The need for a safe haven of calm water was demonstrated to Churchill and his staff on board the *Queen Mary* when they were on their way to the United States to co-ordinate the plan for Overlord with the American president and his staff. Churchill and his advisors all crammed into one of the liner's bathrooms for a presentation by Admiral Sir Dudley Pound while he stood on a lavatory seat. He asked them to imagine the water in the bath was the sea approaching the beachhead. A fleet of boats made of newspaper were launched into the bath and the waves of a storm were created by a junior officer with the energetic use of a bath brush. The paper fleet sank with all hands, so then a Mae West lifebelt was inflated and floated in the bath to represent a harbour into which another fleet of paper boats were launched but within the 'harbour'. The bath brush created yet another storm, but this time all the boats survived. With that simple demonstration the navy illustrated the need for calm water for the invasion fleet to carry the troops and their supplies to the shores of Normandy. From such small beginnings began the project that was to be the centre of the great assault on Hitler's Fortress Europe.

The choice of the Baie de la Seine as the site for the harbours drew a report from the Admiralty stating, 'Nothing favoured the choice of this coast for the construction of artificial harbours.' Maybe that was why the sleepy seaside town of Arromanches-les-Bains was chosen instead. It was probably less well defended and more vulnerable to Allied attack, and thus an easier location to install the prefabricated harbour, than other stretches of the formidable Atlantic Wall.

The Germans had built defences with strongpoints around all the French ports so the choice of the assault was a trade-off between the relative strength of these obstacles against many other difficulties. The rise and fall of the tide in that part of the Channel was exceptional – 24ft when spring tides occurred – promising to create huge problems in the construction of an artificial harbour. Any breakwater resting on the seabed that would be able to give ships the needed 30ft of draft beneath their keel would need to be well over 50ft tall just to reach the surface at high tide. In addition, if an area of calm water were created it would need piers on to which ships would be able to unload their cargos as the tide rose and fell.

Churchill had written a much quoted minute for the harbour planners:

> The pier heads need to float up and down with the tide … the anchor problem must be mastered … Let me have the best solution worked out … Do not argue the matter the difficulties will argue themselves.

And so they did. The problem was given to a sailor, Vice Admiral Hughes-Hallett, whose initial design for the harbours was proposed at a meeting where senior military and naval officers laughed outright at his preposterous idea.

The final shape and size of the harbours, however, was very similar to the admiral's original design – but the devil was in the construction details and they were going to be very complex indeed. The need for a floating wall was discussed, but walls do not normally float so experiments began with other means of creating a sheltered area of water bigger than Gibraltar's huge harbour.

Amphibious constructions invariably have many complications and the huge team of planners began with the basics. They had to study the nature and firmness of the coastal sands and mud on the foreshore and the pattern of the waves in the bay in all weathers. That had to be done under the noses (and guns) of the enemy without them detecting the small parties of army engineers who swam on to the beaches on moonless nights to drill into the seashore for sand, soil and rock samples. One of the Royal Engineers who had swum from a submarine on to the beach regaled us, in the St Ermin's bar, with the story of how he took samples and then lost them on the swim back, so he had to do it all over again.

Scientific tests on the samples enabled the planners to judge what load weight the sand and soil structure beneath the beaches would take and what stresses the waves could put on the structures due to be erected in the bay. I remember another strand of the study, which consisted of an announcement on the BBC asking for any old photographs that the public had of the beaches of France and Belgium – it got 80,000 replies.

Much thought and research was needed to create the stretch of calm and sheltered water needed as a haven for more than 5,000 ships carrying and supplying the invasion fleet across the Channel. A wave study carried out by Lieutenant Commander Lochner showed that a wave's force was only exerted less than an inch below the surface, so he concluded the 'wall' need not be anchored to the seabed. That meant that the wave barrier could float and Lochner began experiments on the village pond with his children's lilos, which they had used at the seaside. He created the breakwater while Mrs Lochner created the waves needed for the test with a biscuit tin lid. The experiment came to an abrupt end when Mrs Lochner fell into the pond, but by then Lochner was convinced that a floating breakwater could create the sheltered water of a harbour. So when Mrs Lochner had dried out the lieutenant commander began to arrange experiments for a floating wave barrier on a much larger scale.

Several types of the floating breakwater, called Bombardons, were designed in Victoria Street. They were 200ft long, 20ft wide and cruciform in shape, and they were constructed in Portsmouth Dockyard. Each looked distinctly unseaworthy. To everybody's surprise, they not only floated but quelled the waves quite well.

However, the Bombardon was just one of three elements to form the breakwaters of the Mulberry harbours. Massive hollow concrete caissons called Phoenix (rising from the waves) were also needed. They measured 200ft long, 50ft wide and weighed on average 6,000 tons. More than 140 of them were built and when they were laid end to end they provided a harbour wall 2½ miles long. They were built in many south coast inlets and the structures, as big as a block of flats, had to be towed across the Channel by tugs and carefully positioned before being flooded to settle firmly on the seabed. They would provide a solid, permanent breakwater and stable moorings for Liberty ships to discharge their cargos on to a dockside. They were more long-lasting structures than their makers ever dreamed as some of the massive caissons can still be seen offshore at Arromanches today – indeed, at low tide I have paddled around them.

More calm water was created by the third component of the harbour, called the Gooseberry. It consisted of a number of ships sunk bow to stern to form yet another breakwater inside the Bombardons. These remarkable engineering constructions protected even more remarkable installations such as the floating pier heads that Churchill had written about and the floating roadways that enabled the trucks and tanks to drive along through the waves to get to the shore.

Two harbours were planned to supply the Allied forces: Mulberry A was to be the American harbour, built to handle up to 5,000 tons of supplies a day, while Mulberry B was a British harbour that was capable of processing more than 7,000 tons. The organisational chart for assembling and constructing the Mulberry harbours and getting them working was incredibly complex. The Admiralty was responsible for towing the components across the Channel and the siting and layout of the harbours. The Royal Engineers would be the constructors and operators of the pier heads, which led to some hilarious stories about co-operation (or lack of it) between the services, all recounted with gales of laughter in the bar of St Ermin's, as described in the preface.

One of the stories concerned a phalanx of admirals facing a bristling rank of generals across the Mulberry planning tables over some issue or other. It was described as being one of the greater battles of the war by an observer.

In spite of – or maybe because of – the friction, the two Mulberries were towed across the Channel and assembled quickly and effectively in the face of the enemy to operate in time to provide reinforcements of men and their equipment for the Allied armies. It was key to the campaign's success that the mountains of supplies and munitions required were available, and because of this it was rare that the advance of the Allied armies was slowed by lack of ammunition, supplies or transport.

The story of the two harbours is told very graphically in the Mulberry Museum in Arromanches, if the reader is able to visit it, and if you are very adventurous you can wade out to some of the caissons that are still where they were placed by the men who put them there more than seventy years ago.

THE ASSAULT

The many tasks that SOE asked the Resistance to undertake to support the Allied assault on the Normandy beaches caused German soldiers on the Atlantic Wall defences to endure a scarcity of ammunition and food, as well as a danger to themselves, as an everyday situation. The dual problem of Allied air superiority and ambush by members of the Resistance behind every tree and every turn in the road had begun to affect the German Army's effectiveness.

Men and women of the Resistance had practised their D-Day tasks in secret many times, either in the safety of the English countryside or in more hazardous locations in Europe in which to harass the enemy. One very effective diversion on the day was Operation Titanic, devised by an SOE experimental station to distract enemy forces on D-Day and involving hundreds of dummy paratroopers being parachuted east and west of the landing beaches. They were dropped before dawn with firecrackers attached to them creating an impression of automatic weapon fire that had the dual effect of alerting German patrols to their presence and at the same time not encouraging them to inspect the parachutists too closely.

The dummy airborne drop was to confuse the enemy defending Omaha beach. This would be assaulted by American troops and paratroopers and hopefully the ruse would assist them in overcoming a strong and difficult beach defence. A whole brigade of that beach's guardians was sent to deal with the airborne landing, taking about a third of the German defence force away from the beach. It was not until well into the afternoon that they found that they had been duped and were wasting precious time before getting back to reinforce their comrades in defence of their shoreline, by which time the Americans had a foothold.

Meanwhile, French civilians watched in awe the remarkable spectacle of more than 13,000 Anglo-American troops parachuting into countryside around the Cherbourg peninsula. The Mayor of St-Mère-Église remembered the night:

All around us the paratroopers were landing with a heavy thud on the ground. By the light of the fires we could clearly see men manipulating their parachute cables; one less skilful than the rest came down in the midst of the flames so sparks flew and the fire burned brighter. The legs of another paratrooper contracted violently as he was hit; he raised his arms as he came down and the giant parachute, billowing in the wind, rolled over the field with the inert body. A big white sheet hung from an old tree covered with ivy with a man hanging on the end and he came down holding on to the branches until he slowly descended like a snake. He tried to unbuckle his harness with the 'Flak' only yards away; they saw him and their machine gun fired its sinister pattern; the poor man's hands fell and the body swung loosely to and fro on the end of the cables.

A few hundred yards in front of us near the sawmill that was on fire a big transport plane crashed into the ground and soon set a second fire raging. The bells in the belfry were sounding the alarm. Now we were in the line of fire of the machine gun in the belfry and the bullets were hitting the ground all around us. It was a lovely night, lit by swathes of moonlight, a paratrooper appeared suddenly and pointed his machine gun at the group by the pump but realised that were French and did not shoot. A German sentry hiding behind a tree let out a yell and ran away as fast as he could. The paratrooper stopped to ask questions but as no one could speak English, he crossed the road and disappeared into the night. The fires lit up the big planes above that dropped their human cargos on either side of our cemetery.

Little by little the night began to dissolve and a milky dawn began to filter through; as the contours became more precise we were astonished to see that the town was not occupied by Germans or British but by Americans. The first thing that we noticed was the big round helmets we had seen illustrated in the German magazines. Some of the soldiers were sleeping or smoking under the trees; others lined up behind the wall and the town weighing building stood with weapons in hand, watching the church still held by the enemy. Their wild neglected look reminded us of the of Hollywood movie gangsters. Their helmets were covered with a khaki coloured net; their faces were, for the most part covered in grime like those of mystery book heroes.

As Allied airborne troops achieved the initial objectives the seaborne forces began their assault in the largest and most complex military operation the world has ever seen. In the first wave ashore there were 57,000 American and 75,000 British and Canadian troops with their supporting armour, artillery and engineers. They landed on five of Normandy's beaches, which they had code-named Utah and Omaha for American troops and Gold, Juno and Sword for the British and Canadians. American troops landing on Omaha came up against a fierce defence at the sea wall, but the absence of many defenders allowed the GIs to get ashore and using the time they had gained the Americans could not be dislodged. The German General Erwin Rommel was widely quoted as saying that during the battle for the beaches following any Allied landings, the initial assault would be 'the longest day' in the struggle.

The many distractions that SOE and its resistance groups created that day, and those following, contributed to making D-Day the successful beginning to the Allies' European campaign. The secret of where, and to some extent when, the Allied troops would storm up the beaches had been kept safe even though there were large numbers of resistance people operating under the Germans' noses who knew the secret. General Rommel was one of many caught unaware that it was the beginning of the 'longest day', as he had gone home to Germany to celebrate his wife's birthday.

I remember how the roads around the embarkation ports had been jammed for miles inland with unbroken chains of assorted vehicles and tanks waiting for their orders to move forward on to waiting ships. The secret of where the assault would be was unknown to them until they boarded their vessels and were given sealed envelopes containing their orders. Only then would they have seen the word 'Normandy', which meant they all scrambled to find a map to identify where the Baie de la Seine was. Also included in the envelope was an 'Order of the Day' from Admiral Cressey, commander of the Royal Navy's Neptune Operation. He addressed his staff and men before D-Day, saying:

> Gentlemen, what Phillip of Spain failed to do, what Napoleon tried and failed to do and what Hitler did not have the courage to try, we are about to do and by God's grace we shall. It is to be our privilege to take part in the greatest amphibious operation in history, a necessary preliminary to the opening of the Western Front in Europe which, in conjunction with the great Russian advance, will crush the fighting power of Germany. This is the opportunity which we have all long awaited and which must be sized and pursued with relentless determination: The hopes and prayers of the free world and the enslaved people of Europe will be with us and we cannot fail them. Our task, in conjunction with the Merchant Navies of the United Nations and supported by the Allied air forces, is to carry the Allied Expeditionary Force to the Continent, to establish a secure bridge head and build it up and maintain it at a rate which will outmatch the enemy. Let no one under estimate the magnitude of the task. The Germans are desperate and will resist fiercely until we out-manoeuver them and out fight them, which we can and will do. To every one of you will be given the opportunity to show his determination and resource, that dauntless spirit of resolution which individually strengthens and inspires us and which is collectively irresistible. I count on every man to do his utmost to ensure the success of this great enterprise which is the climax of the European war. Good Luck to you all and God's Speed.

D-Day was planned for 5 June 1944 when the tides were best suited to the landings, but the invasion fleet was not enjoying good luck or Godspeed as the weather, which had been fine and bright, quite suddenly changed. On 1 June heavy rains reduced visibility in the Channel with heavy seas. The weather forecast for the next three days was getting worse but despite that, on the evening of the 3rd, the troops were ordered to embark on to the waiting armada of vessels. Anybody living on the south coast of England knew what was about to occur as the camps that had been full of soldiers emptied almost overnight and the seaside towns suddenly became ghostly quiet.

Soldiers packed into ships and landing craft were cramped, cold (although it was June) and often seasick as the weather blew half a gale, but on the 4th a report from the RAF meteorological branch was given to General Eisenhower with the news that there would be a break in the weather on 6 June. The due date of the 5th came and went with the men still in their various vessels. An account of one experience came from a private soldier:

We marched down to Southampton to be put on board an infantry landing craft. We put out to sea and we went round and round in circles for about three or four days [it was actually thirty-six hours], in and out, in and out, nobody wanted to stay on board because the sea was that rough, you did not float – you flew. We came back to Portsmouth for refuelling and then we finally did go across to Normandy on D-Day.

The great invasion fleet assembled just south of the Isle of Wight, at a rendezvous appropriately called Piccadilly, preceded by nearly 400 minesweepers sweeping a broad highway almost 30 miles wide and clearing mines right up to the Normandy shoreline. The fleet sailed through the swept channel marked out by dan buoys indicating where the dangerous areas were to be found. This was followed by the tugs towing the monstrous concrete blocks that were to be part of the world's first prefabricated harbour. As the daylight dawned on the 4th a landing on the following day began to look increasingly unlikely as waves lashed the Channel shores, although the weather reports still made the 6th or 7th possible alternatives.

As the fifth day of June approached the agonising decision was taken not to go on that day, so a FLASH signal of the highest priority was sent to all stations to halt the operation and await further orders. In spite of the situation the embarkation was still going ahead. In the great throng of men and materiel at Tilbury Dock a company of Royal Engineers, whose orders were to assemble the Mulberry harbour, boarded *City of Canterbury* as she prepared for sea. Pontoon bridge sections were being towed down the Thames Estuary along with the floating pier heads that would only come together once they were across the Channel.

The one-day delay caused a huge gridlock of ships and the 600 ships and tugs involved in the harbour assembly found it hard to find anchorage for the night. The following morning the weather was due to abate so another FLASH message went round the fleet that Operation Overlord would proceed on the next day, 6 June. The great fleet slowly reassembled just south of the Isle of Wight with their crews nervous of the threat of marauding E-boats. However, the continuing bad weather was a blessing in disguise. Conditions were so bad in the Channel during the night that the *Kriegsmarine* had ordered its flotillas of high-powered torpedo boats to stay in harbour. The presence of hundreds of tugs and minesweepers followed by thousands of all sorts of ships carrying 150,000 men across the Channel was not revealed until next morning. The armada approached the French coast without the kind of mishap that had caused the disaster at the Dieppe Raid and the first ships sighted land without being perceived.

Next morning all the alarm bells rang and the E-boats hurriedly left Cherbourg Harbour to make mischief among the invasion fleet. The Phoenix concrete caissons wallowed in the increasingly rough tide as they floated down Southampton Water and were towed out into the open sea where the E-boats were waiting. An account of the voyage of one of them was given in the diary of Robert Pintar, who was an American Seabee engineer. He had lunch and recorded being 'dressed to go to war' as his ungainly craft followed the invasion fleet.

June 7   got dressed with five layers of clothing plus a rubber tube life jacket. Stopped for lunch and were then given six pork chops and a loaf of bread for our dinner. Went on board the Phoenix base at about 1300 hours with six British soldiers who were to man our 40mm anti-aircraft gun, they were in the bow quarters and we were in the stern quarters. We left our river dockage early that afternoon by a USA tugboat towing us at 4 knots an hour headed for Omaha beach to arrive at dawn on June 8. The six of us Seabees were paired off to stand 4 hour watch each.

June 8   I went on watch at 24 hours with Chief Isaac Willingham. We were the second caisson to arrive by dawn. It was dark; the skies full of planes, ships all around, red skies on the coast of France, sounds of war gave chills up the spine. Standing on the stern deck and watching the tug boat towing us at 01.15 hours I heard a splash and a hissing sound on the port side and saw two torpedoes skimming along the surface that crossed our bow and aft of the tug boat – missed us. The Germans misjudged our slow speed of 4 knots, the tug cut us loose! I was speechless then hollered down below to the four Seabees. Torpedo's-

Torpedo's (May Day all on deck) then ran along the gangway to the bow quarters to alert the soldiers with the same warning. I ran back to the stern and made sure that Chief Willingham's Mae West was tied on tight. At that time we could hear the deep throated sound of the enemy E-boat and two more torpedoes splashing as they were launched. We watched them hissing along the surface in a foam of death towards us. One along our starboard and the other along out port side, both from the stern. Both missed again. By this time I had cut our life raft loose (how dare the Germans shoot at us). We were all on deck now, looking and listening, looking and listening, Harry Winslow and myself were standing on the stern. Off in a distance, dead centre of our stern we heard the splash – splash; one torpedo was off to starboard. Harry and I leaned over the stern rail to watch. The torpedo slammed into our stern with a mighty KA-BOOM. We were about 45 feet above the water. We were blown 20 feet into the air, by the time we landed back on the concrete deck the caisson was listing to port at about 30 degrees and sinking fast. We slid and tumbled on the deck to port and into the cold sea. The sinking caisson sucked us down to the bottom of the English Channel about 25 fathoms deep and ten miles from France. The noises under water seemed me to be made by angels hollering plus the sound of underwater explosions and many air bubbles.

When we came to the surface Winslow and I found the life raft along with three others to float on. Chief Willingham found a case of K rations to float on. All five of those men were strangers to me as we had just been put together as a crew a few weeks earlier. We were all fighting to keep alive. We still heard the sound of the enemy's diesel as it patrolled around us. Chief Willingham was crying out 'God save us' very loudly when out of the darkness came a German E-boat. We could see the skullcap bridge. A machine gunner opened fire and laced the water in front of Chief Willingham and fired from bottom to top. Chief Willingham was gone! The E-boat disappeared into the darkness.

All through the night's early hours we would be silent or whisper. Winslow and I would take turns to hold up two soldiers who did not have any life jackets on – we did not see any life in them, as time passed we were numb and cold and let them slip under! During the time in the water we were drifting towards Cherbourg and Omaha. We encountered many body parts and dead bodies, like fishing bobbers, heads down, feet up, drowned. The sea was full of debris, what a solemn sigh! Harry Winslow lost his hearing and got his leg crushed. All the others were banged up. We watched the red glow in the night and the sound of explosions.

June 8   0635 hours at the coming of dawn we sighted, to the west, a ship and as it came closer we saw that it was a light destroyer, HMS Vivacious. It stopped to pick us up putting its starboard bow alongside us. The crew put its cargo nets over side just as the crew pointed to the eastern sky. We looked up to see a German Stuka Ju-87 D nose over with its wing brakes in position along with its 110 lbs bombs slung under its belly, its two dive sirens screeching.

The crew of the Vivacious along with the survivors were motionless as we awaited the bombs! Two loud KA-Booms that were about 20 feet from the starboard side of the ship as the bombs landed in the water between the ship and us. The concussion blew our legs back under the wooden frame of the life raft. The back of my legs were all shredded. The Stuka came out of its dive and disappeared into the clouds. The crew of the Vivacious helped us up the cargo nets, we were numb and cold, we would not have lasted long. They dried out our oily shredded invasion clothes and gave us a grog of rum and hot tea and for some reason the Captain of the Vivacious notified that we were prisoners of war!

June 9   We turned over to the British War Ministry who treated our wounds and interrogated each of us. We were taken to London and put into a hotel on the second floor quite near Piccadilly Circus. How convenient! [I wonder if the hotel was St Ermin's?] Early that evening we climbed out to the window, down the fire escape and off to Piccadilly Circus. In oily shredded invasion clothes with French invasion money we went into a pub. Did not need money! Soon, some Scotland Yard Dicks were with us. They escorted us back to the hotel and put a guard on the door of our room and another on the window.

Robert Pintar was awarded the Purple Heart medal as a result of the wound he received in the Channel and another later in the war. He was one of hundreds helping to assemble and install the first components of the prefabricated harbour that was operating within a couple of days of the first assault. Fortunately the other components of the harbour did not suffer the attacks that Pintar's caisson had and within days the first ships were beginning to unload their cargo on to the quayside. The men involved recognised that they were doing something unprecedented in history and were all proud of their part in it and the high tension of its exciting days, although many would not admit it. One young midshipman was heard to start declaiming the Shakespearian verse from *Henry V*:

> And gentlemen of England now abed shall think themselves accursed they were not here,
> And hold their manhoods cheap while any other speaks that fought with us on St Crispin's Day.

But he was told to shut up before he was finished and get on with what he had to do. There was the unanimous opinion among the harbour veterans drinking together in St Ermin's bar that they would not have changed places with anyone at that time but would never have admitted it to any outsider.

The harbour began to operate with a few teething problems as expected, the decrepit old ships designated to be sunk bow to stern to form the Gooseberry breakwater were in place (or nearly so) and the Phoenix caissons were coming into place. The British harbour was operating better than planned with 9,000 tons of supplies a day, 2,000 more than the harbours were designed for, but naval officers were apprehensive. They faced two enemies they said, the Germans and the weather; they feared the second more than the first and there was bad news. Ten days after the harbours had begun to be assembled the wind began to blow with such a gale as had not been seen for more than eighty years. It was comparable with the storm that dispersed and destroyed the Armada on the French coast almost 350 years before.

Waves more than 10ft high crashed on to the pier structures and breakwaters unmercifully hour by hour for three days, creating chaos among the newly installed components of the harbour equipment and the shipping that it was supposed to protect in the calm waters. The situation was desperate, as men performed valiantly against wind and tide, which was trying to destroy their work. One American colonel addressed his men telling him what the price of failure would be. He had been told by a British general that his head would be skewered on the end of a bayonet and it would be displayed at the end of one of the floating piers if he did not keep the harbour operating.

The colonel felt that the treatment he was promised would be similar to that of his ancestor, Sir William Wallace of Elderslie, who was captured by the English in the fourteenth century after a failed revolution in Scotland. He drew the conclusion that the English had changed very little since 1300 and he told his men they all had to do their very best otherwise they knew what to expect. Their best was not really good enough in the American harbour as it was almost entirely wrecked, although the British one survived because it was in a more protected part of the bay and, although it was damaged, it was not terminal. The American Mulberry was not repaired, as by then the Port of Cherbourg had been captured after a hard fight. The Liberty ships would soon dock to unload their desperately needed cargos there, in spite of German demolitions.

The storm abated on 22 June and the destruction that it left defied belief, more ships and materiel was lost to the storm than during the invasion itself. General Eisenhower wrote to Group Captain Stagg, who had given the weather forecast before D-Day, saying, 'I thank the gods of war that we went when we did, otherwise we would have made the initial landing in that terrible storm'.

Essential supplies were still flowing through, partly through the damaged pier heads but also over the beaches protected by the sunken hulks of Gooseberry, using flat-bottomed landing craft unloaded by sheer muscle power and the effort of the soldiers on the beach.

The huge amount of work necessary to move thousands of tons of stores and arms was not always appreciated in London. It is worth recounting the tale told to the author of the fate of a visiting War Office colonel, retold several times with relish (and embellishments) in the hotel bar:

> The storm had almost subsided when the harbour was visited by some high-ranking War Office wallahs who were clean and fresh with highly polished boots who came full of praise for what we had done with exception of a certain colonel. He persisted in asking awkward and often pointless questions in an obnoxious manner which annoyed the sleep deprived engineering team who got to dislike him intensely.

They devised a small entertainment for themselves by constructing an officers only latrine about the size of a small wardrobe with the luxury fitting of a corrugated iron roof to keep out the rain. It also had a slit trench dug beside it to provide a refuge for the occupants when the occasional German fighter bomber managed to break through the harbour's anti-aircraft screen.

The engineering team waited until the colonel slipped into the latrine and in a carefully choreographed procedure, one of the engineering team began to operate a klaxon horn placed immediately behind the latrine. This was followed by a medley of voices all shouting 'take cover!' as another member of the team lobbed a couple of bricks onto the corrugated roof, which caused a considerable noise within the closet.

The results exceeded expectations, the rickety door in the closet burst open, the colonel with his cavalry breeches round his ankles flung himself face down in the slit trench, previously filled partially with water. As he lay in the mud at the bottom of the slit trench, the gale that was still blowing (although not as it had been) lifted his shirttail to expose a moonlike bottom protruding from the trench for all to see.

The group of senior officers whom he was with were chatting idly nearby and gazed with fascination at this bizarre picture as the team of engineers rushed to haul the colonel out to the slit trench with many exclamations about the well-being of the colonel.

The lesson to be learned there was 'do not upset the Royal Engineers', as that was not the only time they got their very inventive own back for some slight made upon them; the men in my regiment developed a lively respect for them. The Mulberry harbour project was without doubt one of the great engineering feats of the war; it fed, supplied and armed the greatest seaborne assault force of men the world has seen, before or since. The Allied forces hardly paused for want of supplies or arms and ammunition as they advanced through France to liberate Europe but the supplies position for the German Army was a different matter.

The telephone certainly rang in the Rommel home at first light to tell him of the landings, so he would certainly have issued immediate orders over the phone to activate the plans to counter the assault on the beaches, which his staff had been preparing for years. Unfortunately for him the French Resistance, directed by SOE, were also activating their own plan. They had also been preparing to effectively paralyse the communications and transport of the German Army.

Telephones that should have rung in the German Army's divisional, brigade, regimental and even company offices were silent; Frenchmen throughout their land had been alerted by the BBC broadcast. The first line of the poem heralding the approach of D-Day caused many a Frenchman sleepless nights, cutting wires or moulding plastic explosives into the crevices of telephone poles and electricity substations and power facilities of all kinds.

News of airborne landings began to trickle in to the headquarters of German General Marck at Saint-Lô in Normandy while he was enjoying a birthday party given by his staff, one of whom, Major Friedrich Hayne, tells the story:

At 01.11 hours – an unforgettable moment – the field telephone rang (the land line was not working) something important was coming through: while listening, the general stood up stiffly, his hand gripping the edge of the table. With a nod he beckoned to his chief of staff to listen in. 'Enemy parachute troops dropped east of the Orne Estuary. Main areas Brevilee–Ranvile and the north edge of the Bravent forest. Countermeasures are in progress', this message from 716 Intelligence Service struck like lightning.

Was this, at last, the invasion, the storming of '*Festung Europa*'? Someone said haltingly, 'Perhaps they are only supply troops for the French Resistance?'… The day before, in the St Malmo area, many pieces of paper had been passing from hand to hand or been dropped into the letterboxes; they all bore a mysterious announcement: '*la carrotte rouge est quittee*', in addition our wireless operators had noticed an unusually large volume of coded traffic. Up to now, however, the resistance groups had anxiously avoided open action; they were put off by the danger of premature discovery and consequent extermination.

While the pros and cons were still being discussed, 709 Infantry Division from Valognes announced:

Enemy parachute troops south of St-Germain-de-Varrelle and near Ste-Marie-du-Mont. A second drop west of the main Carentan–Valognes road on both sides of the Merderet River and along the Ste-Mère-Église–Pont-l'Abbé road. Fighting for the river crossings was now in progress. The time was now about 0145 hrs:

Three dropping zones near to the front! Two were clearly at important road junctions. The third was designed to hold the marshy meadows at the mouth of the Dives and the bridge across the canalised Orne near Ranville. It coincided with the corps boundary with the natural feature forming the northern flank but would serve a purpose for an enemy driving south. It is the task of parachute troops, as advanced detachments to from the air to occupy tactically important areas and hold them until ground troops, in this case landing forces, fight their way through to them to incorporate them in the general front. Furthermore in Normandy they could, by attacking the strong points west of the beach, paralyse the costal defences. If it was really the task of the reported enemy forces to keep open the crossings, it meant a landing would soon take place and they were really in earnest.

Erich Marck proved to be an exception among German generals that June morning, he mobilised the 87 Corps almost immediately. Other senior German commanders proved sluggish, their bewilderment and indecisiveness improved by the Allied ruse of dropping several thousand dummy parachutists. Worse still for the German Army, numerous of its commanders were away from their headquarters. General Dollman and others were at Rennes for a '*Kriegspiel*' [a war game ironically enough with the scenario that the Allies would land in Normandy] and General Edgar Feuchtinger of the crack 21 Panzer Division was nowhere to be found. Rommel himself was in Germany, convinced that the weather was too bad to allow an invasion. It was a frustrating experience for German troops ready and willing to encounter the enemy.

Resistance groups attacked telephone exchanges and virtually paralysed the communications, but the German High Command had expected some activity of this nature, although certainly not on such a large scale. Orders had to be sent out by staff car, motorcycle dispatch rider, bicycle and even on foot to army units at all levels to get the army to begin to move; but not as fast as its generals would have liked.

Once their men were on the road they met with many other delays as Resistance men (and women) had ensconced themselves in woods or other cover overlooking the main roads as snipers. Columns of infantry made good targets and staff cars even better ones, so to supply the resisters with weapons, the RAF dropped 10,000 tons of guns, ammunition and explosives into willing hands in the days following the landings.

Unending streams of armoured cars, lorries and occasionally tanks filled the roads leading to Normandy and were held up constantly by tree trunks across the road or other physical obstacles, making any column of troops and vehicles sitting ducks for marauding Allied aircraft. Every fold in the ground or clump of bushes was treated with suspicion by the jumpy soldiers and had to be investigated by an advance guard of cyclists or men on foot.

When snipers did pick off a German soldier or two, the whole column would come to a halt and shred the woods or fields close to the road with machine gun and rifle fire as the snipers melted away. They were keeping to the guerrilla warfare principle of hit and run, while their opponents were wasting ammunition that they would need later against Allied troops at the beachheads – and, even worse, it was costing them time.

As a result, German Army commanders at many levels could no longer depend on the expected arrival of reinforcements in planning the battle they were fighting. Nor could they even depend on using the troops they had as Hitler was still concerned about other landings, particularly in the area of Pas-de-Calais; his 15th Army stayed there for seven weeks before moving down to Normandy.

The SS Armoured Division Das Reich was one of those delayed. It was equipped with the latest Tiger tanks and a fearsome reputation for fighting (and brutality) and had been ordered up from Toulouse, where the division was stationed. The journey was estimated to take three days, despite all the bridges on the River Loire being destroyed – the well-equipped unit had a bridging train that had seen the division across wider, deeper rivers. As Das Reich prepared to move the Resistance people blew up its petrol dump, so the tanks began to be loaded on to trains.

However, derailment was a speciality of the Resistance in that region and all the time there were constant snipers. Rail travel became impractical but the unit had managed to commandeer enough petrol to begin the march to the north, harassed not only by the Resistance but the RAF, whose rocket-firing tank busters inflicted much damage on its men and machines.

The whole division was already in a black mood when one of its popular commanders was shot by a sniper, which caused the whole division to go berserk. An SS team turned up at the village of Oradour-sur-Glane next morning and assembled the whole population of about 700 people in the village square. It shot all the men and boys out of hand and then herded the women and children into the church and set it on fire, posting guards at the doors to make sure no one got out. Demolition teams then blew up all the buildings, leaving the gutted remains of the village that are today maintained as a memorial for the price that France paid for resistance.

The division finally arrived at the front to confront the Allies in their beachheads, seventeen days later than expected, in a state of mind and equipment that would have made them less than effective for the battle they faced. The Das Reich Division's experience was just one of many that were endured by German military formations at the hands of the Resistance, aided by the hunter-killer squadrons of the RAF. The lethal hindrances inflicted on German units were a considerable factor in helping the Allies secure a firm foothold in France and the subsequent actions in the occupied countries on the way into Germany.

Membership of the Resistance Army grew exponentially after the landings, so the new recruits needed training and leadership and this was to be provided by Operation Jedburgh, which dropped British officers in military uniform behind enemy lines. They provided more than support and training for the new recruits as the presence of a British officer wearing British Army uniform in the midst of a Resistance group engendered considerable confidence in those groups and did great things for their morale. In return, the Resistance groups provided unexpected support for Regular Army units. An account of their help given to the 4th Battalion of the SAS unit that parachuted into Brittany is attested by General Eisenhower:

Special mention must be made of the great assistance given to us by the FFI [*Forces Français de l'Interieur*] in the task of reducing Brittany. The overt resistance forces in that area had been built up since June around a core of SAS troops of the French Forth Parachute Battalion to a total strength of some 30,000 men. On the night of 4–5 August, the État Major was dispatched to take charge of their operations. As the Allied columns advanced, these French forces ambushed the retreating enemy, attacked isolated groups and strong points and protected bridges from destruction. When our armour had swept past them they were given the task of clearing up the localities where pockets of Germans remained, and of keeping open the Allied lines of communication. They also provide our troops with invaluable assistance in supplying information about the enemy's dispositions and intentions. Not least in importance, they had, by their ceaseless harassing activities, surrounded the Germans with a terrible atmosphere of danger and hatred which ate into the confidence of their leaders and the courage of their soldiers.

Eisenhower's account of this action that liberated most of Brittany is an indication of the enthusiastic co-operation between the Resistance movement and conventional forces that had not been envisaged by the planners before the landings. Activities by other groups were less 'hands on' in their contributions, which took a more tactical form, such as subversions of military movements and road and rail watching, along with intelligence gathering to help the advancing Allied forces. Those groups kept closer to the principles of guerrilla fighting by avoiding open engagement with the enemy, fading away before the troops were able to react and leaving them to beat the empty air.

Eastern France was particularly chaotic for the Germans. A panzer division took only a week to travel from the Russian front to the River Rhine, but after that it took another three weeks to get to Caen as it ran into bandit country and frequent ambushes. Fighting around the city, which the British had failed to capture, was fierce as the Germans saw it as their important transport and communications hub in Normandy and fought hard to keep it. The delay in achieving the objectives in Caen made life difficult for French Resistance groups. They still had to live under German rule in northern France although some groups had become very active in the drive to capture the city, which unfortunately revealed their identity and position to the Nazi troops.

Two months after the D-Day landings a second assault on the coast of southern France was made with a mixed force of American and French troops in Operation Anvil, which was soon renamed Operation Dragoon. The Resistance helped to clear much of southern France of German troops – although not without a fight – but the operation was not without its detractors. Churchill agreed to the name 'Dragoon' because he said he was 'dragooned' into approving the operation; the landings had strong political undertones for the Free French and their leader, General de Gaulle, based in Algiers.

The ultimate objective of the Anglo-American forces was to drive on to Berlin and defeat the Nazis, but the French understandably wanted primarily to liberate their homeland. The important objective of Operation

Anvil was to capture the ports of Toulon and Marseilles to provide a partial solution to the ever-present problem of supplying the Allied armies in the field.

The unexpected result of Operation Dragoon, together with the American break-out from Normandy, was the speed at which most of France was liberated in a matter of weeks. The landings took place on the Côte d'Azur, with the main landing point in Saint-Tropez and the coast around it with almost 200,000 French and American troops. They outmanoeuvred the German troops facing them, causing Hitler to abandon the south of France and order his troops to retreat north along the Rhône Valley towards the Vosage Mountains; but again not without a fight.

French Resistance in the region was well organised and helped the regular troops in completing a very successful operation, but what it achieved was overshadowed in the public's perception by the Normandy landings. Operation Overlord was seen as the most important assault on the mainland of France, although that was not necessarily so in the minds of the French. Seven of the eleven divisions commanded by the American General Patch in the south were French, who pressed forward with the liberation of their homeland so vigorously that they took 10,000 casualties compared with just over 2,000 American ones.

The forces of the Resistance acquitted themselves really well in the campaign by clearing areas and roads, particularly the road to Grenoble. They made the lives of the German troops retreating through the Rhône Valley miserable with their guerrilla techniques as they harassed the retreating troops at every turn in the road.

The co-operation between the Resistance and the French and American troops was close, as the story of the author's friend, Steve Weiss, illustrates. Steve was one of the first in his unit to go ashore in one of the first landings in Operation Anvil. As a first scout in an American infantry regiment, his team 'bumped' the Germans in a confused action in which he became separated from his comrades. His parents were notified that he was missing in action. He was found by a French Resistance group and he became one of its active members; both he and his carbine represented a valuable addition to its armoury.

Among his other activities in the group he stood guard over the group's 'pianist' during transmissions of coded messages to its controllers. After many adventures with the Resistance, Steve was reunited with his army unit only to be told that he would face a court martial for being absent from his unit. The court heard his explanation, after which he was exonerated, but the French government regarded his exploits highly and awarded him its Resistance Medal for his services, then two *Croix de Guerre* and after that the American Army awarded him its Bronze Star for bravery.

Steve's part in the Resistance group eventually emerged, for which he was awarded the *Légion d'Honneur*, which was presented by the French President, Jacque Chirac, in Paris. Later, in July 2013, he was promoted to the highest decoration that France has to offer, the *Commander de la Légion*, which he received at a ceremony in London's Victoria Street in front of the statue of Marshal Foch.

Steve's awards have been absolutely unique for a private soldier in the American Army, but so were his experiences. Steven Weiss is now a professor in the War Studies Department of King's College in London and is currently conducting research into combat stress experience, which he lectures on regularly at the university.

Many Resistance groups like the one Steve joined were active in the south of France helping American, but particularly French, units by sabotaging the rail network regularly as well as encouraging railwaymen to go on strike as often as possible. Toulon and Marseilles were both taken, even though they were damaged by the retreating Germans, and were brought back to working order more rapidly than the Channel ports. About one third of all Allied supplies and ammunition came through the southern French ports, enabling General Patton to supply his troops in his race to the Rhine as well as food for the populace of France.

The French Resistance was not just a fighting force; it rapidly became also a political one led by General de Gaulle, who installed his followers in the administration of one town after another, as they were taken, to replace the Vichy administration officials. The way that de Gaulle managed the takeover of the administration of France as it was liberated shaped the politics of France for decades after the war.

PARIS

The glittering prize in the Allies' race across France was the liberation of Paris, which the German General Rommel said would be operationally, economically and psychologically decisive – and so it was. The Free French Deuxieme Division led by General Philippe Leclerc had landed on the beaches of Normandy, joined in the American Army break-out from Cherbourg and started on a fast but triumphant race along the tree-lined roads towards the capital. It was racing to claim the honour of liberating Paris and as it reached its suburbs the Resistance Army erupted into the streets to fight the retreating Germans. Even though the resisters were poorly armed, they were inspired by their leader, Charles de Gaulle.

They met an extraordinary situation among the German garrison of the city, commanded by General Dietrich von Choltitz. He was ordered personally by his Führer to defend the city to the last bullet and then destroy Paris with the explosives he had been given so there would 'not be one brick left on another'.

Von Choltitz had a reputation for being a ruthless, brutal commander with a blind obedience to orders but the way he acted in Paris was absolutely contrary to his character and previous performance. His first act on being appointed there was to release 3,000 French political prisoners, among whom were many Resistance and SOE people. He then stopped a number of trains departing from the Gare du Nord crammed with French citizens destined for the concentration camps.

This flagrant disobedience of Hitler's orders was surprising as Choltitz had always been an obedient servant of the Führer. He did not obey this direct order despite the terrible price that disloyalty could carry. The recent bomb plot to assassinate Hitler was the reason why Choltitz had been given command of Paris; the officer he replaced had been involved in the assassination attempt and had met a dreadful end at the hands of the Gestapo. In spite of this dreadful example, Choltitz ordered his engineers to remove demolition charges from electricity and gas installations, telephone exchanges, many public buildings and more than seventy bridges due for demolition as the German Army left.

The Luftwaffe general, Otto Dessloch, then threatened to reduce Paris to ruins by bombing the city at night but Choltitz objected as he said it would be a danger to his soldiers in the city. He asked Dessloch to carry out the attack by day, even though he knew full well that that Allied air forces dominated the skies over France, so the attack by the Luftwaffe's bombers did not happen.

In the final days before Paris fell to General Leclerc, a squad of SS officers arrived at the Louvre Museum to 'rescue' the Bayeux Tapestry from its cellar. The keys could not be found and while the search went on shots were fired from within the museum, which made the squad think that discretion might be the better part of valour and it departed empty-handed.

The fiction of the German defence of the French capital was maintained by Choltitz, who reported back to Hitler that the bridges were blown up, the city was burning from end to end and there was fighting in the streets. The French Resistance, meanwhile, knew nothing of Choltitz's efforts to keep the peace and set up barriers so that gun battles really did begin in the streets. The battle was short, against a not very determined German garrison and the Tricolour flag was soon hoisted over Notre-Dame, the Palais de Justice and the Hôtel de Ville. The city fell to the Allies without great damage and after the war General Choltitz was feted by the French people as the saviour of Paris as he had risked all to ensure the largely bloodless surrender of one of the world's most beautiful cities, almost undamaged.

The tanks and armoured cars of Leclerc's columns of French heroes swept through the suburbs of Paris hindered only by people who waited by the roadside to throw flowers or thrust a glass of wine at the soldiers hurrying on towards the city's heart. American soldiers who spent some time in the city afterwards told each other that they were looking for some Free French girls, but they all seemed to have joined the Resistance movement. In the centre the deserted streets still crackled with the sound of small arms fire in the dying hours of the German occupation as its troops scrambled on to vehicles to escape, always harassed by the ubiquitous snipers. As they went the crowds began to gather in the streets, as recalled by Adrienne Dansette, the French historian, who described the joyous abandon of 2 million Parisians, expressed with a joy of his own:

> From the workshops Montparnasse and the markets of Bercy, from the hovels of the Rue Mouffetard and the shops of the Faubourg Saint Antoine, from the great houses in the Avenue Foch and the hutted camps in the outer suburbs came men, women and children. The people of Paris came up, more and more numerous as they neared the centre, coagulating in dense swarms. By three in the afternoon they had formed a gigantic crowd, crammed in irregular layers on iron chairs, stools, ladders; waiting along a way bright with tricolours for a glorious procession to pass. At the Étoile tanks fanned out to cut the open

space in two, facing down towards Concorde, leaving open the side towards the Champs-Élysées. Generals Koenig, Leclerc, Juin, Admiral d'Argenlieu – the whole High Command of fighting France was there. The police band strikes up; General de Gaulle is coming, 'Vive de Gaulle! Vive de Gaulle!' He reviews the men of the Chad frontier force drawn up in line and lays a cross of Lorraine made of pink gladioli on the sacred stone. 'Vive de Gaulle! Vive de Gaulle'.

No doubt, as official processions always do, this one will drive down the Champs-Élysées – but no. Loudspeaker cars address the crowd down the route: General de Gaulle confides his safety to the people of Paris. He asks them to keep order for themselves and to help in this task the police and the FFI who are weary after five days of fighting. Four tanks lumber forward, Lauragaid, Limagne, Limousin, and Verdelon. Behind them blocking the avenue come forward arm-in-arm policemen, FFI, first-aid men, soldiers in a human chain; a fireman, a postman, a Negro grinning from ear to ear, are among them. Behind, in disorder, come motorcycles, sidecars, overloaded jeeps; then after an empty space an usher in a black coat with a white shirt front and a silver chain, very solemn; behind him at last a throng of people with a few officers half-hidden among them. In the front rank there is one man in uniform, he is a head taller than the rest 'Vive de Gaulle! Vive de Gaulle!' the crowd yells. He walks with a springy almost nonchalant stride and replies tirelessly but without warmth to the cheering with that gesture of both arms. If he notices he is a little ahead of his retinue he slows down to so that he is level with them. To tell the truth people who do not have good seats cannot set eyes on him but cry as confidently as the rest 'Vive de Gaulle! Vive de Gaulle!' Behind him, after two or three ranks of silent officials, a human herd prances, dances, sings, enjoys itself utterly; from it stick out tank turrets sprinkled with soldiers and with girls whose destiny does not seem to be a nunnery, cars crammed full, placards, some of them written in Spanish and a huge banner in the Spanish Republican colours which spreads across the avenue, a crowd within a crowd.

In London, the crowds who thronged to the cinemas to watch the black and white newsreel record of the vast demonstration in Paris did so with almost as much joy as the Parisians, as it signified a major step towards the end of the war. The image of the crowd streaming down the Champs-Élysées with their French hero in the front rank turned into scenes of near panic as shots rang out from a sniper left behind as the German troops left, or rather fled, the city. As one, the throng ducked into what cover they could find with one exception, the general strode forward without pausing towards the Arc de Triomphe applauded by the crowd as they recovered their courage.

It was a great day and the apogee of the French Resistance, but it was all downhill from there as the general walked into his old office in the Ministry of War and found it all just as he had left it in 1940. No one was in charge and the German administration that had kept Paris in chains for years had vanished; chaos was inevitable. All across France old scores were being settled and some new ones created as the internal disputes that had been smouldering for years, but held in check by a German occupying force, blazed into a terrible inferno. For the minor transgression of being friendly with a German soldier some women were beaten and their hair shaved, while many thousands, and maybe even tens of thousands, of summary executions took place for the more serious crime of collaboration with the enemy.

Everyone claimed to have played an important part in the Resistance, many of whom supported their claims with documentation, much of which had been forged by those who had learned the art during the occupation. The incoming Gaullist troops provided provisional governments made up of men with little civic administrative experience but whose qualification was that they supported de Gaulle. The Allies only concerned themselves with their lines of communication as they struggled to reopen the Channel ports, so the communist Resistance groups were outwitted by the Gaullists.

The race was on to replace the remains of the tawdry Vichy administration in the south, whose members disappeared – sometimes with the aid of a summary execution. The south-west of France was in a particularly chaotic state until de Gaulle visited the region and took charge of the administration, also largely supplied by French Resistance men whose purpose was now largely served. The Resistance and its struggle came to an end in France and those who had served in it now turned their hand to the administration of a country that had been ravaged by the invaders for so long. The Resistance turned to the politics of France and the rebuilding of the country, but it was not so in the rest of Europe.

In Belgium, German resistance almost collapsed and the Allied armies swept through the country. With an advance of 200 miles in one day, they entered Brussels in a similarly triumphant way to that of Paris with delirious crowds delaying the advance of the tanks with wine and flowers.

We at home were avid cinemagoers and began to grow used to the triumphant progress of our tanks and men through Europe's great cities recorded in black and white newsreels. We assumed they would forge ahead across the borders into Holland, but we were wrong. Hitler became more and more desperate as the Allies approached the borders of Germany.

Dutch Resistance had been shattered by the '*Englandspiel*' disaster, but SOE had slowly and painfully rebuilt a fresh network of agents. Three Resistance groups were operating in Holland – the *Raad van Verzet*, the *Knock Ploeg* and the *Ordre Dienst*. They formed a triangle covering Holland with more than twenty radio transmitters that became known as the Delta Resistance Network. They reported on the movements of the retreating German Army, marking minefields for advancing Allied units and even identifying the V-1 Flying Bomb launch sites for the attention of the RAF. They became a part of General Eisenhower's offensive and were ordered to hold certain bridges and stop the Germans blowing them up, identifying themselves to advancing Allied troops with prearranged passwords.

The Dutch resisters were unable to contribute much to the Arnhem Battle, although they played a major role in organising the escape of soldiers from the battlefield afterwards. They became an important 'counter-scorcher' movement that saved water and electric power plants from destruction and particularly dock installations in Rotterdam, Amsterdam and Ijmuiden.

The Dutch Resistance was as much the saviours of the infrastructure of its country as it was agents for its sabotage and destruction. General Eisenhower asked administrators and managers of ports, canals and rivers to meet at Eindhoven when it was liberated to arrange the future governance of their country and they came in their hundreds, some even by canoe. The Delta Network not only helped the Allied cause but also the resurgence of its country, so that Prince Bernhardt of the Netherlands officially recognised the members of the Resistance as members of the Dutch armed forces after the surrender.

The war dragged on to its Wagnerian climax for a few months with the Resistance movements in the liberated countries playing less and less of a part in the final acts. The Red Army took Berlin and finally the Nazis surrendered to Montgomery and his army at Luneburg Heath. Those few months were full of drama as first Germany was defeated and then Japan with the dropping of the atomic bomb on Hiroshima. A president had died; Hitler had committed suicide; a prime minister who had led his people through the darkest days of the war was rejected by his people; millions were buried, often in unmarked graves, and many great cities of Europe lay in ruins.

The Red Army had redrawn the Continent's boundaries, which cast the people of eastern Europe adrift, causing more almost 15 million refugees to wander, hungry and cold, looking for a place to sleep and a meal to eat. It was a time of great change and consequently a time for political struggle and readjustment in all things.

The political chicanery in the British intelligence community as the Second World War finished was savage compared with what took place after the First World War, largely because of one maverick agency that had grown to maturity in the intelligence community. They did not like it, and senior people in MI5 and MI6 were desperate to see the nonconformist SOE sabotage and espionage agency vanish in a manner that would leave them to dominate the intelligence field.

There was little recognition in government circles of the achievements that SOE had accomplished in its short, eventful and bloody life, and the public remained unaware of the part it played in defeating the Axis powers. All that seemed to be beside the point now, and there seemed be little place for an organisation that specialised in creating mayhem and sabotage behind enemy lines now that it was thought there was no enemy – little did anyone know what was in store for them!

Agents and desk officers dispersed and went their different ways. Some of them would be recruited into the intelligence agencies that were already plotting the demise of SOE; others went back into either public or private life. A number went into the diplomatic corps to become ambassadors; others became politicians. This was particularly so in France where an FFI armband was a sure passport into politics – three French presidents wore their Resistance Medal with pride.

Most SOE operatives and agents in Britain tried to pick up their pre-war lives in their own country as journalists, lawyers, teachers or farmers, and tried to live a normal life. But it was not easy. Many found it difficult to adjust to the different tempo of civilian life and suicides and divorces were common as they found the relative monotony of domestic life arduous. Odette Sansom, who was awarded the George Cross, married another SOE hero, Peter Churchill, but the marriage broke down as with so many others.

The 'White Rabbit', who was Wing Commander Yeo-Thomas, was awarded the Military Cross, the George Cross and the *Croix de Guerre* by de

Gaulle, but the appalling torture he suffered at the hands of the Gestapo led to his early death. The effects of the concentration camps on the 75,000 men and women who had been arrested as suspected members of the Resistance haunted those who survived the executions and the cremation ovens. One skin and bones survivor was Brian Stonehouse, who returned to London and was taken pity on by members of the SOE administration. They invited him to lunch and ordered a well-done steak. He ran out into the street screaming because he could not stand the smell of burning flesh – no one in London could begin to comprehend what he and his comrades had been through.

The awards of medals and indeed any kind of acknowledgement of what the SOE returnees had done were rare as the politicking of the other intelligence agencies worked against recognition of their achievements. Christine Granville had been awarded the George Cross and an Order of the British Empire (OBE) by the War Office, but it was given reluctantly because she was Polish, and as the war ended she was left stranded in Cairo. She borrowed money to get back to London, where she took a series of menial jobs culminating in being a porter in the Reform Club in Pall Mall. A fellow worker tracked her down and followed her to her flat, where he stabbed her to death.

Agents often became untraceable, sometimes because they wanted to get away and sometimes because the records of SOE were so badly kept and managed. The ad hoc way that SOE had grown in its early days meant that there was little centralised registration of documentation and the tension and demands of wartime operations did not make for a tidy administration. The paperwork shrank to a trickle as the war ended, so the numbers of staff to deal with the mountainous backlog that had accumulated during the intensely busy life of SOE were drastically reduced.

An enquiry was instituted into the tragedy of the penetration of the Dutch Resistance groups by German *Abwehr* counter-intelligence, and the Dutch team came to London to ask for the archives. An examination of the transcripts of wireless transmissions from the radios that the Germans had captured would have established where the responsibility for the security failure had been, but the skeleton SOE staff were gradually closing down the organisation. They had to admit that all the transcripts and records for the Dutch sections' operations had been destroyed, and the debate as to who was responsible for that disastrous lack of security still goes on today.

Aircrews who flew 'Joes' in and out of the remote landing strips in France were better recognised and treated as if they were a part of the Royal Air Force administration, which was much more established, efficient and detailed in its functions. Pilots with many hundreds of flying hours in their logbooks began to man the airlines beginning to spring up in the post-war aviation boom. Even the Luftwaffe contributed some pilots to the growing commercial airlines. Aircrew, both serving and retired, were going to play a central part in the early stages of the next war, which was just beginning even as the previous one was coming to an end.

As the Second World War drew to its close the atmosphere between the Great Powers became increasingly tense. Rivalry grew between them, mainly based on the conflicting ideologies of Russia and the Anglo-American alliance. The two power blocs had conflicting aims for central and eastern Europe: Stalin wanted a buffer zone of friendly states to shield Russia from any invasion from the West; the alliance wanted democratic elections in Stalin's buffer zone.

The differences between them became apparent as two peace conferences were held, the first in Yalta with Churchill, Roosevelt and Stalin, and the next in Potsdam a year later. By this time, Churchill had been voted out of office and Roosevelt had died, and Stalin had the new British Prime Minister Clement Atlee and even newer American President Harry S. Truman as his new partners in the peace talks. They were relatively unpractised and naive in the world of global politics and no match for Stalin's plans to create a Soviet empire in eastern Europe with a mixture of force and stealth. A conflict between the two power blocs and their ideologies directed mainly by the intelligence services of each country would last for more than forty years.

Left: A statue of St Ermin who was the patron saint of Henry VII and stands guard over his tomb in Westminster Abbey. (The 'Minuments' of Westminster Abbey)

Above: The Caxton Bar that was a meeting place for the intelligence community and a place where many espionage plots were hatched and some dispatched by the KGB's double agents in the Cambridge Spy Ring. (St Ermin's Hotel)

Above: Entrance to St Ermin's Hotel, which was a courtyard for horse-drawn carriages for the residents when it was first built in the 1800s, then a car park in the 1950s and now the impressive approach that it is today. (*Eye Spy Intelligence Magazine*)

Left: Hugh Dalton was the Minister for Economic Warfare in the coalition government led by Winston Churchill in 1940. The concept of the Special Operations Executive was put forward by Dalton in his paper submitted to the Cabinet, leading to the formation of the Executive. (LSE Library)

Right: Admiral William Reginald 'Blinker' Hall was an outstanding spymaster who headed the Room 40 Intelligence agency at the Admiralty in the First World War. Its performance was more than comparable to Bletchley Park's during the Second World War. (US Library of Congress)

Left: Winston Churchill seen testing one of SOE's weapons used in 'Setting Europe Ablaze' by his Ministry of Ungentlemanly Warfare, as he ordered it to do when it was formed in the desperate days of 1940. (Author's collection)

Left: Major General Sir Colin Gubbins was the dapper Scotsman who led the SOE from 1942 – during its most critical period in the preparation for the landings in Normandy on D-Day – until after the war in 1946. (Author's collection)

Right: Commander Alistair Denniston joined Room 40 at the Admiralty in 1914 and had a long and outstanding career in the intelligence community. He was a code breaker throughout the First World War and led his cryptographic team through the interwar years to provide a foundation for Bletchley Park's beginning in 1939. (Author's collection)

Left: Arthur Zimmermann was the German Foreign Minister in the First World War and by 1918 his country was losing and it was desperate. In a secret telegram sent to Mexico he offered an alliance if it attacked the United States. Room 40 decrypted the message, which brought America into the war on the Allied side (Author's collection)

Left: The Albert public house that was one of the few buildings to survive the German bombing and the developers in Victoria Street. It was a rendezvous for SOE and MI6 officers that was almost as popular as St Ermin's. (*Eye Spy Intelligence Magazine*)

Right: Sir Mansfield Cumming was the eccentric chief of the British organisation formed in 1909 that later became MI6. He was addicted to disguising himself; the photo looks as though he was in disguise mode when it was taken. (*Eye Spy Intelligence Magazine*)

Above: When the organisation that became MI6 was founded, the building in Melbury Road was its headquarters. (*Eye Spy Intelligence Magazine*)

Above: The beautiful architecture of Queen Anne's Gate hides what was the back door to MI6 headquarters in Broadway Buildings, just round the corner that was the main headquarters of the agency. (*Eye Spy Intelligence Magazine*)

Left: The German *Abwehr*'s equivalent of Bletchley Park in June 1940, which was its main intelligence evaluation centre at Lauf in Germany. It monitored the British army signals from Dunkirk and the French army's despairing calls for help in the Battle for France. (Roethenbach Military Museum in Germany)

Left: The Anglo-American listening post at Teufelberg (the Devil's Mountain) in Berlin that overheard the ceaseless chatter of the Red Army and Soviet Air Force in the Cold War. (*Eye Spy Intelligence Magazine*)

Below: Kim Philby was accused of being a Soviet spy long before his final detection. He was cleared of the charge, so to celebrate he called the press conference pictured here. You have to admire the chutzpah of the man who continued as a double agent for years afterwards. (*Eye Spy Intelligence Magazine*)

Left: Guy Burgess was a self-confessed homosexual (when it was illegal) and a drunkard who proved to be the weak link in the Cambridge Spy Ring. He fled to Russia with Donald Maclean when he had been exposed as a double agent. (*Eye Spy Intelligence Magazine*)

Above left: Rider Street housed one of many intelligence bureaux that MI6 used in the West End of London where Philby started his espionage career in Section V of SOE in 1940. (*Eye Spy Intelligence Magazine*)

Above right: Broadway Buildings opposite St James's Park underground station was the MI6 Headquarters from the 1920s to the 1960s, where much of the dramas of the wartime and Cold War intelligence conflicts were played out. (*Eye Spy Intelligence Magazine*)

Left: The imposing archway entrance to Artillery Mansions, which was an MI6 outpost during the Cold War and known to the author who passed through the arch many times, as did the double agent George Blake, who also worked there. (*Eye Spy Intelligence Magazine*)

Above: The Admiralty Building in Whitehall where the Room 40 intelligence agency that changed the course of the First World War had its home. The window of Room 40 is hidden, as is the window of Room 39 where Ian Fleming operated in naval intelligence in the Second World War. (Snapperjack of London)

Above: Spandau Prison in Berlin where seven Nazi war criminals, including Hess and Raeder, were incarcerated for many years. The photo depicts the British taking over guard duties from the American Army, which is where the author first made contact with the TICOM intelligence team. (Author's collection)

FIVE

THE COLD WAR

Military intelligence concepts and practices were created and formed in the heat of battle in two world wars, largely to serve military purposes, but as the 'hot wars' came to a chaotic end in 1945 intelligence began to change in nature. Cold War tensions and pressures emerged, and a different kind of threat to the world produced a differing need for intelligence with an increasingly political motive rather than a military one. Information and knowledge about the sinews of war became the basis of a long-term political policy rather than a shorter term military strategy. Military force in this era was available and of an overwhelming nature, represented by the atomic bomb as a weapon of war. The prime armaments were no longer guns and tanks, although there were still plenty of those, but information about the activities and intentions of the opposing side in the new atomic age was paramount.

The world's major intelligence services and their people clashed in an epic story of great drama, heroism and even greater deceit as they enacted their parts in a modern version of the Great Game. Germany became the chief battlefield once again, although minor and major skirmishes took place all over the world. The Germanys, both East and West, were the arena for the conflict and the city of Berlin was the prize. Both the Soviet Union and the Anglo-American alliance concentrated on gathering intelligence to ward off the possibility of the Cold War turning into a real one in an effort to make sure they were prepared for the worst.

The threat of nuclear war loomed over Europe and the rest of the world for almost half a century, but the worst was mainly fended off by an intelligence war of special intensity. During the conflict, major espionage and intelligence agencies were created and destroyed as their methods and objectives changed to keep pace with the struggle between communism and the democracies. Enormous bureaucratic and technological systems were built during that time, the effects of which still resonate over old battlegrounds.

The Cold War was foretold over a century before it began, in 1836 by the French historian Alexis de Tocqueville, who wrote:

> There are two great nations in the world, which starting from different points seem to be advancing towards the same goal: the Russians and the Anglo Americans ... Each seems called by some secret design of Providence one day to hold in its hands the destinies of half the world.

A century later, in 1945, Adolf Hitler also predicted the coming clash of the Great Powers in his last political statement made barely a month before he committed suicide in the Führer Bunker in Berlin. The guns of the Red Army were already pounding on the gates of Germany's capital city as he dictated to his secretary in his bunker:

> With the defeat of the Reich and pending the emergence of the Asiatic, the African and perhaps the South American nationalisms, there will remain in the world only the two Great Powers capable of confronting each other – the United States and the Soviet Russia. The laws of both history and geography will compel these two powers to a trial of strength, either military or in the field of economics and ideology. It is certain that both powers will sooner or later find it desirable to seek the support of the sole surviving great nation in Europe, the German people.

The predictions proved to be right, including Hitler's assertion that both sides would try hard to gain the support of the German people in the struggle. Strangely, very few in high or low places on the Allied side in the war saw the onset of the next conflict (or probably even wanted to) and were totally unprepared for the coming of the Cold War – but come it did.

When the Russians overwhelmed the invaders of Mother Russia at Stalingrad they were pushed across the countries of eastern Europe so that the Red Army then penetrated the heartland of its bitter enemy. When the Soviets advanced inexorably across the frontier of Germany in January 1945 their clear objective was to assault the city of Berlin, which filled its population with terror. An avenging horde of 2.5 million men gathered to strike at the vulnerable city and its desperate but inadequate defenders.

The German Army and people expected little mercy from the juggernauts of massed tanks and guns as Russia's generals prepared their soldiers for one final onslaught to end the war. They bombarded the city, whose air defences were almost completely destroyed by bombers of both the Russian and Allied air forces by day and by night. The intensity of what had clearly become a futile resistance by a tattered but desperate German Army required horrific sacrifices by the Red Army. It lost more than half a million men in the final assault that enabled it to raise its country's red flag over the Reichstag.

The civilian population were not spared either. More than 100,000 people, mainly women and children, had perished in the city's endless heaps of rubble, so finally on 2 May 1945 the city surrendered, or rather collapsed exhausted, and the guns fell silent. All transport services, all electricity supplies and even supplies of drinking water had been destroyed, but worst of all any kind of supply of food had ceased to exist. Survivors cowered in their cellars and shelters, no longer afraid of massed artillery or the terrible Russian flamethrowers but instead terrified of the bayonets and rape by the savage soldiers that Goebbels' propaganda had been telling them to expect.

When they first appeared, the Russian front-line troops were often disciplined, courteous and even compassionate to a terrified people, but the second wave of men were of a different and savage breed. The terrible things that happened to Berliners, particularly its women, in the first weeks after the city's surrender directly affected the attitudes and actions of its people when, a year or two later, they were asked to endure their city's siege. Watches were torn from wrists, rings from fingers and homes plundered, to culminate in an alcohol-fuelled mass rape of women of all ages.

The Red Army's assault on the city had terrorised people who were hiding in their cellars. But it was the personal violations that followed that created an abiding bitterness and hatred of the Russians among the Berliners. This would be a major factor in the coming Cold War. It gave them a deep and determined resolve never to be subjected to Soviet rule, no matter what the cost. Russia's soldiers may have thought that it was retribution for the terrible wrongs that Hitler had inflicted on his people. Berliners saw heavily armed men casually violating their women, causing mothers to weep over traumatised daughters, and ruined hospitals with no medical supplies filled with distraught women seeking treatment for their injuries or for syphilis. Suicide rates mounted dramatically and in one medical centre in the city 250 cases of violent rape were treated in one day. Women in the food queues discussed how often they had been raped that week in a most matter-of-fact way.

A memorial was built, dedicated to the Russian dead in the assault on Berlin. They called it the 'Unknown Soldier', but it was universally known by Berliners, particularly the womenfolk, as the 'Unknown Rapist'.

Just a few short years after the Red Army's savage assault on Berlin, the Soviets thought the events were in the past, but its inhabitants had to live and deal with the terrible results. Berlin never forgot the mass violence by Russian troops towards people and property, and this played an important part in the determination of Berliners to resist Stalin as he tried to starve them out of their city.

Germany surrendered on 8 May 1945, which virtually brought to an end the Second World War in Europe and left the Red Army in occupation of most of the countries of Eastern Europe and a large slice of Germany, with the Allies occupying the rest. The Grand Alliance of the United States, Great Britain and Soviet Russia always had stresses and strains in it and conflicting war strategies increased them, but after they defeated Nazi Germany the task of separating the spoils of war began. Each of the victors occupied a zone of Germany: the American one had about 17 million inhabitants and was dependent on the Ruhr for its coal and steel; the British zone included the Ruhr and most of the coal and steel production, but its 22 million people depended on other areas for their food; the smaller French zone's 6 million population was fairly self-sufficient; while the Russian zone was mainly agricultural and its 17 million people were dependent on coal from the Ruhr. Therefore, each zone was to some extent dependent to some extent on the other.

The Allies had agreed at the Yalta Conference that Berlin should also be divided into four zones, but it was 100 miles inside the Soviet zone and Britain, France and the United States each depended on free access through the Russian zone for their road, rail and canal links to supply the city. Soon after the war the Allies clashed over reparations – the Russians and the French wanted maximum payments from Germany as their countries were the most damaged by the war, but the United States and Britain considered that if they took much out of the German economy it would collapse.

Stalin watched the beginnings of economic development with suspicion and mistrust and tried to counter the moves that the Allies made towards economic recovery with some counter-moves of his own. The final straw was when the Allies issued a new currency called the *Deutschmark*. This revalued the currency, which had become valueless; the Soviets promptly started to circulate their own *Ostmark* banknotes. So, two currencies were circulated within Germany, and in particular in Berlin, which caused even worse relations between the two opponents, and in time it got worse – which is about the time I arrived on the scene …

THE BLOCKADE

I was called away from friendly old Victoria Street to join the colours and be decanted into Europe's increasingly difficult situation in the early stages of the Cold War. Orders to join the Queen's Royal Regiment, based in Dortmund, took me to a world of military discipline and to witness the devastation that war had wrought on Germany.

It was the first major post-war trial of strength between East and West, whose lines were being drawn with the help of a speech by Winston Churchill describing how the drawing down of the 'Iron Curtain' was beginning to take place. The evolving perils of the international situation made little impression on the young men of my regiment until we were ordered to provide a garrison for Berlin. To do that, our convoys would have to travel the autobahn for 100 miles through the Soviet-occupied zone.

Our commanding officer's briefing made us begin to realise how volatile the situation was, as he kept on emphasising that we should not shoot, no matter what the provocation. Why should we want to fire on our Soviet allies, we asked ourselves? The looming crisis, caused by what we were told was the intransigence of Stalin, was gradually closing down the route into Berlin. All communications by land, rail and even canal were being constrained in some way but the Allies were resisting the creeping programme of restrictions.

They would finally culminate in the blockade of the city following a difference of opinion between the members at a *Kommandantur* that governed the city, caused by a speech made by Ernst Reuter, the Mayor of Berlin. He asked Berliners to resist the Soviets' moves to take over Berlin. That infuriated the Russian representative, Marshal Sokolovsky, who snatched up his papers, saying, 'There is no sense in continuing this meeting,' and swept out of the room. From then on the *Kommandantur* met infrequently and then only for propaganda purposes.

The noose continued to tighten around Berlin, restriction by trivial restriction. The supply routes, by rail and then road, to Berlin were gradually being curbed. The author's regiment's journey on its way to join the garrison in Berlin was the last road traffic into the city before the road closed:

The battalion formed up on the barracks square in Dortmund at first light, the transport was ordered forward and the convoy advanced in good order. At the Russian checkpoint at Helmstedt, we were cleared without much trouble, giving us access to the autobahn into Berlin. At the bridge at Magdeburg we were told the bridge was unsafe and the road blocked even though Russian vehicles were seen to be using it. After a discussion, much of it in sign language, a harassed Russian sergeant indicated that there was a ferry downstream and we might be able to try it. Our convoy set off down a gravel track to where the ferry was indicated which turned out to be a large flat-bottomed barge. It was attached to an overhead wire by means of a pulley so the barge could be moved across the river through its very strong current. The ferryman had no English and we had little German so we began to negotiate mainly by hand signals: he was encouraged with the aid of many cigarettes and much chocolate to co-operate. Our crossing was glacially slow; our fully loaded three ton trucks were driven gingerly on to the ancient barge one at a time then, helped by the rivers flow, they were floated over to the other bank. Mercifully, none of our precious trucks were lost in the flood although there were some near disasters. There were other distractions as well, a truck full of po-faced Russian soldiers arrived and purposefully took defensive positions around the barge with weapons loaded and sighted. Were they going to take us prisoner – or worse? No they stayed in position for ten minutes or so and then without a word clambered back on their truck and shot off in a shower of gravel. This happened several times during the day which did nothing for our peace of mind or speed of the operation.

As the light began to fade the convoy completed its river crossing and formed up on the autobahn to resume its journey to Berlin, arriving without further adventures very many hours later at the British Berlin Sector Checkpoint. A huge reception awaited us including several generals and other notables; everyone had begun to think that the whole battalion had been put 'in the bag'. As the day wore on they thought a third world war seemed to be in prospect. A lot of debriefing took place as we eventually reached the Olympic Stadium where the battalion was to be billeted to get a meal and some well-earned sleep.

I was part of a small detachment of men that formed the rearguard to the regiment. We were about to start the journey when we received an urgent signal not to proceed and await further orders, which was not unusual in the 'hurry up and wait' style of the army. Meanwhile, we listened to radio reports about the main body of the regiment and were reassured that the incident was fairly typical of the increasing restraints on military and civilian traffic passing through the Russian zone.

Marshal Sokolovsky had ordered even further restrictions on Allied military and civilian traffic travelling on the autobahn, and the following day his chief of staff, General Lukyanchenko, accused the West of encouraging subversive and terrorist elements to travel illegally through his zone. The Russians suspended Allied military train travel, but the American General Lucius Clay decided to test the effectiveness of the restrictions by sending a train through the Russian zone. Orders were given to the train commander not to let any Red Army soldiers board it, so the Russians promptly shunted the train into a deserted siding and left it there for several days until, short of water and food, the commander had to give in.

Stalin had given the Allies signs of his intentions but the siege of Berlin was clearly only just the beginning of a conflict that would prove to be a major trial of the strength of will of the Allies. It would also test the capability of the intelligence communities of Britain and the US, and create the CIA. It would also change the culture of the British security and intelligence community, in which St Ermin's would have a role to play.

All military personnel now had to be flown into Berlin's airports and that included our small rearguard detachment, so a movement order was issued for our party to fly into Berlin's Gatow Airport in a Douglas Dakota aircraft. Those aircraft had been the workhorses of Allied forces during the war and like all workhorses they were treated badly; our aeroplane was in terrible shape, cracked windows, metal bucket seats and not an air stewardess in sight! We occupied one side of the aircraft while high-ranking officers and mysterious gentlemen in pinstriped suits sat facing us on the other.

The first flights into the city such as ours, whose cargo was only meant to supply the garrisons and diplomats in Berlin, became known as the 'Little Lift'. That operation only lasted a couple of weeks but it taught the Allies some valuable lessons about the logistics of cargo loading and clearance. Those early flights took place before the siege really got under way, so passengers shared the aircrafts' spartan interiors with a few tons of eggs, milk and other perishables – but Berlin would need at least 12,000 tons of supplies a day just to survive.

Our battered old Dakota landed into an almost deserted Gatow Airport that was about to spring into life in the days following as a great armada of aircraft began to assemble. The operation was to form the Carter Paterson Operation. This in-joke referred to Britain's house removal company, but the humour soon backfired as the Russians began to suggest that the name implied that the British wanted to remove themselves from Berlin, and it rapidly became Operation Planefare.

The city was unlike any that we had seen before, and no wonder, it had been through a trial of sword and flame that was unimaginable, leaving the population to live primitive lives in conditions that would be unimaginable to anyone who had not seen it. There were almost no emotional feelings left in the people after surviving the trials of war and this sometimes caused them to act strangely. One instance that I saw concerned some concentration camp survivors with heads shaven (because of lice) who were given work in the camps of the occupying armies. They mixed with other workers bearing different kinds of tattoo – the marks on their arms indicated that they had been SS personnel who had possibly been guards in the concentration camps. It was a source of amazement to us that the ex-captives and their ex-prison guards, whose bestial crimes were well known, even acknowledged each other, let alone talked, but talk they did, although I must say I never saw them laugh together.

The city was largely populated by women, many of whom still did not know whether or not they had been widowed or orphaned at that time – a quarter of a million men had been taken prisoner in Stalingrad alone by the

Red Army, of which only 5,000 returned alive to their homeland. A great many other German soldiers captured in Russia suffered a similar fate so there was a great dearth of younger men in the population. It was a sad and desolate city.

The *Trümmerfrauen* (Rubble Women) who had begun to clear Berlin's ruins brick by brick, all by hand, were an abiding part of the scene. It was almost the only work available and Berliners either worked or starved, although it was possible to do both together. They were generally dressed in worn clothes, although occasionally one of them might be seen in a dusty party dress or high-heeled shoes among the ruins. The lady probably had nothing else left to wear as they all heaved never-ending piles of bricks and masonry into waiting trucks.

The rubble took more than twenty years to clear. Much of it was dumped in one huge mound of bricks that grew to more than 400ft high, the Berliners called it the *Teufelsberg*, or Devil's Mountain, and it gradually grew to be a vantage point that dominated the flat Brandenburg Plain around Berlin. It thus became the ideal site for a large Allied listening post to intercept and listen to the radio traffic of the Red Army. The NSA (American National Security Agency) established a field listening station there, as did the British – but more of that later …

Berliners were working for their survival day to day and suffering the deep despond of a defeated people who lived in mortal fear of the Russians: Nazi propaganda had portrayed an avenging horde, and this image proved fearfully correct. It must have been one of the few truths that Goebbels had broadcast to his nation and Russian soldiers did little to assuage that great fear once they arrived in the city. The Red Army had annihilated the armed forces of Nazi Germany, but as the great battle drew to its dreadful conclusion another kind of conflict began to emerge in the minds of the leaders of the Great Powers – particularly that of Stalin. What next?

Soviet policy wanted its revenge on the German people for the damage they had done, the Allies were more forgiving and wanted to resurrect Germany and feed her people, especially since there had been a disastrous harvest that year. They wanted to repair the great number of damaged homes, as well as reconstruct the country's national and local administration as a part of healing the huge economic and cultural wound in the heart of Europe. Stalin's fear of the ghost of a belligerent Germany rising from the ashes led to two varying concepts of Europe's future that created the

Cold War as much as the conflict between capitalism and communism. The two diametrically opposed objectives of the Soviet bloc and the Anglo-American allies that had once formed the Grand Alliance were about to meet head-on in Berlin.

The Soviets held most of the cards in any negotiations for improvement of conditions in the city; they had entered it first and then advanced far beyond into Germany, leaving the city isolated deep in their zone beyond the River Elbe. The city's isolation enabled the Russians to offer only a few canards to the Allies when the three leaders, Stalin, Roosevelt and Churchill, had met to divide Europe up at the Yalta Conference a few months earlier in the Crimea.

The American President, Franklin Delano Roosevelt, wanted to trust Stalin, but had no conception of how steely was the Russian's determination to settle matters for his own benefit. Stalin's strategy at the conference was to demand as much territory he could get and once terms were set he would redraw boundaries to cause huge migrations of people. The redistribution of populations would establish the Soviet claim to territory with scant regard for their needs or suffering, and causing far greater disruption than the immigration problems we face today.

This was particularly true of Poland, whose borders were substantially changed, followed by the forcible transfer of tens of millions from one area to another. It left the Poles with a burning resentment that their country had been 'sold' at Yalta by the Anglo-American alliance for decades afterwards. Roosevelt had tried to win over Stalin in the talks by gently sidelining Churchill. This is why Churchill entitled his memoirs of this time, *Triumph and Tragedy*, after his isolation.

He had expected his usual intelligence briefings to inform his discussions, but intelligence evaluations at Yalta were sparse, mainly due to decrypts of Ultra from Bletchley Park being excluded from the evaluations. It had been decided not to use them for security reasons. Little did Churchill's security people know that Stalin had been regularly reading the transcripts as the NKVD (later the KGB) was being supplied with the Park's secrets by John Cairncross, a senior British civil servant in Whitehall. Stalin had been able to read substantial amounts of Churchill's intelligence reports from its source, so after Roosevelt's death the new American President, Harry Truman, said that Stalin showed no surprise when he was told about the atomic bomb. He was right – even before it was tested Stalin knew about the new weapon from his well-placed agents in the Manhattan Project, well before the bomb was dropped on Hiroshima and ended the war with Japan.

Roosevelt's wide experience of world affairs that had helped to guide the war's strategy was lost with his sudden death, and he was replaced by the totally inexperienced vice president. Truman created a major policy turnaround. Newly elected American presidents are said to have to learn on the job as they are launched into office, but no president ever found himself in the Oval Office at such a critical time and with so little experience as Harry Truman. Decisions he made then almost certainly accelerated the progression into the Cold War conflict as the new president decided that the far-sighted Marshall Plan should come to a precipitous end.

Ships laden with goods and materials to rebuild shattered Europe were turned round in mid-Atlantic to go home. A near bankrupt Britain, which had received some $27 billion in Lend-Lease with little more than $7 billion in contra aid, faced America, which suddenly became the world's stringent financier. A settlement of $650 million helped to pay off Britain's indebtedness and feed its people, but it needed a loan of nearly $4 billion from America, which was offered at an unfriendly 2 per cent per annum over fifty years.

There was worse; at the global conference on the world economy at Bretton Woods, American negotiators demanded that the dollar act as the world's main reserve currency to make it exchangeable against sterling. The run on the pound meant that Britain had to sell all the holdings it had left in America at a hugely uneconomic price. The reversing of American policy, in contrast to the generosity of the Marshall Plan, meant the pound was burdened with problems and Britain lost its main opportunity for economic growth and recovery through exports. Loans were made more difficult to pay off and relations with America reached an all-time low as the negotiations were labelled 'an economic Munich' by the British press.

In a speech in Parliament, Lord Boothby gave it as his opinion that the terms of the negotiations were those usually reserved for defeated enemies. The traditionally pro-American newspaper, *The Economist*, commented, 'It is aggravating to find that the reward for losing a quarter of our national wealth in the common cause is to pay tribute for half a century to those that have been enriched by the war.'

Truman also repealed the joint authority for nuclear weapon development that Roosevelt had signed with Churchill. The Americans had lost their copy of the accord and even though Churchill sent a photograph of his copy to the new president, Britain was excluded from the future atomic research that she had inaugurated.

Nor was Britain the only financial casualty of the break-up of the Grand Alliance. The Soviet minister, Vyacheslav Molotov, had requested $6 billion in American credits for post-war reconstruction a few months before the war came to an end. The Americans made no answer so the matter was brought up again at Yalta, again without response. It was not raised again until Russian troops were poised to engage the Japanese Army on the Russo–Chinese border in Manchuria in accordance with the Yalta Agreement. On this third request the Kremlin was told, to its disbelief, that the American State Department could not trace the request and a golden opportunity was lost for America to invest in Soviet goodwill. The influence America could have had in Russia dissolved into rows over the way that eastern European countries, which became satellite countries in the communist bloc, were treated.

The changing policy with regard to aid money and resources created a breach between all sides in which the secrecy about plans and breaking of agreements was made worse. Due to excellent intelligence the Soviets knew more about the atomic bomb than America's British ally, with whom America had agreed full co-operation for military and commercial purposes even after the defeat of Japan. In short, the early years of the Truman administration were not America's finest hour and the ungenerous mistakes made by the new president helped to lay the foundation for a conflict that would last for decades. Fortunately, Truman quickly learned some lessons in global politics and economics along the way, but much damage had been done that might not have occurred if President Roosevelt had lived. Not that the conflict between communism and democracy would not have occurred, but it might well have taken a less confrontational style and been easier on a nervous world's economic system.

A year before the Yalta Conference was convened to determine global spheres of influence, Churchill, on a visit to Moscow, had offered Stalin 'percentages' of that influence in the Balkans scribbled on his scrap pad. Stalin made some recognition of his proposals, but at Yalta he demanded a barrier of 'friendly' eastern European countries around Russia's borders. The Allied leaders little realised what the word 'friendly' meant, so the democracies were solemnly assured that the people of those countries would all have the right to freely elect their own governments. Those assurances were received with reservations, particularly by the British who became increasingly aware of the differing ideological and political objectives emerging in the newly found peace.

The two ideological camps would split further apart, bringing them into greater conflict when Stalin demanded that Germany pay billions of dollars in reparations but also be stripped of most of its heavy industry. Churchill's reaction was that it could never pay such a bill without the production capacity to earn the money with which to pay it, so huge loans would have to be arranged that Germany would have difficulty in repaying. That could lead to the collapse of the German economy which, Churchill reminded Stalin, was the reason for Germany's pre-war economic difficulties and Hitler's rise to power. Later, it became obvious that the Russians were abrogating their Yalta agreements as the countries under Soviet control in eastern Europe were not allowed free elections.

Russia also accused America of ignoring its commitments from the Soviet point of view, as it was not levying the reparations from Germany to which it was entitled. That did not equate with the Russian objective of keeping Germany poor and, therefore, differences began to sharpen and the conflict began to take shape. To this point the increasing difficulties had no formal name; that was supplied by the author George Orwell. He wrote a piece about the situation, which ended with the phrase 'A peace that is no peace characterised by a permanent state of Cold War', and so the phrase entered the world's lexicon.

Politicians on both sides of the Atlantic took up and used the phrase increasingly, then Churchill created a second defining phrase of the time. 'From Stettin in the Baltic to Trieste in the Adriatic an Iron Curtain has descended across the continent', he told the world. A barrier, both physical and psychological, had been erected between the two sides, communism and democracy, or capitalism as the Russians might have called it.

However, there was a breach in the Iron Curtain's defences. Berlin gave the world's espionage agencies the opportunity to engage in the colossal struggle. The Soviet fortress' breach would prove to be a Trojan horse that was only finally blocked by the erection of Berlin's infamous wall, but until then the efforts of the Allied intelligence agencies and the KGB would be focused on Berlin.

The Cold War had been named and its battlefield defined, but now what was needed was a strategy. That came from an American diplomat,

George Kennan, serving in the United States Embassy in Moscow. From his sickbed he dictated his thoughts to his superiors in the State Department in Washington in an historic document that became known as the 'Long Telegram'. Its significance lay in the analysis of the complex political pressures inherent in the Soviet government's administration. Kennan predicted the nature of the actions to be expected from the Kremlin. He stated:

> Intransigence towards the Allies was inevitable due to huge internal pressures inherent in their system of governance. The Communist regime needed to treat the rest of the world as hostile as the fear of external enemies was indispensable to them. […] Without it they would not know how to dominate their people. They had to inflict the cruelties and sacrifices they felt Communism needed to maintain its grip on its population.

He went on to say that the Allies:

> … must never expect any concessions made to the Kremlin to be reciprocated and further, they could not even expect any change or redirection in any Soviet policy until a string of failures made it evident that the particular strategy was not workable.
>
> The Kremlin does not take risks but is not impervious to the logic of force and can easily withdraw. which it usually does when strong resistance is encountered at any point.

CONTAINMENT

Kennan went on to expound the philosophy of 'a long-term, patient and vigilant containment of Russian expansive tendencies'. Soviet signals intelligence intercepted Kennan's Long Telegram, having broken the American diplomatic code. Stalin was able to read the criticism of Russian foreign policy, which Keenan painted as a malevolent dictatorship 'dedicated to destroy the international authority of our society and its internal harmony'.

It was a hardliner's philosophy. Truman and his State Department were very disturbed by the subsuming of Romania, Bulgaria, and particularly Poland, into the Soviet sphere of influence so the telegram was received with great interest. The American government adopted Kennan's suggestion of a long-term containment policy and that became the key to America's European foreign policy for more than half a century. To implement that course of action a continuous flow of good, reliable intelligence would be necessary to monitor the intentions of the Soviets and so the build-up of American intelligence agencies began.

Truman's determination to maintain the containment of Russia's expansionist policies required him to develop West Germany's cultural as well as economic well-being. In co-operation with Britain, and to some extent France, a keystone to that policy was to maintain a firm foothold in Berlin. America's newly formed CIA confronted the Soviet security services, the name of which would change from the wartime NKGB to become the Committee of State Security (KGB) in 1954. The two intelligence agencies would drive this major intelligence conflict (and an opportunity for book publishers and filmmakers) for half a century.

The future of Europe, and particularly Germany, were the main issues at a conference in Moscow in January 1947 when the Allies proposed the rebuilding of Europe's economy. Soviet Foreign Minister Vyacheslav Molotov was asked for an account of the industrial plant and equipment taken from their occupied zone in East Germany by the Soviets. He, in turn, demanded the unconditional fulfilment of his government's reparation claims and, predictably, after six weeks of prevarication on both sides rejected all the Allied proposals.

The legendary American general, George Marshall, acting as US secretary of state, then visited Moscow for a quiet conference with Stalin to discuss the urgent rebuilding of post-war Europe. Stalin quietly doodled on a writing pad in front of him as he assured Marshall that settling the future of Germany was not one of his main priorities and was no great problem. Stalin's attitude shocked Marshall and convinced him of the importance of finding some form of initiative to prevent the complete economic collapse of western Europe, with or without the Soviet Union.

On his return to Washington he told President Truman so, and as a result the president announced to Congress a policy of support for Europe that became known as the Truman Doctrine. The United States would support the free peoples of Europe and enable them to 'resist attempted subversion by armed minorities or outside pressures, they had to be allowed to work out their own destinies'. The Truman Doctrine included the launch of a massive aid programme with a $13 billion budget over four years starting in April

1948. The huge aid programme, whose rough equivalent value today would be $148 billion, was aimed at modernising business practices and reducing trade barriers. European industry, or what was left of it, used much of the money to buy goods and raw materials from America and Canada whose economies had prospered greatly during the war. The European Recovery Program was popularly known as the Marshall Plan and would prove to be a keystone in rebuilding Europe's sense of hope and self-reliance. It would also widen the chasm of doubt and enmity between the Kremlin's Soviet Bloc and what had once again become the firm alliance between Britain and America.

Marshall's original plan was intended to include the countries under Soviet control as beneficiaries as well as those administered by the Allies. The plan had many facets, but a principal one was to avoid the risk of hunger, poverty and despair driving the people of Europe into the arms of the communists. The Czechs, who were the least committed to communism in its sphere of influence, were eager to accept aid, but that probably accelerated their country's takeover by Stalin, about which more later.

The Soviet Union found such a programme unacceptable as it saw it all as capitalist propaganda, so Stalin banned any of his satellite countries from accepting US aid assistance. From then until sometime after Stalin's death almost all initiatives to improve the economic health of Germany as a whole, and to some extent that of western Europe, were sabotaged or at least disapproved of by the Kremlin in conducting its Cold War objectives.

The gauntlet had been thrown down by Stalin and by picking up the challenge the three main partners in the Grand Alliance that had jointly won the war split into two camps, becoming an Anglo-American group and a Russian Bloc.

Moscow's grip on its satellite countries tightened; the Red Army advance had liberated Romania in September 1944 and its capital, Bucharest, known as the Paris of the Balkans. The city proved to be an attractive posting for Allied diplomats and military personnel, who enjoyed the city's wide, tree-lined boulevards that gave it a relaxed and carefree air that had survived the German Army's occupation. It enabled the Russian liberators and American military personnel posted there to mix relatively easily in the first stages of its freedom. The Romanians had thrown off the anxieties of Nazi occupation as the war passed them by, but the honeymoon with the Soviet administration would only have a few months to run. Russia's secret police (still called the

NKGB at this point) began rounding up tens of thousands of Romanians with any kind of German ancestry to be shipped off to Russia; Stalin needed slave labour to rebuild his country. The head of Romania's government, Nicolae Rădescu, proved too reactionary to serve the communist purpose. He was discarded as the Soviets drove a coach and horses through the Yalta Agreement's commitment to hold free elections.

The communists began orchestrating demonstrations and riots, supported by the press they controlled, to pressurise and destabilise the government. After a mysterious shooting or two the Soviet military issued an ultimatum stating that it felt compelled to intervene in the situation. Stalin's representative, Andrei Vyshinsky, turned up in Bucharest to bully the young King Michael into sacking Rădescu and then he dominated the administration with his own communist nominees. He was quoted as saying, 'Free speech is all right as long it does not interfere with the policy of the government,' so clearly the quality of his governance was not high. The Red Army then played its trump card, rolling Russian tanks out on to the tree-lined boulevards of Bucharest, and Romania inevitably became a part of the communist bloc.

Poland was a more difficult problem for Stalin as there were two governments, one in Warsaw sponsored by the Soviets and the other that had fled to London before the German (and Russian) invasion. Poland's tragedy was that she was sandwiched between Germany and Russia to act as a pawn in their European geopolitical games, as had been the case for centuries. The German and Russian armies invaded her almost simultaneously in 1939 and then, by previous arrangement, carved up her territory between them. The Polish government in exile took sanctuary in Britain and in exchange its army and air force fought manfully for their host, first in the Battle of Britain and then in North Africa and Italy.

General Wladyslaw Anders was the commander of the Polish forces in exile and head of the Polish government in London. He tried to avoid the Yalta sell-out of his country by calling on Churchill to ask him to avoid the great calamity. He was told that the Red Army was the occupier of his country and he could only negotiate with it. But Anders and his government found it difficult to accept that Roosevelt and Churchill were in such a poor negotiating position. Churchill was privately embarrassed, he could not admit that what was agreed at Yalta was uncertain because the poor drafting of the documentation of the agreement enabled it to be interpreted in several ways.

The Polish government in exile in London was invited by the Soviets to Warsaw to further negotiate the future of its country's governance, but as the Russian aeroplane was due to land in Warsaw it was redirected. After some mishaps the Poles found themselves in Moscow Airport and from there it was only a short journey for Anders and his colleagues to find themselves in Moscow's infamous Lubyanka Prison. The reality was that the Red Army was in occupation of Poland and so it was Soviet property.

Other countries slipped behind the Iron Curtain more easily. The annexation of the Baltic States of Estonia, Latvia and Lithuania were fairly easily stage-managed but Czechoslovakia was more difficult. The Czechs relished being Europe's most democratic nation so Stalin waited until 1948 to make his bid to dominate their government and its peoples. A move by the communists to undermine the country's independent police force caused twelve ministers to resign, hoping that would bring the government down and bring on a free election. That did not happen as two non-party ministers, Jan Masaryk and Ludvíc Svoboda, refused and remained in office, thus only weakening but not terminating the government's administration.

The communists then used their control of institutions such as the trade unions and police to seize power and force President Eduard Beneš to appoint a new Cabinet. The new administration toed the Communist Party line so elections were then held with a list consisting only of Communist National Front candidates offering a manifesto approved by Moscow. Shortly after the coup Masaryk, who had become Foreign Minister in a new communist-led government, was found dead after jumping (or being pushed) out of the upper storey window of a public building. With Masaryk's death any possibility of democratic independence for Czechoslovakia within Stalin's sphere of influence had gone. The Cominform (Communist Information Bureau) was created in the summer of 1948 to enforce communist orthodoxy upon the mostly unwilling satellite countries.

The communist bloc was complete and was fenced in with a barrier consisting of hundreds of miles of barbed wire, minefields and control towers manned by men staring across into enemy territory through high-powered binoculars. They could not observe very much from their towers so they had to depend on their intelligence networks to provide the strengths and intentions of the Allies. Eastern Europe's military forces were amalgamated to act as one (well almost) as directed by Moscow through the Warsaw Pact. Meanwhile, the Allies were rebuilding western Europe, and particularly

Germany's economic, democratic and cultural confidence, so Konrad Adenauer, its future president, was asked to prepare the new West German Republic's constitution.

The Federal Republic of West Germany was to be an autonomous and sovereign state, while East Germany remained very much under the Soviet thumb. France dreaded Germany's emergence as a nation almost as much as the Russians, but Truman reassured her government by agreeing to French troops helping to garrison Germany.

Berlin had now become a divided city, within a divided country, within a divided continent, that contained the presence of four foreign armies. The Allies asked Adenauer to complete the draft of the constitution by the summer of 1948. They also proposed to introduce a new currency, created to replace the old, discredited and almost valueless Reichsmark. The new currency was to be circulated in the Allied zones of Germany and Berlin's three Allied sectors. It all fed Stalin's great fear of the emergence of a strong German state with a growing economy and strong currency, which was beginning to take shape before his eyes. The Soviets responded predictably by introducing a competitive monetary system of their own. The Ostmark was the currency to be used in the Soviet zone and her sector of Berlin, but it never caught on with the German people. The new Deutschmark and all the development of the country that went with it would now create, from the Soviet point of view, major problems in the Cold War battles to come.

The political and even the military standpoint of the two sides concerning Germany's future deteriorated almost week by week over a couple of years, until it had begun to reach a critical point. Stalin believed he could force the Allies to reconsider the whole German question by putting pressure on their position in Berlin, which had 2.5 million people isolated almost 100 miles deep inside Soviet territory, making it very vulnerable. The city had been divided at Yalta into administrative sectors designated American, British, French and Russian, each with their own form of military government. Each sector was run by its own military governor – there was the American cigar-chomping, dynamic General Lucius D. Clay; the acerbic and reserved British General Sir Brian Robertson; the flamboyant French General Jean Ganeval; and the tubby and deceptively affable Marshal Sokolovsky for the Soviets. Each ran their sector using their own national resources and were fiercely protective of their country's rights within their own patch of ground. They acted together (generally) in cases of common need, such as water supply, transport, food distribution and energy, through a body called the *Kommandatura*, which dealt with matters that controlled the city's common interest.

As spring turned into summer in 1948 the Russian military and civil administrations began to inflict what the French called 'a war of pin pricks' on the citizens of Berlin and visitors coming and going through the Soviet zone by road, rail or canal. An increasingly less affable Marshal Sokolovsky and his team created all sorts of harassments for the city's administration and supply chain with petty measures and restrictions. Tensions mounted and apprehension grew throughout Germany as storm clouds gathered, but it was Berliners who were particularly fearful. They had reason to be, as they knew they were the foremost outpost of the West. However, they did not, as yet, know the tests that awaited them and what they would have to endure in the coming months.

BERLINERS

Newly arrived soldiers of the city's garrison soon found their way round the city; it was not a metropolis with London's urban sprawl with which most of them were familiar but almost a network of townships. Each had their own *Kiez*, or community, often with wooded areas in between. It was a city of woods and trees for which the people seemed to have a great affinity. The Tiergarten in the British sector was a sizable forest, mainly fir trees, reaching right up to the Brandenburg Gate in the city centre. The gate marked the beginning of the Russian sector and was the entrance into the city's iconic boulevard, the Unter den Linden ('under the lime trees'), which ran on into the mysteries of the Soviet zone and on and on in the direction of Moscow.

All the great buildings lining the city's major thoroughfares were in ruins. Almost without exception every building was a burned-out shell or totally reduced to rubble. The war had reduced the Nazi capital city to a desert of broken, damp-smelling bricks and masonry where the people were reduced to enduring primitive existences in the wasteland.

The young soldiers began to get to know Berliners as soon as they picked up enough language to make themselves understood, although it was only with the simplest patois. Most never mastered the ability to understand the special way of the large portmanteau words that could include nouns, verbs, adjectives and even prepositions in one word. The German language's Lego brick-like (or *Legosteineigenschaft*) ability to put a whole phrase into a single word was not easily mastered. We found Berliners to be a fairly resilient people, confident of their own culture, not unlike the Cockneys of London in the Blitz. American personnel compared them to New Yorkers; maybe there is a similar kind of culture shared by all the world's big cities even if war smashes some of them to ruins.

Berliners shared in-jokes among themselves and enjoyed them uproariously. It was received wisdom, particularly among the British, that the Germans had no sense of humour – this proved wrong. They have their own style of fun, but it did not have the subtlety of British, and particularly English, humour. German humour was (and is) much more robust and obvious. As the political and even military tensions grew grimmer, stand-up comedians proliferated in the city's concert halls that were being repaired as a matter of priority to bring audiences together. To enjoy the black humour that reflected the city's increasingly grim situation.

The difference between German humour and the British variety was mainly one of body language. A British joke could sometimes be so subtle that it could go by with just a wry smile – there were no wry smiles in German humour. Their jokes were known as *schenkelklopfer*, or thigh-slappers, and were often preceded by a signal of some kind, a raised eyebrow or a word that signalled a joke was coming.

Berliners would need all the laughter they could get as the Russians became increasingly intransigent and began to choke the transport and supply routes to and from an increasingly resurgent West Germany and the world. If the worst had happened and those roadways to the rest of the world were finally strangled, the economic and everyday life of the city would shrivel and die. Most of Berlin's inhabitants and even Allied personnel feared that Berlin would be subsumed into the communist bloc, the false dawn of a kind of peace after the war began to fade and few could see that there would be an alternative. The city seemed to be destined to join Russia's satellite countries behind the Iron Curtain – but there was going to be a surprise for all concerned.

Berlin's economy was no joke, its factories had been destroyed, there was no raw material on which to work and create products and the constriction of the city's transport system needed to export goods was another powerful constraint on its commercial prospects. Clearing away rubble was not proving to be a wealth creator and some form of economic activity was needed to help the people earn their bread.

Stalin's attempt to eliminate the Western presence in Berlin by a means other than armed force, following the takeover in Prague that had already sent a tremor of fear throughout Europe but which had resonated most strongly in Berlin.

Serious interference of any movement to and from the city by road and rail was also being repeated in the air. In April, a Soviet fighter 'buzzing' a British passenger plane collided with it and the crash killed everyone. General Clay had cause to wonder if the Russians would try to prevent flights of aircraft through the agreed air corridors to the city's airports. He made it known through his intelligence network that he would be forced to organise fighter protection for flights to escort American aircraft flying on legitimate missions if necessary. Soviet fighter planes would have to fire on his machines to stop them. It responded with the reaction that the move might seem a bit too extreme an action for Stalin. Clay had established the ground rules for his rights to the use of air corridors into and out of Berlin and this would prove critical to the mounting of the great airlift.

As all this was happening my battalion moved into the impressive Olympic Stadium that Hitler's architect, Alfred Speer (now in Spandau Prison down the road), had built as a showpiece for the 1936 Games. The Nazis were very good at impressive events with massed torchlight parades and striking neoclassical public buildings, but the vast Reichssportfeld complex in West Berlin's fashionable Charlottenburg district was one of their best.

The battalion was quartered in the stadium itself but had access to all its facilities within the Reichssportfeld, with every kind of sports facility including an Olympic-sized swimming pool. A maze of rooms, mostly lofty, full of drafts and inhospitable, were the abode of a battalion of men despite its not being designed to accommodate military units, particularly in the coming winter. Traces of other soldiers who had been housed there before were found, German Army helmets, uniforms and boots had been abandoned as rich pickings for souvenir hunters. The Reichssportfeld facilities contained a great *Sportshaus*, used by Hitler for his speeches, along with many other ghostly reminders of the Nazis' 'Strength Through Joy' movement.

Buildings of all sizes were set among the pine woods, intended for indoor tennis, boxing matches and other sporting purposes, and had also stored ordnance of both the German and Russian armies. Shallow trenches scratched in the sandy soil marked the starting point from which the Red Army had launched its final attack on the centre of Berlin. One of the Reichssportfeld's anonymous buildings contained the offices of the SIS (or MI6, as we knew it) station in Berlin. It shared its quarters with the British Control Commission as a form of cover, but everyone knew the secret. George Blake, who was a double agent for the KGB, was a senior SIS officer serving there, but his treachery was a secret as yet unknown to his colleagues.

Other more substantial ghosts haunted the gates of the stadium – black marketeers were selling anything they possessed for cigarettes. It was the common currency, and could buy everything as Germany's paper money had no value, at least until the Allies replaced it with the new Deutschmark. The black market was universal, women sold their clothes to get milk for their babies, old men sold their treasured possessions, and younger ones offered medals, swords and anything military for whatever they could lay their hands on. The author was offered an Enigma coding machine for 200 cigarettes, not once, but several times. Bletchley Park's secrets would not be revealed for another thirty years or so, however, and 200 cigarettes was too steep a price for a funny-looking typewriter – it was almost the price of a Luger pistol!

THE BERLIN AIRLIFT

The last food train had entered Berlin on 21 June 1948 and all barge traffic between West Berlin and the Allied zones was terminated on the same date. Three days later the Soviets suspended all surface communications with the city and two days after that a large part of the city's electricity supply was cut. The water supply to the city was threatened by the reduction of the electric current needed for pumping it. On 25 June the Soviet ADN News Agency reported:

> Because of technical difficulties on the railroad we were compelled to stop, during the night of the 24 June, all passengers and freight traffic between Berlin and Helmstedt and all train traffic has been cancelled. All necessary orders for prompt repair work have been issued. It is impossible to re-route traffic in the Soviet Zone of Occupation.

Lights in government offices in London and Washington burned well into the small hours as politicians began to deliberate and take the stage as the crisis burst upon them. The first to react was Ernest Bevin, the British foreign secretary; he was a shrewd ex-trade union movement man with huge experience of eyeball-to-eyeball negotiations; those talents would be badly needed in the coming months. He saw the need for the airlift as a priority from the very first. He insisted on calling the Russians' bluff; which is more than many other members of the British and American governments wanted to do.

Bevin was on holiday as the news broke, such was the failure of British intelligence and the unpreparedness of the Allied governments, who never sensed the Soviet blockade coming despite all the signs. Bevin's energy galvanised everyone; he held a press conference two days after the siege began, to emphasise Britain's firm determination to stay in Berlin. His statement in the House of Commons received loud support from all members, who cheered him to the echo when he said, 'the alternative was to surrender to the Russian blackmail and that none of us would accept'. As foreign secretary he canvassed the high commissioners of many of the Commonwealth countries and also French Ambassador Massigi for his support. Most of all he worked to strengthen the bond with the United States to make sure that the Americans were fully committed to remaining in Berlin. Britain was the only country to have spoken out decisively at that stage, while in Washington the hot potato was passed from hand to hand until the State Department passed the problem to the White House.

President Truman's desk had a plaque on it saying, 'The Buck Stops Here' – and so it did. 'We stay – period', was the unequivocal response to the questions of his aides and advisors. General Marshall announced the American intention to stay in Berlin on 30 June, adding that the city would be supplied by air transport (although he probably had no idea at that stage how that could be done). For good measure Bevin told the world that if any Allied planes were shot at it would be regarded as an act of war.

The siege had begun, and it destroyed any illusion of Soviet neutralism at a stroke, particularly for the American public. It firmly committed the British, French and United States governments jointly and severally to remain in Berlin, necessitating the airlift and precipitating the formation of the North Atlantic Treaty Organisation (NATO). It was not quite the beginning of the Cold War; that had already begun with Stalin's takeover of the eastern European countries. What the siege did was put the cards on the table for Anglo-American military and political policy decisions. Their objectives had to be rethought almost overnight and the policy of containment of Soviet expansionism was established as a firm and unshakeable way forward. It was a watershed for a military build-up and an intensive intelligence offensive on both sides.

As the siege began few believed the Allied statements that they were determined to stay, least of all the Berliners – actions spoke louder than words and British and French Army families were being sent home. General Clay heard what was happening and stopped any American families from leaving. Large formations of Russian tanks and artillery moved ostentatiously into the regions bordering Berlin and its citizens were sorely afraid.

Clay had been struggling to supply the city with the increasing road and rail traffic restrictions, but now the dice were cast and he needed to know if he could depend on the people of Berlin. Clay went to see Ernst Reuter, Mayor of Berlin and another of the players in the Great Game, to ask if his people would be able to suffer the privations of hunger and cold that they would have to endure as a Continental winter approached. Reuter's answer was as unequivocal as Truman's, 'Do what you are able to do; we shall do what we feel to be our duty, Berlin will make all the necessary sacrifices and offer resistance, come what may.' Clay was satisfied and without referring to Washington issued orders to put all available resources into creating an airlift to supply the city.

The great armada of aircraft, equipment and men required to move the mountains of food, fuel and all manner of goods needed to feed, keep warm and sustain a city of 2 million souls had begun. United Nations dietitians estimated that an adult needed 2,600 calories a day to live an active life but Berliners were only getting about half of that. They would get even less as the airlift struggled to keep up with demand, and the Allied administration began to fear that an already undernourished population would slowly starve to death – and many did. The Russians advised that anyone who wanted to register with them for extra food rations would be welcome. Only a few thousand moved across the border, as they knew there were bound to be strings attached and Berliners knew that the Russian zone was just as short of food as the Allies'. The airlift would only just manage to feed the people as they sat in the cold and dark that winter – if Berliners wanted to have light and warmth they would go hungry. Hundreds froze to death in their homes and the disposal of the dead became a problem. The price that Berliners would have to pay for their freedom was going to be high.

From a standing start the creation of the airlift was an unimaginably difficult task – Allied intelligence indicated that the Russians expected the siege to force the city to evacuate its population by the end of August. All military personnel were by now being flown into and out of the airports of Berlin (one of the first flights in the airlift included a small detachment of the Queen's Battalion rearguard, of which your author was one). The movement order issued for our small party of men to rejoin the regiment and fly into Berlin's Gatow airport mentioned earlier was the first of thousands of men moving in and Berliners, particularly children, being moved out. The mysterious gentlemen in pinstripe suits also mentioned earlier were a part of the mobilisation of the Berlin Station of the British Secret Service. We did not know that the service was rotten to the core; double agents working for the KGB, or NKDV as it was then, were in situ in high places in London, Washington and Berlin. In spite of this, the Soviet Secret Intelligence Service missed forecasting the possibility of an airlift operation as it thought it was not possible to feed a major city by air – but then neither did most people. Berliners, the Soviets and indeed some Allied commanders watched in disbelief as it would take a few weeks for Bevin's determination and Truman's firm decision to get a major air-supply operation into gear, but gradually it did. As the tempo of the airlift increased, so did the spirits of Berlin's people – a little. There was much to do and no time in which to do it. The determination of Berliners to endure the privation would be central to resisting the challenge of the siege, the magnitude of which had never been seen before in history.

Our Dakota aircraft was one of the first to land at Gatow airfield (not airport because it only had a dirt runway) which was nearly deserted when we arrived but only days later was transformed into a frantic hive of activity. The airfield sprung into life as the vanguard of a great armada of aircraft began their immense task and the transformation of the scene was amazingly theatrical. We found out later that details of our flight and indeed every other traffic movement made in air and cargo operations were reported in detail to Moscow by the Russian intelligence service.

Even at this early stage NKVD operatives were incredibly active in observing everything from the edge of the airfield through powerful binoculars. Unfortunately, not only for them but also the huge Allied effort to supply the city, they felt unable to tell Stalin that the Allied airlift was gathering strength; they were sure that Stalin would not want to hear the bad news, so many intelligence evaluations fell on stony ground. Messengers reported to the Kremlin that the airlift was not succeeding and cargo deliveries would not stop Berliners starving – which was almost true. If the siege was seen to be succeeding, or even just not failing dramatically, Stalin might have decided to discontinue the failed strategy a lot earlier than he did. The lack of communication could have been to the Allies' long-term advantage, Stalin's misjudgement would be underlined and emphasised to the world as the airlift gathered its strength. Peter Sichel, the deputy chief of Berlin Operations Base (BOB), commented, 'I always regarded the blockade as a miscalculation by the Russians. They always wanted to see how far they could go and they went to too far.'

The airlift was a decisive defeat for the communists in the Cold War and to have prolonged it only made it more obvious to the world. But it was a close-run thing, Berlin had two airfields that could be used for operational purposes and they were stretched to the limit to satisfy the demands of the city's cold and hungry population. More capacity was needed.

The larger airport was Templehof, in the American sector, and it had been the city's main civil airport in times of peace. It had been a factory making Messerschmitt fighters during the war, then a hospital for casualties from air raids and, later still, wounded soldiers as the Red Army closed in to assault Berlin. The airport was not in very good shape when the United States Air Force took it over from the Red Air Force and structures needed much repair and reconstruction. Building large structures rapidly is an American talent, so a 1,600 yard runway of pierced steel planking was laid with a taxi apron and concrete block hardstanding in quick time.

The facility to unload and handle cargo was desperately needed as Templehof had to deal with the major workload and tonnage of cargo for the duration of the airlift. In its first weeks, more than 14,000 flights landed at the two airfields, flying in just over 70,000 tons of desperately needed supplies. In the following month of August just over 18,000 flights brought in nearly 120,000 tons – but it was still not nearly enough. Food stocks were dwindling by 1,500 tons a day, fuel of all kinds was running out and the public services such as the city's hospitals needed 2,500 tons of coal every twenty-four hours. That was before any allocation of coal could be made for domestic use – and it all came in sacks that had to be manhandled out of the holds of a ceaseless stream of ageing aircraft.

The operation was first designated Carter Patterson by the British, but the Russians soon realised the name was that of a well-known British furniture removal firm. To avoid any implication of a removal from Berlin, the operations name was later changed it to Planefare .

The drumbeat of mobilisation among Allied air forces around the world sounded loudly as aircraft of many nationalities, lifting capacities and technical configurations were on their way from Alaska, Hawaii, Japan and the United States. Contingents of the British Commonwealth air forces were also ordered to Berlin. Startled diplomats in Washington were being offered the use of bases in Britain that they had not even asked for, whose facilities were usually made available very slowly, cautiously and grudgingly. They saw the hand of Bevin in this new enthusiasm for co-operation.

The Royal Air Force had inherited the old Luftwaffe Gatow air training station situated to the west of the city, near to the Soviet zone's border of the city limits. The airfield was found to have no hard, structured runways so 1,500 yards of pierced steel planking was laid. However, the ground was sandy and unstable. A concrete runway was completed in record time as the fleet of Anson and Dakota aircraft needed to land on hardstanding rather than sinking up to the axles of their undercarriages in the winter mud.

Teams of German men and women (many of them ex-rubble women) were rapidly recruited and mobilised into a growing and diligent workforce to unload the cargos of a continuous stream of aircraft as soon as the propellers stopped turning (and sometimes before). The problems were not only to fly the tonnage of cargo into Berlin's airfields but to cope with getting the flow of supplies away from the airfields and into safekeeping. Hundreds, and later thousands, of Germans worked by day and by floodlit night to hump heavy sacks and crates of food and coal to waiting trucks, each with an armed guard.

The problems were many and various, but a principal one was finding the trained personnel for servicing and keeping the hundreds of overworked aircraft flying in all weather conditions. Wireless mechanic, Fredrick Burrows, based at Royal Air Force Manston in Kent was ordered to pack his kit bag and report to Wunstorf Airport in Germany, and this is his account of the event:

Like Noah's Ark we were led two by two (two for each trade) onto a waiting York aircraft and then to Wunstorf. The airfield there had been one of Goering's crack fighter squadron bases and a comfortable enough billet but we were immediately put on to a double shift duty. The airfield was covered in York and Dakota aircraft trying to manoeuvre in a sea of mud but after one or two aircraft bumped into each other and got stuck in the mud the army put down some hard standing. No camera could have done justice to the sight of a whole fleet of Avro Yorks and Dakotas lined up in long rows on either side of the main runway.

Our ground crew task was to inspect every plane before it took off, so by the time we had worked down the line of aircraft ready to take off the first ones were returning from Gatow. There was no time to fix faulty equipment so replacement of components became the normal practice. A standard part of the servicing procedure was a pair of bellows for blasting coal dust and flour from the sensitive parts of the T.1154 and R.1155 wireless equipment.

Some sixty years later, the Avro York serial MW232 aircraft, a veteran of the airlift, was being restored at the Imperial War Museum at Duxford and was found to still have flour and coal dust underneath its metal flooring.

Fred was one of the first to be assigned to the demanding and continuing task described, and this went on for months at a time. The dedication of both flight and ground crew was quite extraordinary; they were all dead tired for months at a time. One of the pilots, Flight Lieutenant Cornish, completed more than 3,000 sorties into and out of Berlin in eleven months. Fred recalls that out in the zone the food was good but they had a job to stay awake to eat it. However, for staff in Berlin's British sector the food was awful – dried fish was a favourite import, along with dried pea soup powder (lightness of payload was the first consideration within an aircraft that was trying to feed a hungry population). Unfortunately, the noxious pea soup took hours to boil up into an almost edible state, taking precious coal to heat it, so the awful pea powder was discontinued. Potatoes in their dehydrated or powdered state were much lighter than the real thing so a large part of our vegetable diet in aircraft cargos contained POM powdered potato. It became a staple of everyone's diet, even being baked into bread, so naturally it became the subject of uproarious German jokes about it being a substitute for cement (also in short supply).

The Americans lived better than the rest of us as a quid pro quo for contributing the major effort to feeding the city. One American soldier casually told us that his steak at dinner was tough – 'Steak? STEAK? Come over to us and enjoy some POM and dried fish buddy!' Most Berliners would have welcomed even our invitation to POM; there were not many overweight Germans in Berlin during the airlift.

Not only was there a shortage of skilled technicians but also equipment at most airfields. In the early months of the lift loading ceased as it grew dark, no floodlights were available, loading ramps were in short supply, and charging dollies for aircraft were at a premium and were being 'borrowed' constantly. As autumn approached snow and icing became an increasing problem, and then as winter approached fog and low cloud made conditions even more hazardous. Pilots were still flying in weather in which they should have long since been grounded.

Pressure on aircrew created a problem for Gatow that Tempelhof did not experience. Civilian aircrew were being hired increasingly and when they came they brought their own aircraft with them, creating fresh problems. At least the RAF had compatible wireless frequencies, spare parts and equipment, but civilian kit was variable and of very uncertain quality. Radio crystals in R/T sets created the worst problem for compatibility. The countryside was scoured for crystals so that 'Civvy' aircraft could tune to a frequency that enabled them to talk to the tower on approach to landing.

Civilian aircrew also lacked the discipline of their RAF opposite numbers, although many had served in the air force during the war. One such was the legendary Retired Air Vice Marshal (Pathfinder) Bennett, renowned for his superb airmanship and, conversely, lack of air discipline. After unloading his cargo at Gatow he would casually take off again and fly round Berlin's airspace revisiting the landmarks he used to bomb during the war. Air controllers in Gatow tower, which was managing an incredibly crowded airspace, had fits of terror and anger by turns as Bennett's aircraft drifted in and out of its air

corridors. No one had the nerve to tell such a renowned and eminent man off, though, so he just kept on doing it.

Not only was there a shortage of men and equipment but there were too few airfields. An additional one was planned at Tegel in Berlin's French sector in the early stages of the siege, and 17,000 Berliners turned out to build a 5,000ft runway, which they did in three months, a month ahead of schedule. The dedicated teams of undernourished workers created one of the many legends of the blockade. Tegel soon became operational, but a 200ft radio tower owned by the Soviet Radio Berlin network was sticking up right in the new airfield's flight path, presenting a danger to aircraft. Many requests were made to the Russians to remove it, with no success, and finally the French General Ganeval ran out of patience and took a demolition team into the Russian sector and blew it up himself. The Soviets were furious and General Kotikev stormed into the French general's office, shouting, 'How could you do such a thing?' General Ganeval's cool reply was, 'With dynamite and French Sappers'. His own countrymen loved him for it, and in Berlin they saw the general's action as a significant commitment to stay in their city – he was their hero.

In Gatow the airlift was going from strength to strength and needed to recruit a growing workforce, many of whom were German Army veterans returning from British and American prisoner-of-war cages. They not only lent muscle to unloading the increasing flow of cargos but also a certain discipline. They tended to gather in groups who had served together – artillery men formed quite a large and noisy group, ex-tank crews formed smaller groups, while quietly disciplined infantry squads went about their work in teams with little fuss but quiet determination.

The groups that I gravitated towards contained smaller clusters of military intelligence men, who often had an almost distinctive cerebral air about them. Veterans of the *Abwehr* intelligence agency seemed mostly to be too proud to get involved in Berlin's new and often strange intelligence scene. Maybe it was too distanced from the discipline of their army service, although some expressed a yearning for employment in a more professional intelligence agency.

German Army veterans gathered in increasing numbers at Gatow and were eagerly recruited to bolster those engaged in the heavy work of unloading tightly packed cargo. Working for the airlift gave Berliners an occupation with some respect and even some pride in helping the city. Workers at Gatow increasingly gained the respect of their German fellows, but probably just as importantly the work gave them two meals a day to sustain them through the long hours and exhausting work. Many still went hungry, though, as they took much of the food home for their children, no matter how much they were told not to do so.

The unremitting effort demanded occasional breaks, so veterans would gather together, as old soldiers do, to sit and talk over old times and comrades they had known. I joined their relaxation largely to practise my German and they accepted the company of an untried young soldier, probably for the cigarettes that he brought with him. The talk was sometimes in English, as several had been prisoners of war in England or America, but gradually a knowledge of German rubbed off on me, more by osmosis than by tuition, to strengthen distantly remembered school lessons. Groups exchanged reminiscences round the embers of wood fires as the winter drew on and the darkness enabled their presence not to be missed too easily. Their recollections became even more interesting as my understanding increased, they even shared photos and papers to portray vivid pictures of how intelligence was gleaned by the *Abwehr* in battlefield conditions.

Many of those stories became the basis of my previous book on the wartime history of signals intelligence from the viewpoint of the German *Wehrmacht*. The fireside chats created a warmth and respect for those men, which I kept up for some years afterwards. Sadly, all are gone now, but they were a fascinating link with the history, art and science of military intelligence 'on the other side of the hill' at a tumultuous time. The extraordinary story of Bletchley Park only emerged with a book published in 1976, but until then the German Army's *Abwehr* intelligence agency men sitting round a small fire in a busy airfield still believed that they were the best. The realisation that there was a far better player in the field hit many of them hard, but some were about to play a new role in the Cold War's intelligence conflict.

My German veterans had watched powerless as the Allies carried out savage autopsies on Germany's intelligence agencies, technical operations and equipment revealed after the war. As the armies of the Grand Alliance occupied a defeated nation they stripped it of any technological assets or developments of value. The Russians took everything they could move – vehicles, machine tools, trams, railways engines and telephone exchanges. Some pieces of heavy machinery that were too difficult to move were sawn into pieces never to go together again and thrown on to railway trucks as scrap metal. Other lighter machinery was just stripped out, with no idea how to use it. I remember a clock case at the entrance of a gutted and empty factory where the works had been taken out but the hands had been left behind.

Everything was shipped off to the east by the Russians as a form of reparation (or revenge). They acted like locusts, stripping out anything remotely useful (and many things that were not) that could have been used for a conquered people's future industrial recovery. The Western Allies stole technology in a more sophisticated fashion; they formed committees that oversaw targeted operations to extract specific German scientific and technical know-how.

Operation Alsos determined that Germany was far behind America in understanding how to make an atomic bomb, while Operation Surgeon targeted the understanding of avionics technology and the jet engine research. Commander Ian Fleming's Commando Assault Unit snatched the entire research archive of the *Kriegsmarine* with literally tons of documents on the advanced design of mines, torpedoes and U-boats. Some of the experiences of his unit, dedicated to snatching intelligence in equipment or documentary form, can be recognised in passages from his James Bond novels written after the war. Operation Paperclip, on the other hand, was an American operation that not only took working models of rockets and the technical studies in order to understand German rocketry research but the development team as well. Paperclip persuaded the German rocket scientists' team, headed by Werner von Braun, to go to the United States and help design the space rockets that would send its astronauts to the moon.

SPANDAU AND TICOM

The various technology programmes were well under way when a cryptanalyst – it may have been American or British (there is a difference of opinion here) – wondered if signals intelligence technology had been included in the programme. So TICOM (Target Intelligence Committee) was added as a latecomer to the reparations programme as the Allies realised that it could be a useful weapon in the fast-escalating Cold War.

It started as a project to seize some German *Abwehr* signals intelligence assets but soon accelerated when Russia was found to be seeking advanced German coding machines. It was realised that finding innovative coding and cipher equipment and material could help the Allies to break Russian codes and give GCHQ a great advantage. British and American cryptographers were hurriedly dispatched to Germany and Austria to find out what they could find. Their task was to comb the captured German signals establishments and interrogate their personnel still held in Allied prisoner-of-war camps in a search for clues in finding those cryptographic riches.

TICOM had become an important signals intelligence operation, not just for its immediate objectives but a less obvious long-term one as well. After the war, Churchill had ordered the destruction of all of Bletchley Park's code-breaking facilities that had created such a bond between British and American code breakers. Britain still had strong assets in signals intelligence but they were ageing and weakening against the stronger American cryptographic efforts, which meant that the United States was beginning to lead the way.

The TICOM operation's results somewhat enhanced Anglo-American co-operation and began to strengthen that bond once again, although not to what it had been. The establishment of GCHQ in Britain as a major electronics intelligence gathering facility confirmed the closer co-operation between the two countries. The achievements of Bletchley Park, which had created the successes against the Nazis, had begun to fade but TICOM operations helped to confirm that it was still there and there was an increasing amount to do in the Cold (intelligence) War.

My involvement in the TICOM operation was unofficial and fortuitous. Up to then I had been involved in low-level intelligence gathering, mainly consisting of clandestinely visiting Berlin night clubs and bars to note the insignia of Russian officers to try and identify their units. Invaluable intelligence was gathered in this operation, such as the Christian names of many of the hat-check girls serving in Berlin's dancehalls.

The introduction to the American TICOM operation personnel came out of an incident while the guard was being mounted at Spandau Prison, housing the seven major Nazi war criminals convicted in the Nuremburg War Crimes Trials. They were Rudolf Hess, Walther Funk and Admiral Erich Raeder, who were serving life sentences, Albert Speer and Baldur von Schirach, who faced twenty years, Konstantin von Neurath, who got fifteen years and Admiral Karl Donitz, who faced ten years' imprisonment.

Guard companies of French, British, Americans and Russians each took it in turn to watch over the ageing gang of war criminals. They had helped to bring ruin and terror to Europe and killed millions of people, but they really seemed harmless enough as they tended their own garden plots within the prison walls, or chatted idly in the sunshine while leaning on their garden hoes. Soldiers armed with Sten guns were posted in towers on the prison walls surrounded by an impressive electrified fence containing a 50,000 volt electric charge that was a perfect symbol of Cold War politics.

The cultural attitude of the Soviets and the Allies to the prisoners differed greatly, as you might expect. The Russians strongly advocated immediate, and probably exquisitely painful, execution of the seven for their crimes, while the Allies saw the Nuremburg Trials as a more judicial process in which allocation of the measure of guilt was made before determining a suitable punishment. The Soviets were astonished at the leniency of the sentences for the seven. To the Russians anything less than death for the terrible crimes to which the prisoners had been party was unacceptable. They felt that the verdicts should have reflected the suffering of the millions of victims of the invading German Army that had invaded their country. The Allies had not suffered in the same way and were seen as having a softer attitude, even promising the rehabilitation of an aggressive German nation once again. Maybe the high electric fences at Spandau were to keep the Red Army out …

As the sentences were handed down at Nuremburg the problem had arisen as to where to incarcerate the Nazi seven. The unanimous conclusion was they needed to be kept under the control of all of the four powers jointly. Berlin was the only place in Europe that truly offered the opportunity for a system of joint occupation and control. The seven were sent to Spandau as a temporary solution, to begin their prison sentences as the sole occupants of a prison built to accommodate 600. The temporary arrangement lasted until Hess died in custody forty years later.

The Allies did not like the situation, but suffered it in relative silence while the Soviets made louder and louder pronouncements from the high moral ground about the wickedness of the war criminals. The airlift changed the attitudes of the four powers co-operating in guarding the prison. It had become a symbol in the city, sharing the guard duties at Spandau was one of the few joint operations left. It preserved an illusion of the Allies and Russians working together – if this failed, what other arrangements would also fail? Changing the Guard was a spectacle that became the public affirmation of a shared duty that the Allies liked better than the Russians, whose popularity was plummeting as the airlift progressed.

Not everything went without incident for our guards, however. A Sten gun was an unreliable weapon, but light and easy to carry with a simple automatic mechanism so all the guards carried them on prison duty. As the guards were relieved they would parade in the prison courtyard, fortunately away from public view, and on this occasion someone dropped his Sten set on automatic with a full magazine of ammunition. The gun fired off all the rounds automatically, swathing down the guard. Bullet wounds are not trivial matters, even though they are sometimes dismissed as flesh wounds – bullets hit flesh at the speed of sound and with a force of 2 tons to the square inch, usually punching a small entry hole in the victim. The impact on the body makes them begin to tumble, tearing the tissue as they go, and invariably a bullet's exit wound is more serious than the entry, particularly if it impacts on bone.

In a moment, the British guard at the prison effectively ceased to exist. Alarms went off all over Berlin; set off not only by the Russians but the French as well – the four-power arrangement almost ceased to exist that day. There were many red faces in high places as the Soviets made high drama out of the British dereliction of duty. The panic took a while to subside and guard changes became less formal. The American soldiers on guard relief were sympathetic, they were no strangers to firearms accidents themselves. We chatted easily with them and one or two showed a passing interest in the connections with our German signals intelligence friends at Gatow. Informal invitations were exchanged and we visited our new American friends in their sector, which was much enjoyed, mainly due to American hospitality.

Our hosts included some TICOM team members who talked about their task, so the conversation turned once again to the German intelligence veterans at Gatow. TICOM operations had been under way for some time but were beginning to run down; the major objectives had been achieved but there were some investigations still to be cleared up. The US Army was also running down after the war and a great many of its personnel were returning to the States, and this left the TICOM operation short-handed. They needed help and wondered, could our friends help?

An informal visit to Gatow followed and after much negotiation the German veterans were hired, not with money but cigarettes, which were more valuable to our German friends than the almost valueless German paper money. Even more valuable was the gift (or bribe) from the Americans of a few jars of real coffee. My ability to communicate with the group meant that I was included in the deal and in the following weeks the German veterans earned their cigarettes by indicating sites, finding several ex-signals intelligence men and two women secretaries. My contacts were of such interest that the TICOM operation took on a brief new lease of life and the activities were reported to our superiors. My report caused a stir and the matter was referred upwards to General Robertson's staff at the Military Governor's Office. A staff officer seemed very interested in what the Americans were doing, so the whole matter then became semi-official, i.e. 'Go ahead, but if you get into trouble we do not know anything about it'.

Semi-social outings (with American food) were arranged, some of which were interesting. The Führer Bunker in the Reich Chancellery garden, just inside the Russian sector and under the shadow of the Brandenburg Gate, was one. The site of Hitler's cremation was known and pointed out by a Red Army sergeant, although it was officially denied later as it was in the Soviet interest to maintain that the 'bogey man' lived and was still a threat to the world. The unimpressive concrete entrance to Hitler's massive underground emplacement was pockmarked with bullet holes and the interior was lit by an unreliable, flickering electric light system. There was not a torch among our group so none of us ventured much past the steel door into the dimly lit interior.

The Reich Chancellery was a different matter. It was a huge hall with an impressive hole in the roof letting the sunlight stream in, and a deep bomb crater in the centre of the marble floor did little to detract from its grandeur. The 20ft-high bronze doors, one of which was off its hinges, led into to Hitler's study. His sanctum was a smaller room with a monolithic black marble desk whose drawers had been ransacked by every soldier who had visited the Führer's den.

A scattering of spectators wandered in the ruins, mostly in Red Army uniforms. One stout female Red Army major challenged our group in halting English. We rapidly withdrew to safety beyond the white line painted on the roadway, which defined the edge of the British sector – it was easy to find yourself in a Russian jail for a night or two just by being in the wrong place, as boundaries between the Russian and Allied sector were often unmarked and indefinite.

Some Americans who joined the group did not seem to be army, although a couple of soldiers were G2 intelligence. When the German veterans met the group they had homed in on the intelligence people before I even realised who they were. Our veterans soon engaged the Americans in deep conversation, some of which needed my interpretation, and soon it became obvious that the exchanges were touching on sensitive subjects. Some of their conversation centred on the Gehlen Organisation, which the veterans had mentioned before, and from the looks on their faces we were going to hear more about again. I certainly did, as I was going to witness the beginning of a fresh chapter in international intelligence in the Cold War.

SIX

BERLIN

Local intelligence in both the American and British sectors, and the Berlin situation in general, was poor as the crisis developed. My tour of the dance halls to identify the units of the Russian soldiery was a small part of the effort to improve it. Newly arrived detachments of both British and American military intelligence units arrived in the city to face a well-established opponent who was a past master at the intelligence game.

British intelligence had been running down its military establishments as the war finished and our people had seen little reason to keep their military intelligence antennae active as the hostilities ceased. It also did not help that there was little exchange of information between the British and Americans, as the relationship between them had always been that of friendly (and sometimes not so friendly) rivals. They both sometimes played their cards close to their chest; particularly the Brits, who were a naturally secretive bunch. At a national level everyone was aware that knowledge is power and the British had begun with the edge on the Americans in intelligence, particularly in signals intelligence.

The Americans were quick learners and were catching up fast. They still had some way to go, however, as the British had a long record of success stretching back to the revelations they had made to the American president about the interception of the Zimmermann Telegram in 1918. The alliance would soon need to co-operate again and regain their intelligence skills as they faced a powerful adversary in the KGB, and they would need to improve to guide their decisions in the coming confrontation.

Berlin's position as a base from which to monitor the activities of the Russian-dominated nation states was ideal for the development of several major intelligence networks that would drive the Cold War clash of ideologies for decades to come. The city grew rapidly into the espionage capital of the world aided by very heavy funding from the budgets of a multitude of intelligence agencies and their governments on both sides of the Iron Curtain. Berlin's new-found a role as a strategic listening post deep in the heartland of Russia's eastern European vassal states would earn it much money as well as a certain reputation. It became a training ground and channel for agents and spies of both sides, to be launched into enemy territory as East and West stood eyeball to eyeball across the border of a divided Germany.

An estimate of the number of countries maintaining espionage presences in the city varied greatly – above twenty well-funded major agencies was one estimate, plus half a dozen others, depending on which agency was doing the counting. The main players on the Allied side were the American BOB in Clayallee, the British SIS (MI6) station in the Olympic Stadium and the French Deuxieme Bureau complex in Quarter Napoleon. The intelligence community in the city employed thousands of legitimate agents and many tens of thousands more who acted as their informers or scouts, according to semi-official sources. A host of anti-communist agencies operating in nightclubs, coffee houses, or even in their own well-appointed offices, sought to sell secret information to anyone who would pay their price. That fee could range from the cost of a good dinner to an exorbitant cash payment, but the information rarely came with any kind of guarantee.

There was a rough social division between the various kinds of intelligencer. The professionals were always 'intelligence officers', while the rest were labelled 'agents', or worse. In the world of smoke-obscured mirrors an intelligence officer could turn into an agent for the other side if he (or she) was turned, while some of the less established agents were known to the professionals as the '*hundert mark jugen*' or 'hundred mark youths'. They were used for errands of varying degrees of danger or discomfort, and this collection of dubious and sometimes violent individuals was pitted against the huge communist espionage machine based in the Karlshorst district of Berlin.

The Soviet intelligence operations, measured against the Allied ones, easily outdistanced them in the Cold War's early years. The espionage scene in Berlin was a chaotic mess of competing intelligence organisations, individuals and interests of all shades that emerged as the airlift began and the expansionist nature of communist intentions became clear to the world. Even the KGB directorate described the city quite openly as an 'espionage swamp', even though it owned many of the alligators. The many agencies, and particularly the individual agents who promised much and often delivered little, made its secrets and rumour mills turn even faster.

The Cold War had changed many aspects of intelligence, but particularly its application; in 'hot war' conditions the battlefield evaluations are of little use without them being backed up by force. That axiom no longer applied in the same way in Europe's Cold War because the conflict was never allowed to deteriorate into the use of substantial force since intelligence gave prior warning of worsening situations. The technology available to the espionage agent had developed over the years, but the need for a clear intelligence picture of the enemy's intentions remained.

The difference between intelligence in war and peace, therefore, is that in wartime it directs, or more probably suggests, how a commander's forces can best attack the enemy that faces him. In times of peace (or lack of a hot war) gathering details of a potential enemy's order of battle and objectives becomes a precautionary measure rather than a hostile act. As the airlift progressed it was essential to ensure that the Red Army was not going to attack the sparsely manned Berlin Garrison, whose only protection was the fact that an act of war implied the use of nuclear weapons.

Intelligence operations to gain knowledge of Soviet intentions and the strength and capability of the Red Army was of crucial importance to Allied leaders in a policy of peaceful (or maybe armed neutral) containment of Russia. In the first three decades of modern intelligence from 1914, the reports and evaluations that landed on the politicians' desks were almost all of a military or naval nature. From 1945 the purpose of intelligence evaluations had become much more political with the sabre-rattling posture of investment in aircraft, ships and men being used incessantly in a propaganda war that was peripheral to the intelligence one. It was to convince the enemy (and the public) that your country and its forces were ready for any potential enemies' attack and of our ability to counter it. Intelligence operations of a special intensity were carried out by both sides, all in a defensive posture, although operations on either side never quite assured anyone of their enemy's intentions. A misleading intelligence evaluation could result in the outbreak of war; not just an ordinary war but quite possibly a full-blown nuclear holocaust. The value of good intelligence was in reliably reading the enemy's mind and his intentions in a volatile and dangerous world.

Communist culture was largely ignored by the Western Allies until its repressive political offensive against the people of Germany in general, and Berlin in particular, became evident. The Allies' complete lack of preparedness for the Soviets' espionage onslaught left them needing time to build their own intelligence network to combat Russia's. The result was that the Russian and American agencies facing each other both sponsored another agency of their own, each with German roots.

The two agencies that developed were the Gehlen Organisation and the Ministry for State Security, or the Stasi, as it is known, both of whom faced each other with even more dedicated fanaticism than their parent organisations. They were both driven and sponsored by the reflected ambition that spread the dedicated culture of their KGB and nascent CIA parents.

Soviet policy to contain and delay the reconstruction of the German state was designed to help serve the ambition of communism and to spread its ideology around the globe. The Soviet intelligence agencies were monolithic and ponderous in operation but able to outperform the Allies in Europe, who were outnumbered and underfinanced in the beginning, although that would change. The great limitation of the upper reaches of the Soviet intelligence service was that its officers were unable to convince Stalin of the truth of any intelligence evaluations that did not agree with his own fixed conclusions. A dramatic lack of open-mindedness to trust the evaluations that the Soviet Leader was offered led to the fear that if the intelligence officers offered the wrong advice their freedom, or even lives, might be forfeit. That was the fatal weakness of Russian security services.

Stalin's faults in the acceptance of intelligence evaluation were similar to those of Hitler, but with the difference that the Russian controlled his secret service with a rod of iron, unlike the Führer who gave too much of a free rein to his and yet still did not believe it. Intelligence evaluations are only of value if received by decision makers with an open mind and not contrived (or in Hitler's case rejected) to fit into their preconceived conclusions. Churchill was particularly good at the use of intelligence reports because he had much experience of their use in the First World War when he was involved in creating Room 40.

Stalin's murderous and suspicious character caused him to make huge errors of judgement, but he used his instruments of power and terror to enforce them. They consisted of a triumvirate of powerful institutions with which to control his country and colleagues – or, rather, underlings. The bodies were the Communist Party, the Red Army and the Committee for State Security (KGB), which was the Soviet secret police. It started as the Cheka in 1917 after the Revolution, as the all-Russian Commission for Combating Counter-revolution and Sabotage, and then became the OGPU for a few years before it became the People's Commissariat for Internal Affairs (NKVD) in 1924, with the notorious Lavrenty Beria at its head as the Cold War started, and later the NKGB during the war. As the Cold War started in 1946 it was renamed again as the Ministry of State Security (MGB), then the Ministry of Internal Affairs (MVD) and finally the KGB, but all the organisations had much the same overall function – repression at home and subversion abroad.

Global intelligence was the responsibility of the Soviet Foreign Intelligence Service (SVR), whose 1st Directorate was dedicated to the collection of foreign intelligence against capitalist countries and their policies, and technical knowledge. The KGB, on the other hand, was the main instrument of repression at home (the occupied countries of eastern Europe were regarded as 'home') and had been incredibly effective at subjugating its huge population. Its role in Germany would later be delegated to the Stasi, but still under the rigid control of the KGB and backed up by the might of the Red Army.

Soviet Russia had a very successful espionage and intelligence operation centre in Germany from well before the war, and even during it, so the expertise that sprang from that experience was fully used in post-war Germany. Specialist groups of the Soviet intelligence service advanced into Germany with the Red Army to link up with agents that were already in place as the war came to its end in May 1945. More than a month before Russian troops entered Berlin, Stalin had devised a framework for a Soviet espionage network within which to operate throughout Europe and particularly Germany. The Karlshorst Residency, taking its name from the district of Berlin of the same name, started intelligence operations even before fighting had ceased.

Colonel Aleksandr Korotkov was a highly experienced intelligence officer who had served in the NKVD station in Berlin before the German invasion of the Soviet Union in 1941. He had helped to run the 'Red Orchestra' espionage network in Germany, which was probably one of the most effective spy networks in history. Korotkov was given very few staff and even fewer resources with which to take the first steps in a methodical plan for the development of an intelligence network to cover Germany, but based in and concentrating on Berlin. The appointment of an officer who was familiar with the German scene was a very good one: it got the Soviet intelligence network off to a flying start, with his residency already being in contact with various Soviet agents. Numbers of them had worked undercover in the Nazi administration and provincial government before and during the war to keep Moscow informed on the Nazi war effort.

The Residency began recruiting additional agents, mainly coming from the newly formed 'bourgeois' parties such as the Christian Democrats, who were ordered to report on British and American personnel in areas of joint control. Evaluations and plans for the gathering of intelligence from West Berlin and the Western zones of occupation went on apace.

The preparation for Soviet intelligence networks in Germany stands out in stark contrast with that of the total lack of preparation of the Allied intelligence network. The Allies had built up the wartime Office of Strategic Services (OSS) in 1943, which had close informal links with Soviet intelligence. Those links were much closer than General William (Wild Bill) Donavan, head of OSS, could have imagined. The Soviets had penetrated the OSS comprehensively at all levels, from field officers to State Department staff, with their own spies and were very well informed about all its plans and programmes.

President Truman knew nothing of the infiltration by Soviet agents but decided to disband the OSS as the war had come to an end anyway, which was well for the future of American intelligence operations. Wild Bill did not realise that the OSS was not fit for purpose in providing the main weapons of the coming conflict. They would not be guns and tanks, but information and intelligence, and a security service needed all the confidence and assets it could muster.

The American military had learned the value of intelligence from the British and the huge achievements of Bletchley Park in the war, but now it believed the conflict was over. There seemed no point in maintaining the effort so the Allied intelligence system was being run down and professional staff were being reduced to peacetime levels, which were very low indeed. American operatives were left to administer a service for which there seemed to be no clear future in sight, although the British still had an interest in the European scene as they were closer to it and did not trust the Russians as the Americans seemed to do. They were keeping an eye on Soviet military and economic activities using their ever-reducing staff (although it was not as reduced as the Americans because, for them, the job was done and they were packing up to go home).

What was left was mainly the G2 intelligence sections of the American and British armies, primarily because they were an established part of their army's command structure and not because they had any clear objectives. The Allies were in for a shock.

The Allies discovered that they were facing a highly professional Soviet intelligence service with a continuing history and experience going back as far as the British one, but with much clearer objectives. Its spies were everywhere, often in surprisingly high places, and had penetrated most of the areas of decision making in Allied government circles. Soviet agents were eventually found at every level of American government and they were well enough connected to obtain minutes of British Cabinet meetings within days of them taking place. The archives of the KGB in Moscow after the Cold War finished revealed a continuing series of disclosures that now show how effective Soviet intelligence was at the time.

The methods of US Senator McCarthy may have been repulsive, but his conclusions seem to have been right – there were indeed 'reds under every bed'. A comparison with Allied intelligence services on both sides of the Atlantic showing that they were underfunded, poorly staffed and without a secure future was an invidious one. The Allies, or at least the Americans, did however have the advantage of outstanding leadership in the master spy Alan Dulles as head of the agency and Richard Wisner and Richard Helms, who were serving in the agency and succeeded him.

The German agencies used by both sides to help fight their intelligence war verified Hitler's words, 'both powers will sooner or later find it desirable to seek the support of the German people'. Both the Gehlen and the Stasi secret intelligence organisations were created to support their own side at about the time of the airlift. Both contributed substantially to the intelligence conflict that would shape and to some extent conclude the Cold War, and one at least would survive to become a world-class intelligence agency.

GEHLEN

The story of Allied intelligence began with a German general, Reinhard Gehlen, who was destined to help change the face of intelligence in the Cold War and his extraordinary story is worth telling. He was born on 3 April 1902 into a family with a military tradition. His father, Benno Walther Gehlen, served in the Prussian Army and achieved the rank of lieutenant colonel. His family crest carried the motto 'Never Give Up', which Gehlen boasted he carried through with him for the rest of his life. In his autobiography, *The Gehlen Memoirs*, he wrote that there was little to distinguish his childhood, education and upbringing from others in his country, but he was a child of his time, growing up in a household with a militaristic tradition.

He had the deep-seated conviction that the German Army was unbeatable by any other country in the world, in spite of the Armistice in 1918. The sense of superiority over other countries of the world was held strongly by the German nation, but was particularly so towards the Russian people and their culture. The prejudice against the Slavic people was based on the illusion that they were weaker in intellect, willpower and resolve than any other nation. They were seen as being animalistic and inherently inferior to the Germanic race, and there was worse – they were communists, and this struck at the heart of the Gehlen family's beliefs. They hated the socialist philosophy as it represented an attack on the standing of the officer corps of the army, industries' upper-class management and even royalty and the Kaiser.

German generals who planned the invasion of Russia agreed with this ideology and, mirroring the thinking and pronouncements of their leader, Adolf Hitler, they discounted the Red Army as a leaderless and inferior fighting machine. His pronouncements that 'Russia is ripe for collapse and the Russian is an inferior soldier' were widely accepted and there were some grounds for his saying so. In 1937 Stalin began a purge of the officers of the Red Army and one in four of them went to the Gulags, or worse.

The victims included many who had been battle hardened in the First World War, and the experience had not been a happy one for them. At the beginning of the First World War in 1914 Russian armies suffered a catastrophic defeat at the hands of a single, smaller German Army commanded by General Paul von Hindenburg at Tannenberg in East Germany. The German general's interception of the Imperial Russian Army's uncoded wireless transmissions gave him a crucial intelligence advantage in the battle, enabling him to almost destroy two Russian armies.

The comprehensive defeat of the Russian military forces virtually knocked Russia out of the war until the communists took power after the Revolution in 1917, and indeed that defeat was in part a reason for it happening. The Soviet government was compelled to sign a humiliating peace treaty at Brest-Litovsk in Poland and those memories caused Hitler and the German general staff to completely underestimate the effectiveness of the Red Army.

The planners at the German *Oberkommando der Wehrmacht* (OKW), or Armed Forces High Command, calculated that the campaign in 1941 would take just weeks. In that time they expected to conquer the largest country in the world; but it soon became obvious that the Russians were going to be a tough nut to crack. Owing to the German generals' overweening confidence in the outcome of its assault their army made little preparation for intelligence operations and the army's G2 intelligence arm shared the over optimism of its superiors.

The lack of good forward intelligence against the enemy was not seen as an important matter as the panzers swept over the Steppes on the offensive, but as Russian resistance stiffened and the advance slowed they thought again. Information on Russian Army units and their strengths and movements proved hard to come by as Soviet Russia's closed community proved difficult to penetrate. Very little hard information came through Germany's allies.

Japan had a little military information, mainly concerned with army formations posted on Russia's Pacific borders, but these were of little use to the German military planning on the eastern European front. Finland had fought the Red Army for three months and the OKW felt it should have had some good evaluations of Red Army strengths and order of battle on the Northern Front. That data was grudgingly shared as the Finns did not trust the Germans and the intelligence evaluations were unconfirmed.

As the German Army went on the defensive against the Red Army the need for better information on what the Soviets were up to became urgent.

General Franz Halder, who commanded the German Army on the Russian front, ordered his staff to provide intelligence reports that would deliver a clear picture of the Red Army order of battle. The Foreign Armies East (*Fremde Heere Ost*, FHO) was formed and as the campaign progressed Gehlen was put in command of the new intelligence branch.

The need for better intelligence became paramount to General Halder, so the new FHO commanding officer, Colonel Gehlen, was then appointed head of the general staff branch of FHO and spent most of his waking hours evaluating the military and economic strengths and weaknesses of Soviet Russia. Gehlen had passed out of the War Academy with distinction, particularly in the special classes on Soviet Union matters, and had prepared himself well to become Hitler's wartime intelligence chief in Russia. He had been involved in the planning of the annexation of Austria, the invasion of Czechoslovakia and later Poland and became Halder's principal ADC (aide-de-camp) in July 1940. His interest in eastern Europe helped him plan the build-up of forces in Romania to attack Yugoslavia and Greece as a prelude to Operation Barbarossa – the invasion of the Soviet Union.

During November there was a brief interlude when Gehlen attended a conference with Halder on Operation Sea Lion, the invasion of Britain. In his memoirs, Gehlen wrote that he 'gained the impression that Hitler did not take Operation Sea Lion seriously but regarded the entire plan as nothing more than an elaborate but very effective means of deceiving the Russians as to his real strategic intentions in the East'. Gehlen was pleased when the invasion project was dropped, most probably because he was anxious to get back to planning Operation Barbarossa. The lack of ships to mount a successful landing on England's south coast had been such a problem that Halder assured him that Sea Lion would not reoccur. Gehlen then resumed his work on the completion of Barbarossa. In his memoirs, Gehlen was convinced that Hitler was correct in taking his decision to attack the Soviet Union. He was sure that Stalin would soon attack Germany, although Hitler undoubtedly got the direction of the campaign wrong.

Gehlen met his Führer's deadline of 15 May 1941 for the finalisation of plans for Operation Barbarossa, although he had reservations about the intelligence data analysis methods of *Abwehr* intelligence, which he felt were without any systematic process of evaluation. Gehlen learned a lesson from this and established a team of analysts to collate the streams of intelligence coming in from many sources to ensure that clear deductions of intelligence were made. Such methods were rare in the German *Abwehr* agency practice, unlike the established custom in British intelligence circles of confirming all facts from several different sources.

Gehlen served his apprenticeship in intelligence, and this made him an outstanding figure in the field, which led him to meet Hitler, whose glaring blue eyes had a magnetic effect on him. He felt strongly that his leader was incapable of assessing the dimensions of major operations in time and space and weighing them against the means at his disposal. Gehlen compared Hitler to the similar views expressed by the wartime Chief of the Imperial Staff, Lord Alanbrooke, in his arguments about Winston Churchill, but there was an important difference. Churchill was an enthusiastic amateur strategist and extremely stubborn in arguing his ideas but always open to persuasion; he then rewarded his colleagues for their persistence with friendship and enduring loyalty. That was unlike Hitler who, when someone argued consistently with his plans, or even worse were proved right by events, soon found ways of getting rid of them. The difference between the styles of the two leaders was a major factor in the shaping of strategy in the way the war was fought. Hitler's fault proved to be his undoing when he was planning for the invasion of the Soviet Union.

The preparations for the invasion needed a jumping-off point in the Balkans so a pact had been signed in Belgrade between the Yugoslav government and Hitler in March 1940. In return for neutrality it would give the German Army the base that it required for the offensive. However, neither Hitler nor the Yugoslav Prince Regent Paul, who signed the agreement, had judged the mood of the Yugoslavian people correctly. Days after the signing the Yugoslavian Army took over the centre of Belgrade and Yugoslav Radio announced the immediate exile of Paul. The 17-year-old King Peter II ascended the throne and the coup was greeted with enthusiasm by his people. The document that Paul had just signed was torn up in public.

Hitler was furious, as only he could be, and orders went out to his commanders in the *Wehrmacht* to 'destroy Yugoslavia'. Operation Marita was prepared by Gehlen, followed by the invasion of northern Greece. Operation *Strafgericht* (Punishment) was launched against Yugoslavia with the Luftwaffe making an aerial attack on Belgrade and killing 17,000 men, women and children because they had frustrated the Führer's plans. German panzers then advanced rapidly through Yugoslavia and took Zagreb, then a few days later they were in Belgrade to accept the surrender of the Yugoslav Army. King Peter and his government fled to Egypt.

The German invasion force then passed through the Monister Gap in the mountains of Bitola on Greece's Bulgarian border to attack the Greek Army and the British troops who were supporting it. The British General Maitland Wilson was able to follow the moves the German Army was making with the aid of Ultra intelligence reports from Bletchley Park. He knew his force was too weak to hold the panzers so he began to withdraw his forces, but they delayed the Germans with a stand made at Thermopylae. The bulk of Maitland Wilson's men withdrew to the coast to be evacuated back to Egypt and others to the island of Crete.

The campaign had not gone exactly as Gehlen planned, but it had gone very well so far – then things began to go wrong. The German Army had swept through Greece driving the Greek and British armies before them, and its next objective would be the island of Crete, which was in a strategic position at the eastern end of the Mediterranean. Many Australian and New Zealand troops who had been evacuated from Greece had found their way on to the island to reinforce the small garrison. The battle for Crete heralded a new era in airborne warfare and was the first one to use the Ultra intelligence from Bletchley Park and its sister signals intelligence establishment based in Egypt.

A heavy German air and seaborne assault was made on the island but at such cost of the lives of his elite airborne paratroopers (*Fallschirmjäger*) that Hitler never used airborne assaults again. The heavy losses suffered in the German battle plan were due to Allied commander on Crete General Freyberg's men knowing from Ultra reports just where the dropping zones of the German paratroopers would be.

The Greek campaign was a disaster for the British, but it was a pyrrhic victory for Hitler as it had far-reaching effects on the overall conduct of the war. The German High Command expected to take Crete quickly and without much loss, but the heavy casualties suffered by the paratroops who had been earmarked for the next operation (the invasion of Syria) was a huge blow. The British got to Syria first and attacked the Vichy French troops, who were friendly to the Germans. However, the attackers also contained Free French troops under General de Gaulle. It was French against French – no wonder the American press called it a 'mixed affair'.

Churchill's decision to send troops to aid the Royal Greek Army was a gamble – was it to protect the southern flank of his ally Russia and maintain the supply route into Georgia through Iran? Certainly it gave the British the time to occupy Syria. The popular historian, John Keegan, said of the Greek campaign that he considered it to be a turning point in the war. Hitler's close confidant and friend, Leni Riefenstahl, whose film of the 1937 Olympics had made such a stir in pre-war Europe, reiterated the Führer's view when she revisited the Olympic Stadium when I was there. She quoted him as saying that if the Germans had not got embroiled in the Greek–Italian campaign the war could have taken a different course.

Hitler's offensive into the Soviet Union had been delayed for several critical months by the Greek campaign, so that the invaders were unprepared for the bitter fighting in the even more bitter Russian winter. The German invasion would have been a number of weeks earlier, before the cold weather set in, so the opinion held by Gehlen and other senior German officers was that in that time they could have conquered Leningrad and entered Moscow as well as Stalingrad. Gehlen would have been chomping at the bit as the fighting in the Balkans and British actions in Crete delayed the next step into Syria, but he had finalised his Operation Barbarossa plan for presentation to Hitler in early May.

On 21 June the German tanks broke down the structures that marked the Soviet Russian borders and swept up the surprised soldiers manning their inadequate border defences. Gehlen's lifelong ambition was to be achieved, or so he thought, as the panzers advanced 600 miles into the Soviet Union, putting more than 50 million Soviet citizens under Nazi rule.

General Gehlen, as he had become by then, was at the head of the most important military intelligence section in the German Army at a most critical time on the Russian front. There was an FHO intelligence agency in the West, based in Paris, but it never reached the same level of importance as Gehlen's Eastern Agency, partly because the German Army's attack on the Soviet Union that was planned to last only a few weeks was beginning to go awry.

Another serious long-term problem became apparent in the top secret rearmament plan of the United States, the magnitude of which was evaluated by the FHO largely just by sifting through reports in American newspapers. This was an example of Gehlen's use of publicly available information that enhanced his intelligence evaluations. This novel technique would be used to very good effect by his organisation in the future Cold War. Using the same techniques, he concluded that the US Army build-up of troops in

Britain in the year, based on the availability of shipping space, would be restricted and this would rule out the possibility of a major landing by Allied forces on the European coast in a Second Front for the next twelve months. American forces would only begin to appear in moderate strength in 1943, but the German High Command should expect increasing numbers of troop movements to reach a peak in 1944.

This good news for the German generals was generated by Gehlen's unique method of intelligence analysis, but his principal target in intelligence evaluations remained the Soviet Union. The strength of the Russian armed forces, and the strengths and weaknesses of the Soviet economy that sustained them, was his main interest and he had an important question to answer.

When he was appointed to his post the quality of Gehlen's reports improved out of all recognition but, as he said in his memoirs, it was not by black magic but by application, thoroughness and expert knowledge. The use of public domain information mixed with secret source material was beginning to be Gehlen's speciality, and he now used this to answer the most pressing question of the German High Command. It desperately needed to know what manpower reserves Russia had and if the Red Army could continue to find fresh divisions to put into the front line for its country's defence.

The received wisdom, from the intelligence the other generals were getting, was the comforting conclusion that the Red Army's supply of new recruits would soon be drying up. Gehlen reached a different conclusion using his own intelligence techniques; starting with the published population census for Russia in 1939 giving a figure of 170 million people in the country. The natural growth of the populace would probably have increased by 1942 to about 199 million people. The German Army had overrun an area where their records estimated that about 66 million Russians were living, of which an estimated third would had been evacuated or drafted into the Red Army. The Soviet Union was a relatively young nation, with almost half of its population being below 20 compared to that of Germany, where fewer than a third were under 20 years old. The high mortality rate in Russia among the older age groups meant that an increasingly high proportion of young men would be available for military service in future years. The proportion of Russian women in the population was high, which meant there was a large pool of female labour to be employed in war work. (I personally observed a surprising number of women in Red Army uniform in Berlin, mainly in artillery units.)

Using detailed Russian published statistical information as a basis for his calculations Gehlen estimated that Stalin could have a manpower reserve of about 17 million men on which to draw. Further calculations using other sources of data, both open and secret, confirmed that the accepted view was wrong and there was a huge reservoir of young men that would be available for service in Russia's armed forces.

Gehlen was not the only one to use publicly available information to reach surprising conclusions. The journalist Chapman Pincher, who recently died, disclosed many facts that deeply disturbed the British intelligence community. They tried everything to find out where he was getting his information from, even down to bugging some of his workplaces and finally putting D notices on his newspaper, the *Daily Express*, to restrict him from disclosing facts that they wanted to keep to themselves. After he retired, Pincher told the world with glee that he got a great deal of his information from publicly available information mixed with a bit of confidential stuff that his readers gave him.

Gehlen's news was not welcomed by the German generals as he presented his detailed evaluation, even though the report he gave them also revealed some better tidings for them. Research showed that although the Soviet Union was not going to suffer from a shortage of men with whom to hold up the German advance in front of Moscow and Stalingrad, it did have a dwindling supply of vital raw materials. For instance, the Soviet Union would have expected to mine 200 million tons of coal in the year in which the German Army advanced through the coal rich Donets region. However, the German occupation of that area had cut Russian coal supplies by more than 80 million tons, causing a severe shortage for the Russian railways that traditionally consumed about half of the country's coal output, with heavy industry in the Volga region, the Urals and Siberia consuming the rest.

Coalfields in the Urals and south-east Russia might produce enough for those distant factories in the east but for the important western industrial conurbation around the Volga River there was no local fuel supply. It had to be shipped 1,500 miles from eastern coal fields in railway engines using precious coal to get there and as a result several steel mills in the west would have to close down. The railway system and its overworked rolling stock had begun to show signs of wear and tear, while coal-powered ships carrying materials to the factories on the Volga waterways were also suffering. Coking plants essential for the production of iron and steel had been overrun by the Germans so that iron ore production had dropped from 40 to 13 million tons, slashing production of pig iron and steel to very low outputs. Manganese, tungsten and molybdenum ores needed to produce high-grade steel were also in short supply due to lack of transport and the threat of the German Army advancing over the deposits of those minerals. The report, using Gehlen's unique method of mixing military intelligence and economic data from the public and more secret sources, heartened his superiors considerably.

Petroleum production was not a problem for the Russians as they had been stockpiling huge amounts of it beyond the Urals, but the shortage of oil was a great concern for Hitler. General Halder urged his Führer to concentrate on attacking and taking Moscow as it was the nerve centre of the Soviet Union's armed forces and its economy. Hitler insisted that the primary target for his panzers should be the Caucasus oil fields in southern Russia. It was his solution to the increasing need for oil to lubricate the wheels and tracks of his military machine.

The generals, meanwhile, poured over their large scale maps of Russia in order to understand why the advances of the panzers over vast distances of the tundra to seize oil supplies were meeting such stiff resistance. They were ordered to launch an attack, not only on Stalingrad and the Caucasus but also an all-out attack in the north on Leningrad. Hitler's offensive was on a grand scale right across the whole of the Russian front but both General Halder and his intelligence officer, Gehlen, were unhappy about the scale of the grandiose plan. It would leave the north flank of the army exposed and the situation in Stalingrad was very disturbing as the elite military formations of the German Army were about to attack the city. Its flanks were guarded by the armies of Germany's uncertain allies, with the Hungarian Army on the left flank and the Romanian Army on the right. The Italians, in position in the rear, faced determined resistance from the Red Army.

The savage battle for Stalingrad raged for five months and was almost at a stalemate until the Soviet General Zhukov attacked the German allies on both of its weak flanks. The Red Army encircled the attacking force and took well over 100,000 prisoners, including their commander, General Fredrich Paulus. The action destroyed a major German Army formation that had started Hitler's invasion of Russia with a strength of more than 300,000 men.

Stalingrad is generally thought to be the turning of the tide in Hitler's invasion of the Soviet Union, but German military intelligence estimates said that the real turning point was the Battle of Kharkov, fought earlier in the campaign. Although the German High Command claimed victory in that battle, its army lost so many men that it did not have the strength to bring the assault on Stalingrad to a successful conclusion and so it was seen to be a turning point.

The Soviet campaign ended with the Red Army planting its flag on the roof of the Reich Chancellery in the centre of Berlin. Gehlen's part in these tumultuous events was to create an intelligence network of agents and informers planted carefully in Russia, Ukraine, eastern Europe and even East Germany, that would serve him well in the Cold War that had yet to come.

Gehlen's many espionage operations, planned and organised to gather intelligence, included the recruitment of Russian deserters and prisoners of war who could be used in the fight against communism. There were quite a surprising number, some of whom were senior officers in the Red Army. One of these was Lieutenant General Andrei Andreyevich Vlasov, who had been captured and passed on to Gehlen for interrogation. Vlasov had been a commander in the defence of Moscow and was a Soviet hero well known throughout Russia, which made his defection very painful for the Red Army and the Kremlin. It had been his ambition to lead a National Army of Liberation against the communist leadership that he so hated.

While still a prisoner of war he put his name to a proclamation in the form of a leaflet appealing to Red Army soldiers to defect and the response was immediate. Tens of thousands of them surrendered to German units within the first few days. This grew into the 'Vlasov Movement', which promised to recruit an army formation to face their comrades in a bid to free Russia from communism. The movement was objected to by Hitler based on his view that Russians were inferior beings and only to be defeated and crushed by the superior 'master race'. One captured Red Army officer who was interrogated by senior army officers was asked why the Red Army still resisted the German invaders so resolutely. 'You came as conquerors and not liberators,' was his brief answer.

The Red Army engaged the Germans in one great battle after another across the Russian hinterland, the borders of Poland and beyond to East Prussia as Gehlen became increasingly disenchanted with Hitler. He was not the only one: the bomb plot in July 1944 nearly killed Hitler, but the assassination failed mainly because the German military culture did not lend itself to the kind of plotting that was needed to succeed. The arch revolutionary Lenin said, as he was being transported across Europe in a sealed train to Russia, 'If the Germans wanted to start a revolution they would buy a railway ticket first.'

By a small miracle, Gehlen survived Himmler's bloodletting after the bomb plot, which put him into competition with the Gestapo, which now counted intelligence as one of its responsibilities. That was an unhealthy place to be in Nazi Germany, but he escaped with his life as he was in hospital at the time with a case of blood poisoning. Not only had he survived but he was still in command of military intelligence on the Eastern Front with his encyclopaedic knowledge of the Red Army's order of battle and the state of the Soviet economy.

With the end of the war in sight the general was planning his future, in common with many other senior figures in Germany. He evacuated his family with the help of his second in command, Major Baun, and forged documents to the comparative safety of West Germany, where they narrowly avoided the great air raid and firestorm of Dresden. Gehlen had filled trucks with military and economic intelligence documentation gathered during the Russian campaign, which he drove into West Germany, safe from Russian hands. He was convinced that as soon as the war was over the alliance between the Anglo-American forces and the Russians would collapse and they would be fighting each other – and Gehlen was almost right.

The Cold War took a little while to develop, but it became increasingly obvious that Stalin as an autocratic dictator would find Western democracy unacceptable. Gehlen and his small group watched events and took stock of their dossier of military, economic and industrial intelligence, as well as their network of spies and agents still in place in Russian-occupied territory. They were certain that the Anglo-American forces would desperately need an intact and working intelligence service when they would inevitably come to face the Red Army. Their array of espionage assets included equipment and short-wave radio sets, and agents who Gehlen had trained, installed and controlled with a small army of agents.

The agents were to be found in most regions that the German Army had occupied in Ukraine and Poland, but especially in their own territory in East Germany and numbered into many hundreds. Their talents were well known to Gehlen, who had instructed them to lie low after the war until further orders. The network was an impressive one and backed up by detailed documentation of their findings and evaluations of the order of battle of the Red Army, Navy and Air Force. The intelligence picture and its administration was very comprehensive and Gehlen and his comrades were sure that the Western Allies would accept their entire package; they only had to accept his terms.

Gehlen microfilmed his documentation in triplicate and each set of microfilms was stored in separate steel containers labelled *Geheime Kommandosache* (Secret Command Matters). Weeks before the end of the war, Gehlen had chosen a hideout high in the alps above the snow line where he had rented an alpine hut accessed by a long bumpy dirt road – a place that was perfect for his purpose. In a place called Elends-Alm, or 'Misery Meadow', they buried their espionage archives. They would help to shape the Cold War and waited there for the Allies to come and be shown the value of the intelligence records. Every morning they scanned the valley below with binoculars for a sign of the forward elements of the American 7th Army, but they were slow in coming. They were wary of ambush in the mountainous terrain and had reports of some SS units active in an Alpine fortress around Berchtesgaden that made them even more so. Gehlen and his fellows waited restlessly as they heard the news that the Russians had taken Berlin and the Führer had committed suicide. Hitler's successor, Admiral Doenitz, was going to negotiate with the Allies so it was evident that the end was near, but Gehlen still waited even though there were now signs of American troops in the valley.

He did not want to give himself up to the first wave of troops as they would only put him into a prisoner-of-war cage and move on; nor even the second, as those formations would not contain a general officer who Gehlen needed to talk to about his treasure trove. Then things were taken out of his hands by a dairyman who suspected that Gehlen's group were SS officers in hiding. As he had suffered at the hands of the Nazis, he told the first American army patrol he came across. On 22 May 1945 Gehlen and his principal colleagues descended from his Alpine retreat and surrendered to American forces, where he announced arrogantly to his captors, 'I have information of the highest importance to give to your government.'

'So have they all!' snapped an irritated army captain at a United States Army post in the town hall of a small town called Fischhausen, near Salzburg, where he had been sent to be interrogated.

It was not the red carpet treatment that Gehlen had expected. He found that he was talking to a young lieutenant who was very sceptical about the stories told by the many captured German officers he was interrogating. Gehlen told his story and was promptly locked up for several days until a more senior officer was able to interview him. He was equally as dismissive. A report from that meeting eventually went to the intelligence officers of higher rank with whom Gehlen was desperate to speak so that he could get them to understand the importance of what was being said.

He finally met the American Major General Edwin Silbert, who was an intelligence professional of the same calibre of Gehlen with an understanding of the experience and material that Gehlen had to offer. They talked at length, but Gehlen did not disclose where the steel canisters were buried although he gave a lengthy description of their contents. He also described his grand plan of an intelligence agency that he would direct in operations against the Soviet Union using the data and details of agents stored in his steel canisters that were still buried in the mountains. The Americans also had a secret; they were talking to Lieutenant Colonel Baun, Gehlen's colleague, to weigh up which of the two men and their potential intelligence agencies would be the better bet. Baun offered to start espionage operations without delay against the Soviet Union and the two spy chiefs started to bid for American sponsorship, but Gehlen played his trump card – he had the contents of the steel canisters.

The treasure was unearthed by American soldiers working under Gehlen's direction. They uncovered one container after another and heaved them all on to their waiting army trucks. The convoy transported them to an old Luftwaffe interrogation centre at Oberursel to meet a team of intelligence officers, who sorted out the contents of the steel canisters under Gehlen's direction. The significance of the material immediately became obvious to General Silbert, who brought the archive to the attention of General Eisenhower. The appearance of the material and its implications were particularly timely as relations were being increasingly strained between the Western Allies and the Soviets over a number of matters. The Russians were looking for Gehlen and his staff, to demand what had happened to the intelligence archives that were in the steel containers.

The Americans had begun to realise the value of the intelligence weapon they had in their hands but had to counter the increasingly intransigent demands of the Soviets, so they were evasive. Silbert sent out a notice to the commanding officers of the many prisoner-of-war cages in Germany to find any members of Gehlen's intelligence team. Several were traced and brought together despite increasing pressure from the Russians, which only confirmed the value of Gehlen's team to the Americans.

General Silbert was now being hard pressed by Red Army intelligence officers to send any former *Abwehr* intelligence officers he had in custody to them for interrogation. The general still gave them an evasive reply, telling them he held a few but he had not finished their interrogation so they would have to wait. In return he asked about the senior *Abwehr* officers the Russians were holding and seemed to be refusing to give up to Silbert's men to interview. Indications that Soviet agents were beginning to infiltrate the American military establishments as civilian clerks and cleaners increased the pressure on Silbert and he made the decision that Gehlen had to be removed from Germany.

Gehlen was told that he would be flown to the United States to put any necessary information required by the American intelligence chiefs before them and he could select three of his officers to help him in his presentation. He selected Lieutenant Colonel Herre, who had been responsible for recruiting Russian agents, Major Schoeller, who evaluated reports from those agents mainly based in Russia, and lastly Major von Hymens, an expert on Russian industry, armament production and supplies.

The transport of the four men had to be kept in a rigidly tight security operation as the Soviet spies were growing increasingly busy around the compound where they were being kept. Gehlen and many of his fellow FHO officers were being held at an American Army camp in Oberursel near Frankfurt and General Silbert knew that several Russian agents had been caught trying to penetrate the wire fences of the compound. Getting the four on board an American aircraft in German Army uniform would have been difficult, and even if they were in civilian clothes, so Gehlen was told that he and his companions would travel in US Army uniforms. He agreed, but characteristically demanded that his uniform should be according to his rank. The quartermaster's store produced a field service uniform and sewed a general's star and badges on to it, which Gehlen donned with visible pleasure. His colleagues had to be satisfied with a captain's insignia.

Thus attired, they were driven to a US Air Force field in the middle of the night. They flew across the Atlantic in the beginning of August, barely three months after Germany had surrendered, to take their part in a fresh chapter in military intelligence. Gehlen's arrival in Washington coincided with the grave crisis concerning the lack of America's intelligence operations and so he spent almost a year being interrogated by senior US Army officers on intelligence matters.

Although he was still a prisoner of war of the Americans, Gehlen had made a gentleman's agreement with General Silbert at Oberursel before he left for Washington. The terms are quoted from memory in his book *The Gehlen Memoirs*:

> A clandestine German intelligence organisation was to be set up using his existing structure to continue gathering information in the East just as it had been doing before. The basis for this was our common interest in a defence against Communism.
>
> This German organisation was to work 'for' and not 'under' the Americans, but jointly with the Americans.
>
> The organisation would operate under exclusively German leadership, which would receive its directives and assignments from the Americans until such time as a new German government was established in Germany.
>
> The organisation was to be financed by the Americans with funds which were not to be borne from the occupation costs, and that in return the organisation would supply all intelligence reports to the Americans.
>
> As soon as a sovereign German government was established, that government should decide whether the organisation ought to continue to function or not, but that until that time the care and control (data referred to as 'the trusteeship') of the organisation should remain in American hands.
>
> Should the organisation at any time find itself in a position where American and German interest diverged, it was accepted that the organisation would consider the interests of Germany first.

The last of the six points may raise some eyebrows, since it may be seen that the American representatives had gone overboard in making concessions, but this point, more than any other, demonstrates Silbert's great vision. He recognised that for many years to come the interests of the United States and West Germany should run parallel.

Gehlen went on to write that this was the 'key to our [German and American] success – right from the start was that we had concluded an agreement strong enough to stand all the difficulties that were to beset it in the years that followed'. He admired Silbert as a general who took the bold step of requisitioning the intelligence experts of a former enemy for his own country, in a situation that was fraught with political pitfalls. It was very much to the credit of everybody concerned on the American side that they were able to find the psychological basis and the climate of mutual trust for the launching of this unique venture.

Gehlen had negotiated the terms of this extraordinary agreement while still a prisoner of war and now he and his group had been flown to America to seal the deal and establish its budget. The first year of the new intelligence operation cost the American taxpayer $3.4 million (the dollar had approximately fourteen times the buying power of one today) and the investment would prove well worthwhile. As Gehlen arrived in Washington the official policy was that the Soviet Union was a friendly nation, although many American generals strongly disagreed. General Patton wanted to rearm the *Waffen* SS and incorporate it into his own US 3rd Army 'to lead them against the Reds', and told his own government so. As a result he was relieved of his command.

There were serious exceptions, however. General Bedell Smith, who had been Eisenhower's chief of staff, thought that the Soviet Union was the country of the future and that the British were through – and told them so to their faces. Truman could not hide his annoyance with the socialist policies of the new British government and its new Prime Minister, Clement Attlee, who had replaced Churchill. Nor could the strong and forthright views of the new foreign secretary, Ernest Bevin, please the Americans, although they would have reason to be grateful to him as the Cold War began in earnest.

The American establishment, its military and its people were about to learn a hard, slow lesson about their relationship with Stalin's Soviet Union. General Bedell Smith, who was Eisenhower's hatchet man during and after the war, was sent to Moscow as the US ambassador to the Kremlin, where he became entirely cured of his view that the Soviet Union was the country of the future and that it would be his country's natural ally.

In the meantime, the CIA was being formed as a part of the changing attitude towards intelligence within the American administration. Intelligence operations had not had a very happy history in the interwar years as President Coolidge's secretary of state, Henry Stimson, had closed down its cryptographic office with the remark, 'Gentlemen do not read other people's mail'.

As a result, the American government had no centralised intelligence service for more than twenty years and the only active intelligence available was from the G2 branch of the army and A2, of the navy. There was no co-operation between them at all, until the shock of the surprise attack by the Japanese on Pearl Harbour in 1941 spelt out in words of fire the need for a centralised intelligence system. President Roosevelt subsequently created the Office of Strategic Services (OSS) in 1941 as the centre of American wartime intelligence to the fury of both the existing agencies. At its head he appointed Colonel 'Wild Bill' Donovan, who had served in intelligence in the First World War. He freely admitted that he had used the British SOE as his model in his operations.

As the war came to an end Roosevelt planned to use the OSS to centralise all the American intelligence agencies but the plan was leaked to the press just as the president died. America's new President Truman had sacked Donavan and terminated the OSS so the existing agencies and State Department picked up what bits of the OSS they found useful. It was a fortuitous move, as the OSS was shot through with communist spies and informers although nobody knew that at the time, so American intelligence was ripe for a fresh beginning.

The increasing threat of the Cold War had convinced Truman of the need for a centralised intelligence system, even though he had eliminated any central source of intelligence by abolishing the OSS. The president identified the Soviet threat early on and listened to advice from Donovan and Admiral William D. Leahy, who helped to hammer out the details of the new agency. Taking the views of the military services and the State Department into consideration along with the FBI, Truman established the Central Intelligence Group (CIG) in January 1946. Unlike the security and intelligence agencies of Britain or the Soviet Union, the CIG was democratically sanctioned and the new agency was put under legislative scrutiny.

Congress passed the National Security Act of 1947 and under its provisions America's National Security Council and the CIA were formed. The act was a broad one and tasked the CIA with co-ordinating, evaluating and disseminating intelligence that affected national security as its duty. The agency was to provide strategic warning of threats and also conduct important clandestine activities with little of the usual restrictions of fiscal and administrative procedures in order to protect covert operations.

Rear Admiral Sidney W. Souers was appointed to be the deputy chief of naval intelligence, the first director of the CIA and principal intelligence advisor to the president. His advice was only targeted on one thing, the urgent need to develop the best quality intelligence on the Union of Soviet Socialist Republics as his first directive. He needed to see how that could be done and was impressed by an outstanding Federal Bureau agent, Leon G. Turron, who remarked in 1939, 'The British have a real intelligence service; America has virtually none'. The previous intelligence leader, William Donavan, had already admitted that he had modelled the OSS on the British Secret Service and now Souers looked to it again for a role model.

Some of the British methods came from Winston Churchill, who was determined, in his own words, to make the Americans 'face the strategic facts of life'. Allen Dulles, its future director, spoke of the long history of MI6's quite effective performance. The British were keen to cultivate the view, and from its inception the CIA focused on the development of co-operations in signals intelligence know-how and technology, which is still evident, albeit in a modified form today. Bletchley Park had penetrated virtually the whole of the signals intelligence system of the Third Reich during the war and much of the Japanese one as well. What it had not done was to penetrate the Russian codes and networks of the KGB – well, why would it? After all they were allies. But now the need for an understanding of the Soviet intelligence system was urgent.

Gehlen had negotiated his agreement with the US Army's G2 intelligence arm, who had flown him to the United States in August 1945 with his two colleagues for questioning. He was kept at Fort Hunt military base, near Washington, where he was treated with respect and served by white-coated orderlies as he conferred with President Truman's national security advisor and a team of senior army officers. He first met Allen Dulles there, who would soon become head of the CIA and with whom he became a friend and co-operator in a relationship that would mould the future of the agency and shape global intelligence.

Gehlen gave his cross-examiners the impression of a professional military intelligence operator during the ten months of his gruelling interviews. His mastery of the maps, flowcharts, statistics and other documents defining the economic and military strengths and weaknesses of the Soviet Union impressed his interrogators. Finally, he was flown back to Germany from the

United States on 1 July 1946 and twelve days later he was discharged from prisoner-of-war status.

That day marked the formal birth of the Gehlen Organisation in Germany and the appointment followed of 350 agents, who became a reconstituted and functioning espionage network funded by and under American control. Gehlen's mandate was to continue to gather information about the Soviet Union from his base in Pullach, south of Munich, in an anonymous 25-acre factory site under the innocent title of the South German Industrial Development Organisation. The new agency was referred to as 'the Org' by intelligence community insiders and was given a budget of millions of dollars by the American government. Gehlen began to reconstruct the network of agents that he had been running during the war in eastern Europe, which in turn began to refresh the body of intelligence with which he had so impressed the American Army.

The people to whom he now had to report had changed. Now the Org's paymaster was the CIA and not the army, and Gehlen's contact man there was Deputy Director Allen Dulles, whose past seems as obscure as some of Gehlen's agents. Dulles knew Berlin well during the 1920s as a diplomat but had left government service in 1926 for the greener pastures of private business. He became a lawyer in W.A. Harriman & Co., along with his brother, John Foster Dulles, who was destined to be the future American secretary of state.

By the middle of the 1920s Germany had begun to recover from the effects of the Great War and its post-war economic collapse and the great German industrial firms were beginning to look like attractive opportunities for wealthy British and American investors. The firm of Sullivan & Cromwell, which had the Dulles brothers as partners, would represent those investments whose assets partly financed Hitler into power. There has been much speculation of how much the Dulles name was involved in the subterfuge and financing of the early days of the Nazis coming to power but what it undoubtedly did was to give Allen Dulles superb contacts at high level in Germany. He used them in his next appointment at the OSS, while living in Herringasse in Zurich during the war, and until the OSS was dissolved by Truman.

THE CIA

General Bedell Smith, who had been appointed head of the newly formed CIA, recognised the talents for intelligence work exhibited by Dulles, and he asked his deputy to supervise the Org in its new role in the Cold War. The link between the CIA and the Org was well established by the time Allen Dulles was appointed head of the CIA following Bedell Smith's resignation in 1947, so the centre of power in intelligence was moving away from Broadway in London.

By this time the Gehlen Organisation was firmly established in its role as the agency acting as the eyes and ears of the CIA in Germany's espionage battlefield. Dulles' reputation as an international spymaster grew as his work at the agency developed; he got on well with Gehlen, another global spymaster, and the two agencies co-operated, but they could not have had more different characteristics. Gehlen, as the secretive *éminence grise*, was unknown by the public and never knowingly photographed, while Dulles was an extrovert and the life and soul of the party with many well-published affairs of the heart.

The two agencies were close. The Org helped to midwife the newborn CIA and it, in turn, loved what Gehlen's evaluations were saying as it increased the importance of the agency. The reports of the activities and intentions of the Russian military had to be of great value to Washington, as the CIA was spending more than $200 million on intelligence, much of which went into the Org's budget. The evaluations that the Org was producing were just what Dulles wanted for his master in the White House to hear, so it is said that he put Gehlen's reports almost verbatim on to CIA letters heading for submission to Truman. These cloak-and-dagger exercises maintained the pressure of the Cold War, which cost the American taxpayer more than $8 trillion over half a century, so there was concern about the accuracy of Gehlen's assessments.

On the other hand, the flow of intelligence about the USSR kept the Cold War at least below boiling point and enabled both sides to read the minds of the other. The simple outcome of it all was that the CIA was able to report to the Oval Office regularly, 'there is no indication of Russia mobilising to attack us in the next 60 days' – so it can be said that the effect of the intelligence conflict was that it gave peace a chance.

That was not the way that it looked to us in Berlin, as the siege tightened and the tension rose in the MI6 station in the Olympic Stadium until it reached almost hysteric proportions. Gatow Airfield was suffering from a matching tension but in a more well-ordered way. However, I noticed that my group of German signals intelligence veterans was continually getting smaller. I asked why, and was told that they had been recruited by the Org in the American zone. I hardly recognised the term, but soon began to understand its implications as Gehlen began to establish his organisation in the city. Among the men who had gone were several I had previously had long and heated discussions with about the value to Germany of Hitler and the Nazi regime – their views surprised me as the lack of benefits to their country lay visibly in the ruins of their city.

There were clearly still convinced Nazis among us, and it was my first inkling of the Org's policy to recruit ex-Nazi intelligence personnel from the *Sicherheitsdienst* (SD) intelligence arm of the Gestapo. Their agency had been the direct competitor of *Abwehr* military intelligence during the war and they were a brutal part of a murderously cruel organisation, but Gehlen's assurance to the Americans that he would not use ex-Nazis in his organisation was not kept and that eventually became public knowledge. The fact that our Nazi veterans went off to Pullach showed us that he had broken that promise, but he had his reasons; the SD were skilled intelligence operatives and they were a rare commodity. Gehlen's attitude was rather like that of Dulles towards Gehlen himself. 'He is on our side and that is all that matters,' the CIA chief explained, invoking the exigencies of the Cold War. Gehlen had to have the best and most experienced intelligence men that he could find for his organisation – if they were ex-Gestapo that came second to the pressing task of engaging the Soviets in their intelligence conflict. So the Org was using ex-Nazis in becoming America's foremost intelligence source in Europe, casting a sweeping influence over American foreign policy.

Turning a blind eye to war criminals and high-ranking Nazi officials was not confined to the recruiting practices of the Org, the United States had Operation Paperclip. It was the US State Department's code name for the secret importation of more than 5,000 scientists and technicians who were convinced Nazis into America simply by rewriting their records to get them through the immigration procedures. While German war criminals were being chased in Germany, President Truman's National Security Council in

Washington issued a classified directive sanctioning the use of those Nazis who would collaborate with American needs and interests. The German newspaper, *Frankfurter Rundschau*, commented, 'in the Gehlen headquarters one SS man paved the way for the next and Himmler's elite were having happy reunion ceremonies' – so, Paperclip was working well …

Two of Gehlen's most notorious hirelings were Franz Six and Emil Augsburg, both of whom were being sought by the American Army's Counter-intelligence Corps for war crimes. Their use to Gehlen, and therefore the CIA, was that they had the knowledge and experience to reactivate spy networks in the Soviet Union and eastern Europe. Unemployed German intelligence veterans were hired to revive the old network, and in fact Augsburg became so successful at it that he moonlighted for several other intelligence agencies, including the French Deuxieme Bureau. As tensions increased between the Soviet Union and America, the Org depended more and more on Gehlen's reports – and they were not the only ones. According to one estimate, the Org generated 70 per cent of all of NATO's intelligence about the Warsaw Pact forces of eastern Europe.

British security people in the Olympic Stadium and London were not so keen on the findings coming out of Pullach, maybe it was because the Org was not their asset, or maybe it was because their innate conservative instincts left them feeling uncertain. Research accepted by the CIA with such enthusiasm was not received so eagerly in Broadway. Gehlen realised that his evaluations had to be of good value to his sponsors in Washington to justify the $200 million from the 'black' budget being paid to him by the CIA. The only way that kind of expenditure could be justified on the cult of intelligence in peacetime would be to maintain the threat of an enemy at the gate, poised to attack the outnumbered Western forces.

That was exactly what the military and intelligence community wanted. President Truman ceased the post-war cutbacks to the military budget and increased expenditure on weapons research and the purchase of equipment. The threat was certainly evident. The forces of the Allies were outnumbered, as I was able to see in Berlin – the British Brigade garrison was not much more than a couple of battalions of 1,000 men each and American strengths were not much greater. Gehlen's estimate was that there were 208 Soviet battle-hardened divisions stationed between Berlin and Warsaw, which showed that the odds were certainly overwhelming, but it was time to check the figures.

The Teufelsberg (Devil's Mountain) built of the rubble of Berlin still dominates the surrounding countryside and was an ideal place to put a station to listen to the chatter of the Red Army. Two huge wireless dishes, one American and one British, swept the horizon picking up the messages from the ether. The British dish sent information back to the Olympic Stadium for analysis and the answer the British got from the dish was that there were not 208 divisions facing them but 120, although that was still a huge body of troops, tanks and artillery, albeit almost half what Gehlen was telling the Americans.

The two great listening stations set up by the Allies to collect the signals intelligence are still there as museums and the story of the formations of the Red Army and their strengths that were revealed in the intelligence can still be seen in its exhibits.

The estimates and evaluations of the Org were being questioned. The CIA did not want to know about it – Gehlen's story was effectively increasing its budget by hundreds of millions of dollars and American forces were being prepared for a Russian offensive that never came, at least not in Europe.

Allied preparations for a confrontation did not deter the Soviets from exerting massive political pressure and launching an espionage initiative of their own aimed at both the Allies and the West German government. It reached an intensity that disturbed governments and people in the Allied zones of West Germany, and most of all Berlin, as the Cold War progressed. The KGB acted with alacrity in rounding up land owners, teachers, doctors, police officials and other dissidents who were labelled as either Nazis or undesirables and sent for 're-education'. It was not necessary to build new educational establishments for the purpose; old concentration camps such as Buchenwald and Sachsenhausen were still there to be used.

It has been estimated that from the time the Red Army entered Berlin until the end of the airlift in 1950 more than 200,000 people were sent to those camps and more than a third of them died there. For the rest of the population, the rationing system was an effective way of maintaining order and discipline among the masses with an allowance of 2,500 calories a day for the upper crust and manual labourers who were working for the state. The bottom layer, including any unemployed, undesirables or old people, were allowed just 1,250 calories, which was hardly a sustainable daily ration.

Some other kinds of 'undesirables' telling unpleasant truths about communism lived in the Allied sectors of West Berlin, beyond the reach of the KGB – or so they thought. People who were vocal in protesting against the Soviet regime could be 'snatched' (a euphemism for kidnapped) by a small team of anonymous and violent men, bundled into a car and driven at high speed into the Russian sector to just disappear. The abduction of protestors was not limited to Berlin, a dissident, Oliviu Beldeanu, was kidnapped from West Germany by a unit specialising in the practice.

Nor was a snatch limited to German nationals; targets could be British or French personnel (but rarely Americans, for some reason). One incident I recall involved Douglas, an RAF radio technician at Gatow whose job was to log into the transmissions of Russian pilots overflying East Germany and Poland. He was a Russian linguist who had been taught the language in a government programme involving more than 5,000 national servicemen who had to go through a punishing course of instruction to reach a level of competency in the language. Douglas would feed back the interceptions he made at Gatow to GCHQ as a part of its evaluation of the order of battle of the Soviet Air Force. That made him a security risk, so he was strictly forbidden by his commanding officer to cross the border into Soviet territory. Of course, when he did the KGB nabbed him for questioning.

I found myself in a similar position when I was said to have crossed an unmarked boundary (I was not sure that I had), bundled into a small cell and asked a few questions by an overweight Russian official in perfect English. I was held for a few days while they decided that I was of no value. There was no official release or exchange of prisoners, I was not important enough for that. They just left the cell door unlocked in my rather ramshackle jail.

THE STASI

There was more repression on the way for the people of Berlin as the Ministerium für Staatssicherheit, commonly known as the Stasi. It was formed in 1950 as the security service of the Deutsche Demokratische Republik in East Germany. It has been described as one of the world's most effectively repressive intelligence agencies whose main task was to spy on East Germany's people through a vast network of citizens acting as informants in a way that was more insidious than the methods of its sponsor, the NKVD.

The Stasi employed well over quarter of a million people during the Cold War, mainly recruited from East German Army conscripts who were instructed to root out the class enemy. A former Stasi colonel who served in its Counter-intelligence Directorate estimated that the number of informers employed by the agency would top 2 million if you included occasional informants.

The surveillance files on millions of East Germans were laid open after reunification in 1990 so that any citizen could inspect their own files; that archive is maintained by the German government. The files were created by full-time officers of the Stasi, many of whom were posted in industrial plants to report on the effectiveness of workers in contributing to the economy. A tenant in every apartment block was an informer of the *Volkspolizei* (or Vopo, as they were known), whose duty was to report on any relative or friend that stayed the night in another's flat. They were known to have drilled holes in hotel room walls through which Vopo agents could film the incumbent's actions with special cameras.

The Stasi had a close association with the KGB, who maintained liaison officers within all the Stasi departments; they had the reputation of being even more repressive than the Gestapo. The Stasi were reputed to have one full-time agent to about 150 East German people while the Gestapo at its peak employed one secret policeman to about 2,000 in the population. The Stasi infiltrated every aspect of the people of the German Democratic Republic to the extent that, in some cases, a spouse even spied on and reported his or her partner's activities. The Stasi's repressive regime operated right up to the time that the wall came down and when it did the records that were found in its headquarters were full of friends and relatives betraying each other. The building in Berlin's Normanstrasse is now a museum and a monument to the awfulness of the repression that the sponsored agents of the KGB did so well.

The success of the Stasi was such that the KGB used it as a proxy for international tasks such as helping to set up a security network in Cuba and others in Africa, including Ethiopia, Angola, Yemen, Syria and Nasser's Egyptian State Security organisation. The Stasi not only assisted others in setting up repressive police networks, it also engaged in its own espionage and sabotage in foreign countries.

One Stasi practitioner specialising in the sabotaging of ships was Ernst Wollweber. He served in the German *Kriegsmarine* in the First World War and had been active as a communist agitator in the seamen's unions afterwards. He was sent to prison in Sweden for sabotaging many 'fascist' ships. When the communists took power in East Germany, Wollweber was appointed head of the Stasi by the general secretary of the German Democratic Republic, Walter Ulbricht. The two men later clashed and Wollweber resigned. After reunification he managed a living as a translator in Berlin until his death.

Wollweber may have been a dab hand at sabotage but the Stasi's greatest spymaster was Marcus 'Mischa' Wolf, whose career in espionage spanned thirty-two years – most of the Cold War. He was sent to Berlin with Walter Ulbricht's team to act as a journalist reporting on the Nuremberg Trials, which convicted the seven war criminals that were then incarcerated in Spandau Prison. He was a founder of the Stasi's foreign intelligence service and was 'the man without a face' to the Allied intelligence agencies for most of his career.

As an intelligence chief he achieved great success in penetrating the government, political and business circles of West Germany with his agents and informers. His most notable coup was to place Günter Guillaume in the office of Chancellor Willy Brandt of West Germany as one of his closest advisors. Guillaume's exposure as an East German agent was the cause of Brandt's resignation and is seen to be Wolf's greatest espionage success, although there were many others.

He retired a few years before the end of the Cold War but as reunification drew near he fled to seek asylum in Russia, which was denied. He had to return to Germany, where he was arrested and tried for his part in the Stasi's long record of repression, unlawful detention, coercion and bodily harm, for which he was convicted. He was sentenced to a term of two years' imprisonment but it was a suspended sentence, which caused uproar in the newly formed West German state. He died in his sleep in his Berlin home in 2006.

Berlin's most extraordinary intelligence situation concerned Otto John, who was the first head of the Office for the Protection of the Constitution – West Germany's domestic intelligence service and roughly the equivalent of MI5. Herr John was involved in the plot to assassinate Hitler on 20 July 1944 but avoided being caught and executed in the Gestapo's bloodbath that followed. British intelligence helped him to escape and got him work in the BBC German Language Service. After the war he helped to present evidence at the Nuremberg War Crimes Trials. He was therefore a candidate for the high office that was given because he was supported by British security, even though it was against the will of the German Chancellor, Konrad Adenauer.

Almost four years later, after a ceremony to remember the conspirators of 20 July, he disappeared only to turn up again in East Germany three days later. He said that he had decided to defect to the East because he did not agree with the policies of Adenauer's administration. He criticised the plans for remilitarisation of West Germany and the appointment of ex-Nazi figures such as General Gehlen, and so became a figure of protest on all the policies of Adenauer's government.

Less than a year later he reappeared in West Berlin, where he was immediately arrested. During his interrogation he claimed that he had been drugged and abducted by the KGB. He claimed that he feared for his own safety while he was kept in East Germany and was made to say the things that he did. He was not believed and was charged with treason and sentenced to four years' imprisonment, which he tried to get set aside right up to his death in 1997.

The reason for his disappearance and reappearance is a long-standing mystery. Was he abducted by the KGB in the well-established way? Or did he abscond? And then how did he come back? Was he released, or did he escape? It is the most enduring of the many mysteries that surround the time of Berlin's spies.

THE BERLIN WALL

The world's 'spy capital' lost its title at midnight on 13 August 1961 when East German soldiers pulled up in trucks at numerous locations on the borders of the Allied sectors of Berlin. They unloaded rolls of barbed wire and within a few hours they had established a barrier right around the perimeter of the Allied sectors, with guards every few yards. Soon the barbed wire was replaced by a wall that cut Berlin in two.

There were many reasons given by the communists for creating the wall, or rather the necklace of barbed wire. The real one was to stem the number of refugees crossing the open borders between East and West Berlin. Germany's Democratic Republic was haemorrhaging its inhabitants at the rate of 300,000 a year. Millions of refugees had crossed to the West since the communist state was founded in 1949.

Berlin's U-Bahn (underground train) had previously crossed the city's boundaries without hindrance and was a well-established escape route for refugees fleeing the communist regime. East German people were voting with their feet in large numbers and the ones that came were the ones that had been important to the community – doctors, lawyers and academics were a high percentage of the flood. The people, mostly families, were well aware that Vopo patrolled the train's carriages to stop and turn back travellers, particularly family groups carrying overstuffed suitcases and trailing young children, before the train passed into the Allied sector. I used the U-Bahn regularly, and on coming face to face with such groups in the crowded carriages I would see the fear flash on their faces as they saw a uniform, which then vanished as they realised that the British one was not a danger to them.

Khrushchev joked with the East German leader, Walter Ulbricht, saying that he would soon be the only person left in the country and Ulbricht was not amused. The exodus was the reason for the wall, but it came as a surprise to the West, despite CIA warnings that a Soviet repetition of the 1948 Blockade had been mentioned in intelligence evaluations throughout the 1950s. The agency's Russian double agent in Moscow, Oleg Pencovski, found out about the plan days in advance but was unable to warn his agency handlers, and so President Kennedy, who was told the following morning, decided that nothing could be done.

The overwhelming emotion in MI6 offices in London was relief, as the refugee problem had become critical with more than 5,000 people crossing the border every day. Among them was a KGB officer with his family who crossed only a few hours before the miles of barbed wire were laid across the face of the city. Closing the border defused an increasingly critical situation and we could not challenge it anyway as the barbed wire, and later the wall, were built just within East German territory.

This was not the attitude of the Berliners, however. They acted with fury against what they saw as the complacency of the Allies, which they showed in a demonstration of hundreds of thousands at the Brandenburg Gate in central Berlin. Willy Brandt, the mayor of the city, angrily demanded action but the

Allied military commanders were unable to respond. As the days passed it became evident that no positive action would take place immediately.

Refugees could no longer cross as they wished, although a few brave souls did try and many lost their lives in highly published attempts to do so. All the Allies could do was reinforce the garrison with extra troops. Little could be done for the East Germans, but Berliners in the West were heartened with the arrival of American Vice President Lyndon Johnson and their hero, General Lucius Clay, who had been the leader in the airlift. The Americans had good reason to take a firm stand in the airlift as Penkovsky, the CIA's spy in the Kremlin, told them that if they backed down in the crisis another would be immediately created.

The Berlin Wall was something the Allies could do nothing about, but the next test occurred at Checkpoint Charlie, which was the strictly controlled official gateway through the Berlin Wall. East German border guards attempted to obstruct an American diplomat's access to East Berlin on official business, so the American sector crossing was immediately reinforced by all twenty-four tanks that could be mustered by the Allied garrison. The Soviets responded with the same number of tanks from the armoured divisions that surrounded the city, following which Kennedy and Khrushchev took two days to negotiate a stand-down.

In retrospect, the building of the wall was a watershed in the Cold War as the German Democratic Republic could not keep an increasingly restive population walled up in East Berlin for ever. It changed the opportunity for espionage in the city and no longer offered Allied intelligence operatives free access to the hinterland of East Germany, although the city was still a good listening post. The destruction of the wall would finally mark the end of the rule of communism but the eastern Europeans would have to wait thirty years for it to happen.

SEVEN

LONDON SPIES

In the mid-1950s I was back in London and trying to make sense of the life I had left a few years before. This is not an uncommon feeling for a returning serviceman leaving the close comradeship of an army life for the relative seclusion of a civilian one. The aura of London was not dissimilar to that of Berlin with the ruins gradually being cleared, releasing the damp smell of disturbed rubble.

I thought that our city had similarities to the one that I had just left – but I was mistaken. The Edwardian mustiness of 28 Victoria Street that I had once found intriguing was not as appealing as it was. Sir John Gibson, whom I revered, had passed away and my Mulberry harbour friends no longer visited us. I was unsettled, so what better than to go for a drink in the bar at St Ermin's, although I missed the old company that I had enjoyed there as well. I got to know the barman quite well …

I needed a new direction, before my habits made me too much of a solitary drinker, the chance for which came one lunchtime with a friendly face from my Berlin days at the bar. Lennie Brewer had been a desk officer at the MI6 station in the Olympic Stadium where I had been stationed. I had brought him one or two helpful pieces of information that I had picked up about some things the Americans were doing in their sector. We had regularly gone swimming in the stadium's Olympic swimming pool and became friends, but in London we avoided talking about his work and what he was doing in the city, and I knew better than to pry.

Later on, I saw him going into Artillery Mansions, the monumental block of Victorian flats on the far side of Victoria Street from St Ermin's. It was built on the site of Henry VIII's artillery grounds where the use of military ordnance was practised in mediaeval times. The flats had (and still have) an imposing entrance entering into a secluded courtyard with a fountain at its centre, behind huge iron gates that give the mansion a pleasant air of seclusion. I assumed that he worked there, which was a surprise as I'd thought all the security services were now based in Broadway, but I soon realised that was not the case.

We began to socialise, and with respective girlfriends of the time went out on the town, as well as meeting in St Ermin's bar where we talked a bit about the Berlin days but skirted round what he was doing in London. I confessed to Lennie my growing dissatisfaction with what I was doing at No. 28, which he acknowledged with a little concern and then turned the subject to other things.

In one of our now regular meetings in St Ermin's he asked me again if I was still dissatisfied with civil engineering, to which I replied firmly that I was (I was recovering from a bad morning with one of the ageing draftsmen). Staring at his nearly empty glass, he said quietly, 'Well I might have something for you,' at which I bought him another drink and we arranged to meet again in the bar. At our next meeting he gave me no clue as to what was on offer but we walked across Victoria Street and he guided me through the great iron gates of Artillery Mansions into an inner courtyard and past the fountain playing in the sunlight. I was certain that Lennie was still involved in security work and that I was probably going to be seen for something similar, as this was the way that the security services recruited people. It was in the days before the Cambridge Spy Ring was 'blown' (which made everyone paranoid about security and introduced positive vetting for new recruits).

We passed by a doorkeeper with just a nod from Lennie, after which we came into some rather dingy offices and a meeting room where three men, one an army officer, came to be seated behind a trestle table. Introductions were made and they all began to ask me questions in turn in the typically taciturn military style of inquisition with which I was familiar from my army days. Lennie, who had been hovering in the background, walked out with me when the interview (if that is what it was) had finished and at the iron gates said rather cryptically, 'and now we wait to see'. The iron gates swung shut behind me as I walked back to No. 28.

Some weeks passed with no further contact, not even a drink at the bar. I concluded that the visit was a non-event. However, a telephone call at No. 28 from Lennie dispelled that assumption and the following afternoon we both passed through the iron gates of Artillery Mansions again to meet the army officer (whose name I never did find out). He described the terms of my engagement in the service as if I had already agreed to join and then flourished a sheet of paper, saying, 'sign that'. It turned out to be a copy of the Official Secrets Act. I told him that I had already signed one in the army. 'Well sign it again', he said abruptly and disappeared down the corridor, never to be seen again by me.

Lennie, who was hovering in the background (he turned out to be a great background hoverer), took me with his hand on my shoulder to a closet with a well-used desk and a few papers on it and said, 'you are on my team'. The whole thing took less than half an hour and I was left in front of my desk where the papers turned out to be a list of staff and their telephone extensions. Sitting in my uncomfortable plastic chair I stared at the ceiling trying to resist the thought that ran through my head, 'Come back Paulings, all is forgiven' …

ARTILLERY MANSIONS

The Victoria Street block of flats, misnamed 'mansions', was one of the more active research departments of the service, undertaking tasks and errands for a surprising number of shady characters who came to see us in the course of their assorted mischief making in eastern Europe. The department in which I worked took up the whole of one of the floors of the mansion and was engaged in what we euphemistically called 'technical operations'. That included remote or covert listening devices, and you would be surprised at the number, size and shape of those bugs and their ability to pick up transmissions. Even as long as seventy years ago, no conversation was safe.

The 'research' involved the creation of cover stories for an agent's imagined life, starting with a birth certificate that needed to stand up equally to the scrutiny of an inquisitive policeman or a practised Stasi interrogator. The agent's cover story, with photos of him from an early age and record of schooling and employment, along with other aspects and incidents in their 'lives' were invented and backed up by documents that not only sounded convincing but could stand official scrutiny.

My task was helping to provide 'dodgy documents' to go with any agent's package that we created. I was put in charge of a dog-eared collection of eastern European and Russian passes, identity cards, tickets and other papers. The items were used as masters for any copy we had to make of documents we might have to 'produce' as a part of an agent's cover story, so the quality of the forged document was important. I won my spurs in a small but significant correction to one of the items, which was a checkpoint pass. I recognised that it was a clear forgery of a pass that I had regularly used myself in Berlin. It would often be used when crossing the Allied–Russian border in the city so I was very familiar with that document.

I knew that our master copy was printed on the wrong kind of paper, and said so. Although only acting as a master from which to copy, its reproduction would have been an easily detectable forgery. Alarm bells rang. That particular document, which had been issued to agents in the cover story packages for East Germany, was immediately withdrawn, and as a result I was asked to verify the nature of other master documents or papers among our collection of dodgy documents.

I found a few others that were questionable, so I became the hero of the hour and became established as an authority on the authenticity of papers within just a few months of joining the team. Lennie was delighted because he had the accolade of recruiting the right man, while I was appalled at the largely unjustified mantle of expertise that was thrust upon me. It was all based on the detection of a couple of forged documents that now meant that my approval carried the stamp of authority on the documentation of agents in the field, the detection of which could mean imprisonment for them, or worse. I threw myself into the subject and went on a steep learning curve until I knew that I might not be an expert but I did know more about the subject than anyone else on the station.

SPEAKING RUSSIAN

The floor above the 'Dodgy Documents' Section was occupied by Russian interception operations. They did not have much to do with us operationally, although I could not be sure due to the 'need-to-know' security practices. We did get to recognise some of their people, however. Some were national servicemen who had been directed into the JSSL (Joint Services School for Linguists) programme run by the British armed forces in the 1950s. The programme trained more than 5,000 conscripts from all three services who had been selected to learn to speak and even write Russian in an intensive course of language training. It was created to satisfy the increasing need for interpreters, intelligence and particularly signals intelligence officers during the Cold War and was intensively coached by an exotic group of mainly White Russian tutors. They included a monk, a Russian prince and a Russian countess, who was always dressed in mourning black for the Tsar and his family.

The training in the early years of the scheme was held in a Cambridge college, with lectures and exercises being held for eight hours a day, five days a week, and demanding tests at the end of each week. Failure in two consecutive tests meant that the student would be dropped from the course and 'returned to unit', which would mark the student as a disgraceful failure.

Many of the trainees continued to use the linguistic and related skills they had learned later on in civilian life, particularly in the cultural sector. Writer and actor Alan Bennett, dramatist Dennis Potter and director of the National Theatre, Sir Peter Hall, were all students of the scheme. There were students who became representatives of finance and industry as well. Eddie George, later to be governor of the Bank of England, and industrialist John Harvey-Jones were both students. The programme has been said to have created a generation of young and influential Britons who had a knowledge and respect for the culture of Tolstoy, Pushkin and Pasternak's Russia.

My first meeting with graduates of the school had been at the Gatow Airfield in Berlin where they were RAF technicians trawling through the Soviet Air Force frequencies, listening to Soviet pilots who were always chattering over their radios a great deal. Douglas, who I mentioned earlier, was one of these technicians and he and his comrades worked in a remote building full of chunky radio receivers near the East German border. They spent tedious hours ensuring that the Cold War stayed at least cool by monitoring routine messages from Soviet aircraft controllers and their charges as they flew over East Germany. Years later, I visited Gatow and found the old building empty; the young men plotting vectors of distant aircraft with pencils and maps had been replaced by spy satellites and Gatow Airfield now contained Russian MiGs in an aircraft museum.

The JSSL programme, which promised to be such a significant asset for the Allies, attracted the attention of Soviet intelligence, particularly as a number of MI6 officers became students. The Soviet spy, Geoffrey Prime, was a graduate of the scheme and the British intelligence officer, Guy Burgess, who was a double agent for the KGB and later defected to Russia, was tasked to obtain information on the programme.

I was to be given another opportunity to go on the course (I had been failed earlier on it due to an indiscretion), but the programme was beginning to be run down and finished at the end of the 1950s. The KGB was busy in almost every other corner of the British intelligence community actively recruiting agents, although in the case of Geoffrey Prime they did not have to work very hard to recruit him at all. He was one of the RAF technicians in Gatow concerned with monitoring the movements of the Soviet Air Force when he volunteered his services to the Soviets by wrapping a message around a stone and throwing it out of the train window at a Russian soldier as it travelled through the Russian sector. This unlikely method of becoming a traitor to his country worked, and Prime was soon sending the KGB much information on a regular basis. However, his real value to it was when he joined GCHQ, but more of that later.

Other agents had been recruited much earlier and nothing shows the long-term planning of Russian intelligence as much as the history of the Cambridge Spy Ring, who were recruited in Trinity College the 1930s. The best-known trio within that ring were Burgess, Maclean and their leader, Philby, all of whom had rendered service to Britain in SOE, as already described. As the war finished they had to make a decision about their divided loyalties and chose to continue acting as double agents for the KGB. Leaking Anglo-American secrets served the unintended purpose of strengthening the Grand Alliance during the war by confirming to Stalin that the real intentions of the other war leaders were just as they said they were. The Russian leader feared that his allies would make a separate peace with the Nazis to gain a territorial advantage in the campaign.

Members of the Soviet spy ring not only gathered information about the Nazis during the war; they also interpreted the reactions and real intentions of the Allies in London and Washington. The intelligence they passed secretly to the KGB confirmed what both Churchill and Roosevelt were saying publicly – they would not make a separate peace with the Nazis. Such a move could have enabled them to gain territorial advantage for their armies so the Cambridge spies were able to assure Stalin's suspicious mind that it was not the Allies' intention. They were able to say, with an authority that Stalin would believe, that the American or British governments did not intend to enter into a surrender agreement that would be to the disadvantage of the Soviet Union.

As the war finished Stalin's doubts disappeared and he pressed home the advantages of the Red Army's occupation of eastern Europe and a large slice of Germany. The value of the Cambridge Spy Ring changed as their place at the centre of Britain's security service had become a powerful weapon in the armoury of the KGB in the emerging Cold War.

ALL SPIES TOGETHER

Burgess, Maclean and Philby had all acted as senior officers in the formation of SOE from early in the war and had served their country well, as already described. Now they faced the question, should they betray their country – the answer from each of them was 'yes'.

They had all been recruited by Soviet intelligence in a policy of recruiting young undergraduates in Cambridge (and I assume Oxford) to act as sleepers in the Soviet espionage network. The first to be approached was Philby, who had already applied for membership of the Communist Party but had been turned down, which could have been the cue that led his recruiter to him. The party did not want 'toffs' in its membership, but it was just what the new recruiting policy of Soviet intelligence needed and Philby was soon enrolled by Arnold Deutsch, who acted as an undercover KGB recruiting agent. As soon as Deutsch was sure of Philby he asked him to recommend any other 'candidates' who might be interested. Deutsch was given Philby's close friend Maclean's name and also Burgess, whom Philby recommended but only with reservations.

Burgess was a brilliant, complex and flawed individual whose homosexuality was openly flaunted to every likely man he met and whose drinking bouts led to a constant stream of complaints about his outrageous behaviour. These were almost all the attributes that you would *not* want to have in a secret agent, but when Maclean hinted that he and Philby had been recruited Burgess began to badger both of them to enrol him. By constant entreaties he overcame their reservations and so he became a part of the espionage team that would change the nature of the British security services. The trio was not what the KGB strategists in the Kremlin would have found ideal, they liked their agents to live separate lives and not know each other, but these three would be part of a team that would penetrate the heart of MI6 for more than a decade.

As the three came down from university they found jobs in the media, Philby in journalism in a news magazine entitled *Review of Reviews*, Maclean went to Paris, while Burgess landed a job with the BBC in the Talks Department. They all began networking among London's great and good, but none of them as effectively as Burgess, who used his BBC contacts and resources to further earn the KGB's trust.

One of the tasks it gave him was an early attempt by Moscow Centre to get him to penetrate MI6. One of its officers, David Footman, was invited by Burgess to give some broadcast talks, during which he cemented their future friendship. Other contacts in Burgess' network led to an extraordinary situation as he became close to men who were close to the centre of government, one of whom was Joseph Ball, a friend of Prime Minister Neville Chamberlain.

As Hitler threatened Europe's peace he had entirely hoodwinked Chamberlain, who was convinced that he could talk the Führer round to 'peace in our time', while many of those around him saw things very differently. The prime minister was following a policy of appeasement, which was an absolute anathema to his principal undersecretary at the Foreign Office, Sir Robert Vansittart. He was taking a very uncivil servant stance and campaigning against his master's appeasement policy, to the extent that Chamberlain did not trust him to be discreet about his negotiations. Chamberlain was right – Vansittart was feeding information to Winston Churchill, the principal adversary of appeasement in the House of Commons.

Chamberlain was communicating with members of the Anglo-German Fellowship and others of like mind. He ignored the usual line of communication through his principal civil servants and instead used Sir Horace Wilson as one of his close advisors. Burgess was asked to be a courier for the missives from Chamberlain to various parties who supported his policy of appeasement in which he discussed the situation and strategy for his policy. MI6 was engrossed in learning more about the situation as it needed to know the direction of British foreign policy, which it was convinced would soon lead to war.

What the appeasers did not know was that Burgess stopped off at a flat in St Ermin's Hotel on the way to deliver the messages to get all the correspondence copied by a footman and passed back to Vansittart. What none of the conspirators knew was that copies were also going to the Russian Embassy to keep it abreast of the developments in central Europe.

Burgess was now building his reputation in the British security services in Broadway in London and also in the Kremlin. His career was going from strength to strength at the BBC as well, and he was now the producer of an influential radio talk programme called *The Past Week*, which put forward the case against appeasement introduced by Winston Churchill. A series of talks were to be given by opinion makers on aspects of the international crisis, but Churchill suggested that the talks should be at least postponed because of the deepening trouble. Burgess telephoned him to try and persuade him to carry on and Churchill invited him down to his home at Chartwell to discuss the matter. The ensuing discussion impressed Churchill with Burgess' grasp of world affairs. After dinner they talked at length and at the end of the visit he was presented with a book, signed:

To Guy Burgess from Winston Churchill to confirm his admirable sentiments
September 1938

Burgess said afterwards that the evening was a high point in his life – to be trusted by a politician that he respected may have helped with his decision to resign from the BBC, added to a growing resentment that it was accepting government interference in the talks he was producing. An invitation from the War Office to join MI6 probably made the decision easier and his acceptance made him the first of the Cambridge Spy Ring to become an intelligence officer in the British intelligence community.

Burgess, Maclean, Philby, Blunt and Cairncross had all been recruited as Soviet agents during their student days with the intention of penetrating the intelligence community. Once Burgess had achieved this, the others in the ring soon followed. From his office on the 5th Floor of 2 Caxton Street, Burgess pulled strings to get his friend Harold Philby, always known as 'Kim', a job in the agency.

Anthony Fredrick Blunt managed to get recruited into the security services himself as he was seconded from the Intelligence Corps, in which he held a commission as a captain, to act for MI5. He was made responsible for liaising between his new service and the SHAEF, where his task was to safeguard the secrets of the D-Day landings. They were being planned in Norfolk House, in St James' Square, but as they progressed Blunt shared all he knew with his KGB controllers.

Donald Maclean was a high flyer in the Foreign Office, tipped to be an ambassador at a very young age and recruited into acting as an agent for the KGB at an even earlier one. He was also homosexual and a heavy drinker. Burgess was a drinker in a class all by himself and a libertine whose excesses of all kinds were causing hackles to rise in the Foreign Office. Surprisingly for the time, they were not enough to get him a dismissal from his post but it was probably because he was a part of the old boy network.

John Cairncross was the outsider in the ring who worked, to some extent, independently of the others. Although he knew Blunt and Burgess at Cambridge he claimed that he was unaware they were KGB agents. Each of the members of the ring leaked volumes of secrets to the Kremlin, so claims have been made as to which of the agents was most successful for the KGB. His Soviet controllers have suggested that Cairncross was the most effective of their agents. Of the 5,832 documents that he fed to the Soviets between 1941 and 1945, according to Russian archives, many were stolen from Bletchley Park and smuggled out by the suitcase full. As a result, his information enabled the Red Army to assess the order of battle for the German Army facing it before the decisive Battle of Kursk. He pledged that it enabled them to decisively win the most important battle of the war on the Eastern Front.

Threats of discovery to the members of the spy ring, individually or together, could come from a number of directions. The most immediately dangerous was the disclosure of their activities by Russian defectors. The first real danger for Kim Philby came from a Russian diplomat, Konstantin Volkov, a vice consul who threatened to defect from the Soviet Embassy in Istanbul. He approached the British Consulate for asylum in Britain and in exchange offered to identify three Soviet agents within the British Secret Service. These were two Foreign Office men and a head of a counter-espionage organisation, and so the offer was accepted with alacrity.

However, the defection arrangements made by the security service were disastrous. Volkov demanded that the arrangements should be made with the use of diplomatic bags carried between Istanbul and London because the ciphers used to transmit information had been broken by Soviet cryptanalysts.

The arrangements were being made using the slow carrying of documents by diplomatic courier.

Meanwhile, Sir Stewart Menzies called Philby into his office in Broadway to show him the details of the defection, which all but named Philby, Guy Burgess and Donald Maclean as the spies. Philby read the dispatch without turning a hair and offered to go out to Istanbul to finalise arrangements to bring Volkov back to London. In the meantime he informed his KGB controller of the intended defection. The inevitable happened, with a report of a heavily bandaged man being helped on to a private plane for Moscow and then nothing more being heard of Konstantin Volkov.

His disappearance was put down to the Russians finding out about, or at least suspecting, a possible defection by means unknown. Poor old Volkov would never have suspected that his defection would be put in the hands of the British security service officer he was about to denounce and who would make sure he would never live to tell the tale. Following this, Philby was awarded the OBE and offered a posting in 1947 as a head of the security section of the British Embassy in Istanbul.

After a couple of years in a post that where he would not have had been able to find much information of use to the Russians he was appointed to the plum job of SIS representative in Washington. He was given responsibility for liaison with the CIA and the FBI headquarters, which gave the KGB direct access to the most closely guarded intelligence secrets of the Allies.

Burgess was also posted to Washington and had made a nuisance of himself to the Americans and his own embassy with his excessive drinking and undisguised homosexuality (still illegal at the time), always excused to his hosts with the plea of diplomatic immunity.

Meanwhile, American cryptanalysts were working on breaking a Russian cipher that was known as Venona. This would lead to an outstanding signals intelligence code-breaking achievement that had begun to develop during the war. The code was encrypted by the use of a one-time pad system that was slow and ponderous, but very secure as long as the encoders stuck to the procedure. The Allies had monitored, recorded and filed away huge amounts of script that the Soviets had transmitted since 1940 in the intercepted Venona code, although they had not been able to decipher it. That was largely because they were concentrating on the decryption of German Enigma and other codes, but as the war ended and the Cold War began the significance of the Venona transmission scripts changed. Now the Russians were the foe and what they had to say in their signals was of prime interest to the Allies.

As the war with Japan ended, more than 100 American cryptanalysts became available to break the Venona code. Repetition is a very common way for code breakers to break into a cipher and the Russians had made the mistake of running out of one-time pads during the war, instead repeatedly making the use of the same pad more than once. Slowly the code breakers began to make progress in clarifying the messages – and what they found amazed them. Lists of the personnel involved in the Manhattan Project were found, and highly classified material from the US War Department and Treasury, as well the OSS, indicated that the government administration was riddled with KGB spies.

The Soviet encoders never referred to an agent by name but rather by the code name he had been allocated, so it would take some detective work to identify the agent behind the code name. The cryptanalysts had identified a Soviet agent based in the British Embassy in Washington in 1945 who was known as 'Homer'. He was passing secret information to Moscow. The information was passed to the British in Broadway, who immediately began an investigation and, from hints contained in Venona such as that Homer was married and other details, the suspects were narrowed down to a few – the most likely being Donald Maclean.

Both the American and British security services thought their intelligence from Venona was secure so they did not want to quote it as a source for their suspicion that Maclean was a KGB agent. They would need further collaborative evidence to convict other traitors, but they would not realise until later that in showing Philby the Venona transcripts they had already 'blown' their secret. The disclosure would have sent a shiver down his spine as it was a clear indication that further decryption of the ciphers would reveal him as a traitor. But first he had to do something about his fellow spy. Philby alerted his KGB controller to Maclean's danger and was asked to plan his flight to Russia, but the difficulty was to find someone to assist Maclean with his defection. Verona contained the seeds of the destruction of the Cambridge Spy Ring.

Meanwhile, Burgess' behaviour, which had always been atrocious, was getting worse. Oliver Franks, the British ambassador in Washington, had little time for his extraordinary behaviour. In a trip down into Virginia, Burgess, accompanied by a young black man, was stopped three times in one day for driving at more than 80 miles an hour while drunk. When questioned by the State Police he claimed diplomatic immunity, not only for himself but also his driver. The officer did not accept it and the driver was taken before a Justice of the Peace and he was fined. The offence came to the notice of the governor of Virginia and then the British Embassy, but that was not the end of Burgess' disastrous trip.

Burgess' path to self-destruction continued as he got into an argument with the grandson of President Roosevelt, who was a senior member of the CIA. They got into an argument over the Korean War in which the two men came near to blows. The matter came to the notice of Allen Dulles, who was deputy director of the CIA, and he related the whole affair to Bedell Smith, the head of the agency. The British ambassador had to suspend Burgess, who took a week's holiday, in which time he was briefed by Philby about the plan to help Maclean make his escape to Russia before he was interrogated by MI6. He was given specific instructions as to how the getaway should be made and how he should help his colleague in his escape but Burgess was strictly instructed that he should not go with him.

In response to Burgess' conduct, the ambassador sent him home to London to face a board of Foreign Office and security officials. It was a strange time for all concerned because the alarm bells were ringing for Burgess' colleagues. However, there was no sense of urgency to get to London where the danger lay. So relaxed was Burgess that he sailed on the *Queen Mary* rather than go by air, and it took five days to get to Southampton during which time he was usually drunk. As he disembarked he was met by Anthony Blunt who knew nothing of the threat that Venona had created for 'Homer'. When he was told he reported it to his own Soviet handler who confirmed that Maclean would be welcomed in Russia if he decided to go. Burgess went on to report to Maclean at the American desk in the Foreign Office, as a diplomat might be expected to do on returning from the Washington post.

Maclean immediately told him of the terrible trouble that he was in. It was going to be difficult for him to escape to Russia, even though the Foreign Office investigators still could not believe one of their own people was a spy. Some of them were still busy investigating the embassy's chauffeurs and cleaning ladies. He was being shadowed by two 'followers' who were making themselves more obvious than they should have done. The security service's intention was clearly to put pressure on its suspect, who was in turmoil about the situation. They planned to question him formally when he arrived after the weekend, but Maclean's defection plan timing on that Saturday would beat them to it. Burgess had booked cabins on the cross-Channel ferry, *Falaise*, so the two of them boarded at Southampton and reached Saint-Malo on a bright morning in May, to vanish without a trace. They would not be heard from again for some years.

Broadway's letting one suspect escape was made worse by the fact that not one but two diplomats had disappeared. The effect in Broadway and the Foreign Office was described by someone in Artillery Mansions as a 'major intelligence earthquake'. The immediate reaction among the senior members of the service was to not tell the CIA what was happening, particularly as it had been increasingly critical of the British Security Services' performance.

The British Embassy in Washington received the news of the disappearing diplomats from London overnight due to the time difference between Britain and America. The news was broken to Philby the following morning, and he feigned horror at the flight of Maclean, which turned to real horror when he was told that Burgess had gone with him. Few intelligence officers knew of the 'Homer' investigation so suspicion would fall on those that were in on the secret and Philby was one of that limited number. He braced himself for an investigation as he waited to be recalled to London by his colleagues in Broadway. But he was not the only one to be panicking, Blunt was as well.

Blunt managed to involve himself in the investigation to deflect suspicion, and even hid evidence. He had helped to search Burgess' flat in New Bond Street, where he found a letter that could have incriminated Philby and promptly pocketed it. Later, more papers were found dating back to early in the war. These involved Cairncross and caused him to be put on the suspect list along with many others. He was put under surveillance with a tap on his telephone, on which he was overheard talking to a Soviet Embassy official.

The absconding of the two diplomats had many repercussions, causing governments to re-examine their security and liaison procedures; but most of all it caused almost all senior staff to reconsider the trustworthiness of their friends and colleagues. The morale of the Foreign Office staff was extremely low as they began to realise that their own trusted operatives could be traitors.

Then, when the situation reached rock bottom it got worse. The papers got hold of the story. The *Daily Express* broke the story and ran it with screaming headlines causing journalists to comment that every day was Sunday in newspaper sales. The atmosphere of deep and frenetic distrust deepened. Anyone who had spoken to either of the two diplomats had to prove their innocence of being a 'pinko', let alone a communist in their early life, and even then many remained under a cloud of uncertainty.

In Artillery Mansions the atmosphere of distrust was beginning to cool down as nothing positive had been heard of the two diplomats, but suspicions touched the highest in Broadway for long afterwards. Everyone was under suspicion, even those at the very top. The MI5 director general, Sir Roger Hollis, was a suspect accused even by colleagues such as Peter Wright, who left MI6 to write his book on the internal workings of the agency. Much of the controversy came from journalist Chapman Pincher, who wrote the books *Their Trade is Treachery* and *Too Secret, Too Long*. He accused Hollis and other senior security officers of being KGB agents. The solution came when the Berlin Wall came down and the collapse of the Soviet administration enabled scholars and archivists to search the Kremlin's archives; the records show no trace of Hollis being a KGB agent.

The continuous criticism eroded confidence in the British security services, not only among the public but also among their allies. The CIA was particularly affected because Broadway was far from frank in its discussions and briefings with the Americans. Herbert Morrison, the British foreign secretary, stated in the House of Commons that Maclean had not had access to secret information, even though the American State Department knew that the diplomat had a pass to roam freely in its atomic research establishments.

The Russians watched silently from the wings as the alliance between the intelligence communities was stretched almost to breaking point by doubt and scepticism. The Burgess and Maclean affair was the third body blow to American intelligence suffered as a result of the failure of Britain's security breaches. The first two were the atomic spies. The atomic bomb was the trump card in the Cold War and I believe that it was Stalin's overwhelming consideration in not giving the Red Army orders to roll its tanks into the Western Allies' sector in Berlin.

There was one limited attempt, however, when a Russian armoured column advanced across the Allied border to be faced with a similar unit of our own, including my regiment. It was left with no alternative but to fight or retire, so, after five hours of eyeball-to-eyeball confrontation, the Red Army withdrew. The incident brought us the nearest to conflict since the Second World War, until the time President Kennedy faced down Khrushchev in the Cuban Crisis. The threat of the atomic bomb saved us from a more difficult situation that day, but that threat was be lost due to the Soviets' atomic spies. Allied intelligence evaluations estimated that it would take years for the Soviets to create a working bomb – but they were wrong, the British atomic scientists Alan Nunn May and Klaus Fuchs, who were scientific spies, gave the Soviet scientists technical and practical information enabling them to be ready to set off the first Soviet atomic bomb years ahead of the time expected by the Allies. They could not work out how the Soviets did it until they decrypted some of the Venona transcripts revealing enough clues to identify the atomic spies.

Klaus Fuchs was German born, but a British naturalised citizen, who joined the British Atomic Research Project as a theoretical physicist and from there joined its team to work on the Manhattan Project in New York. Fuchs had made contact with an American communist, Harry Gold, and through him comprehensively betrayed the secrets of the atomic bomb to the Soviets, making it the most serious atomic secrets leak in the Cold War.

He was not the only spy, atomic or otherwise, to betray his country. The gradual decryption of Venona revealed 349 Soviet agents active in the United States, many of whom were never discovered. Fuchs had become head of the Theoretical Physics Division of the British Atomic Energy Research Establishment at Harwell, and that senior position gave him special access to the secrets of Los Alamos and the Manhattan Project. It enabled him to advise the Soviets on a cheaper way of making an atomic bomb using plutonium rather than the more expensive enriched uranium used by the Americans; not only did it make the bomb cheaper but also enabled the Soviets to produce them faster. Soviet scientists were also able to use experience gained in developing the atomic bomb to develop a hydrogen bomb to match Truman's 'super bomb' within nine months – it used lithium, which did not have to be refrigerated, unlike the American one.

Clues from the Venona decrypts were gradually homing in on Fuchs, but he was finally exposed by a friend, leading to his arrest when at the Royal Air Force Intelligence Centre in Shell Mex House in The Strand. The CIA badly wanted access to Fuchs to question him, but British security put a block on it, which annoyed the Americans intensely. However, when they did talk to him they were able to identify a number of Soviet agents working in their own nuclear research projects. MI5 continued questioning him for some weeks before he admitted his guilt. When he was finally charged he believed that he would be shot for atomic espionage but instead he was relieved to receive a sentence of fourteen years.

Fuchs was not the only atomic scientist spying for the Soviets. Another, Igor Gouzenko, uncovered by a cipher clerk in the Soviet Embassy in Ottawa, defected to the Allies and gave them a list of twenty KGB agents working in America, as well as British nuclear scientist Alan Nunn May. He was a friend of Donald Maclean and was working on Canada's atomic bomb project when he was offered a post in King's College in the Strand. On his return to London he was arrested by MI5 and jailed for ten years.

The Russian bomb that had been developed with the help of the atomic spies could be carried by a conventional bomber, unlike the American one that needed to be refrigerated. The atomic age followed by the thermonuclear one were both ushered in by nuclear spies, with the Soviet scientists having created a weapon that was superior to the American one. A remarkable achievement for Russian intelligence and espionage.

VENONA

The Cambridge Spy Ring was living under the threat of detection during the gradual decryption of the many thousands of Venona ciphered messages being worked through by American cryptanalysts. Unfortunately for the Soviets, they did not know which of the transcripts had been decoded so they could not specifically warn any agent that they were in danger of discovery. They were sure of 'Homer's' peril, however, so the defection of Burgess and Maclean focused suspicion on Philby, who was still in the British Embassy in Washington.

A team of security officers were sent out to Washington for a 'chat' and Philby was removed from his post in the embassy. This was in liaison with the CIA, as the Americans were very suspicious of him and did not want him back. The investigatory team consisted of MI5 officers; the traditional vicious feuding between the two agencies meant that Philby did not have a very responsive hearing. Nevertheless, the old boy network came into play as some of the Foreign Office elite still could not accept that 'one of theirs' could be a traitor. They could not find any evidence to convict him, but the

CIA did not accept that the suspect was innocent so he was asked to resign with a substantial financial handshake.

However, he was soon back in a field post in Cyprus. MI5 continued to pursue the investigation with vigour, and this was completed several years later, resulting in Philby's unofficial trial in Broadway. It was unresolved so he was returned to the field, this time in Turkey. MI5 persisted with the investigation and four years later a member of parliament, Colonel Marcus Lipton, named Philby as the 'third man' in the Burgess and Maclean affair, which caused the government to make a statement. The foreign secretary, Harold Macmillan, on the advice of MI6, told the House nothing had been proven against Philby.

All this was the subject of a one-sided discussion in Artillery Mansions, so when the grapevine announced that he was back on the MI5 payroll with the cover of correspondent in Beirut for the *Sunday Observer*, a cheer went up. The close association of the British national press with the security services enabled Philby to stay there as a journalist making contacts, official and unofficial, for five years. His life there seems to have been fairly stable until a major in the 1st Directorate of the KGB, Igor Golitsyn, defected from his post in the Russian Embassy in Helsinki to the CIA in America. He was released by the Americans to come to Broadway for a briefing with Dick White, who had recently been appointed director of MI6, in which it was confirmed that Philby was indeed a Soviet agent. As a result, Nicholas Elliott, who was a friend of Philby, was sent to interview him in Beirut and got him to confess to being a Soviet spy. Another interview was arranged but in the meantime he vanished. Some six months later the Russian newspaper *Izvestia* announced that he had been granted asylum in Moscow.

The Kremlin would not have been too upset when Philby was first suspected as the 'third man' after Burgess' defection and thereby reducing his effectiveness. It had a new agent in MI6: George Blake, who was born with the surname Behar in Rotterdam in Holland. After his father died he was sent to live with relatives in Egypt and attended the English School in Cairo, where his gift for languages became apparent. After two years he returned to Holland just at the time of the Nazis' invasion of the country, which caused his mother and her two daughters to escape to England.

Blake decided to stay and finish his course at school, after which he joined the Dutch Resistance in which he gained a reputation for courage and cunning. However, that attracted the attention of the Gestapo. He fled from Holland and passed through France and Spain to escape to England, where he changed his name to Blake and volunteered for the Royal Navy. He was seconded to SOE and trained with it.

He was posted to SHAEF, where he was commissioned and set to work translating and interpreting the huge number of German language documents that were being captured by the Allies. As the war ended he was posted to Hamburg to evaluate the technology of German U-boats and to interrogate their commanders at an early stage in the TICOM programme. He performed his tasks well and worked with ruthless efficiency until the programme came to an end. He then returned to England and because of his talent for languages was invited by the Foreign Office to study Russian at Cambridge University. When his course was completed he was enrolled in the Foreign Service and posted to the British Embassy in Seoul in Korea just in time for the outbreak of the Korean War.

Blake and the rest of the diplomatic staff were captured and the Communist Army took them, along with 700 American Army prisoners, on a death march – only 250 survived. The history and reason for his conversion to communism is uncertain and has several versions. One of the most dramatic is that when he tried to escape from the tormented column of prisoners on the death march, Blake was caught and stood before a firing squad on the charge of being a spy. As the rifles were loaded he shouted in Russian that he was not guilty of being a spy and the North Korean officer in charge of the firing squad, who understood Russian, stopped the execution. Blake was taken aside to discuss the rights and wrongs of the war and afterwards subjected to an intensive brainwashing programme about the communist ideology, to which Blake was said to have succumbed.

The many stories about his conversion vary, but they all contain some aspect of him being subjected to brainwashing. The Korean War was the first time that a combatant would try to systematically convert prisoners to its own ideology. The procedure was particularly aimed at better-educated men such as Blake. It had begun to work on him, but it was not apparent to his friends on that terrible march that the experience was to be a turning point in his life.

OTHER SPIES

Blake and his diplomatic colleagues were not released until the ceasefire in 1953, when they were flown home via Moscow and then Gatow Airfield to be feted by the Foreign Office and treated as heroes. He had upheld the highest traditions of the Foreign Service, he was told, and was appointed to MI6, which normally only accepted British-born members. It seemed his record in Korea made his case an exceptional one – it was a fatal mistake for MI6.

Blake integrated well into the service and began work in 2 Carlton House Terrace, which is still one of the most elegant residences that the service inhabits, with a marbled hall and classic curved staircase lit by classically designed chandeliers. The building gives the visitor the sense of a more serene age and in it Blake began his career as a double agent for the KGB by photographing every document he felt would be of interest to his Russian handlers. It was at the beginning of his career in espionage as a double agent that the opportunity occurred that would make his name in the Kremlin.

The operation that the British called 'Stopwatch' and the Americans called 'Gold' was intended to tunnel under the Soviet territory border in Berlin to tap the underground telephone cables connected to Moscow. A CIA and MI6 meeting was convened to discuss the most important telephone tapping project that they had ever undertaken in Berlin. It was to eavesdrop on the Red Army communications in the Soviet zone. Top CIA men brought top secret documents to the meeting describing how a tunnel would be dug to connect to the Soviet cables. Confidential conversations between high-ranking Soviet officers and intelligence men would be overheard, in what would be the intelligence coup of the Cold War – and Blake was taking the minutes …

The resources and manpower that would be needed to record, translate and evaluate the potential intelligence output of the tunnel were recorded, as well as the engineering resources and methods required to build it. British personnel who had been taught Russian in the JSSL scheme would be used for the translations and the co-operation between the CIA and GCHQ would be close. The technical aspect of connecting the listening devices to the Russian cable were going to be tricky, they thought, as they did not want any 'noise' on the line to alert the Red Army telephone operators to the link-up.

What the intelligence people did not know was that when the minutes were typed a copy would go to the KGB at the Russian Embassy in London long before the work began. However, it was a classic intelligence problem for the Soviets. If they made any move to change the Russian telephone traffic that the CIA was tapping into, it would mean that questions would be asked by Western intelligence about the tunnel's security. Any enquiry might compromise the safety of their star agent at the heart of British intelligence; they did not want to risk disclosing that they had a secret source of information in Carlton Gardens. For that reason, they allowed the telephone tap to operate unimpeded for eleven months, generating copious amounts of telephone conversations ranging from the pointless to the confidential and even secret – that was a measure of Blake's value to them. His espionage activities continued until he was notified that he was to be posted to Berlin, but before he went he was to marry Gillian Allen, who was an MI6 girl.

Blake arrived in the espionage soup that was Berlin. The MI6 station was based at the Olympic Stadium in the offices of the British Control Commission, placed to administer Germany until it recovered enough to become the Federal Republic. The commission was a perfect disguise for the agency's officers. They did not need to use the usual diplomatic cover as their people got lost among the hundreds of commission staff coming and going in the stadium, so I cannot recall having met him.

The MI6 offices connected to those of the commission were intensely busy and had a number of briefs to operate in the espionage capital of the world. One was technical and scientific intelligence and was concerned with listening techniques (the Berlin Tunnel was one of these). Another was to estimate the order of battle of the Red Army, in which I was involved as a very junior operative and at which the station was very successful. The third was political intelligence and the recruiting of agents – which was Blake's responsibility. He was able to operate very well in that sphere as he had access to the KGB headquarters in Karlshorst, which fed him enough to keep the Olympic station happy. In fact, they gave him the names of some low-value agents to boost his reputation among his colleagues.

The MI6 offices at the stadium were not very secure so Blake's opportunities to copy or photograph the contents of the MI6 files in its office were immense. He was said to have given the KGB more than 5,000 images of his agency's secret documents. He was assured by the KGB that none of the men and women that he had betrayed would be tortured or executed and he seems to have believed that, but there was much evidence that Blake's work caused the suffering and death of a great many agents.

Movement and contacts were very easy for him as he was able to contact his controller just by taking the U-Bahn (underground train) over the border into East Berlin. It was some years before the wall was built so access to the Russian sector was simple, although officers in the security services were usually warned not to go into East Berlin. Blake had been given one of the forged identity cards created by MI6 to present to passport control at Checkpoint Charlie, where there was invariably much interrogation and checking. The Stasi were very punctilious about such tedious and time-consuming formalities, the reason may have been a form of job creation, or at least justification, but probably as much for its nuisance value.

Guards were obviously given a standing order to let him through although they were probably instructed to play-act being difficult to some extent to show onlookers that he was not given any special treatment. Blake had taken photographic images of all card index entries of the many CIA and MI5 agents in place in Soviet administrations and military posts in eastern Europe and delivered the film to the KGB at Karlshorst. He had betrayed a particular thorn in the side of the East Germans, Robert Bialek, who had been a senior member of the Stasi. He became a valuable defector to the West as he began making German language broadcasts back to the East from the British sector comparing life in the Eastern sector and zone with that in the West. He was a marked man by the Stasi so his security was administered by MI6 and was very tight, but he was lured away with Blake's help to a party and walked into a trap in an unusual way. He was then kidnapped, as were so many prominent anti-Soviet men who lived in Berlin, and driven over the unguarded border, never to be seen again.

Blake's reputation grew among his KGB handlers, who wanted to enhance his value in the eyes of MI6, making him even more valuable to them as a highly placed agent. The Allied security services had not been able to penetrate the KGB's security network so it was decided in the Kremlin that it would provide an opportunity for them to do so. The supposed double agent would, of course, be a 'plant' by the Soviets. It came through one of the many 'hundred mark youths' who populated the espionage underworld of Berlin, Horst Eitner, who was one of those Blake had cultivated as a part of his network in the name of MI6.

Eitner, who was also working for the Gehlen Organisation, was trying to keep his financial head above water with a family to support and knew nothing of Blake's link to the KGB. He used the cover of a Dutch news reporter named DeVries (Blake's real name). Eitner put the KGB's pretended double agent in his way as part of a carefully choreographed dance of the spies, which then connected to Blake. Blake then played his part by carefully grooming the double agent, who Eitner had introduced him to under the name of 'Boris' and was highly placed (but not too high) in the communist hierarchy. He was a senior interpreter at high-level Soviet discussions on economic matters and often accompanied senior Soviet people on negotiations between government departments in Russia and also her satellite countries in eastern Europe.

The senior security people in Broadway could not believe their luck. They told Blake to cultivate Boris carefully and as a result the badly needed intelligence about the economic strength of all parts of the communist bloc began to flow back to London – all edited by the KGB. The inflated estimations of Soviet economic strength were used as the basis of Allied strategy and would have been the origin of many decisions in London and Washington during the Cold War. It also explains why the collapse of the Soviet empire's economy, leading to the fall of the Berlin Wall, was such a surprise to everyone in the West.

Internal political pressures from Khrushchev's old guard as a result of increasing economic difficulties were becoming uncomfortable for him and he was looking for a diversion, which finally came with heavy rain in Berlin. It was the reason for revealing the secret tunnel in Berlin, which the Allies had been using to listen to the telephone conversations of the Soviet military between East Germany and Moscow. The CIA and MI6 had been listening continuously and transcribed the contents of almost 450,000 conversations between many thousands of people, on subjects great and small, for almost twelve months. The astonishing thing is that the KGB knew the exchanges were taking place and did nothing about it.

Now it had a reason to do something. The heavy rain gave it the reason to act when water began to seep into the connections of the cables, causing them to short out and requiring urgent attention. The signals engineering team that was probably KGB began to dig. Blake had been forewarned by his handler about what would happen so he would have been very apprehensive about the outcome. The engineering team dug steadily down until it found the Berlin Tunnel. The American listening team had vacated so quickly that its kettle was still warm.

Preparations for the discovery of the tunnel had been included in the design by the American engineers. The Russian engineers came up against a steel door barring their way. Written on it in both English and German was the legend, 'You are now entering the American sector'. The Russians stormed at the Americans in simulated rage and they made much fuss about the intrusion into Russian, or rather East German, territory although there was not much of a distinction to be made.

Parties of schoolchildren were conducted around the tunnel to see how the 'evil capitalists' treated the sovereign territory of the peace-loving communist states. The fury in the Soviet press did not make much impression on the media in the West; in fact, they rather enjoyed getting one over on the Russians. However, that would change when they found out the truth about the betrayal of the secret tunnel.

Blake heaved a sigh of relief when no leakage of secret information was found and his social and intelligence life went on without a hitch. He was told that his next posting would be to Lebanon, but for the time being he would be working in London. He and his wife and children went to live in Bromley, from where he commuted to the MI6 station in Artillery Mansions.

I was working there, but I cannot remember him because he was probably on the 2nd Floor (I was on the 1st) doing different things. The next floor up was full of linguists, of whom he was one, speaking Russian, German, Dutch and studying Arabic. He had, by all accounts, a natural talent for languages as many Dutch people have. He was still a spy dedicated to working for the KGB and must have picked up good intelligence as he was only a stone's throw from Broadway, and he also knew where to find his friends in the bar at St Ermin's, which was even closer.

He must have lived the routine life of an ordinary businessman, catching the train to Victoria Station to arrive in the office sometime about 10 in the morning (we kept gentlemen's hours) to a cup of coffee and begin his daily office work. What he had that the rest of us did not was the unimaginable burden of his double life. He had to keep a regular rendezvous with his handler to hand over what secret information he had gleaned from his colleagues and documentation since his last 'drop'. To make those connections he would have to use a technique known as 'tradecraft' in Broadway, which consisted of a tedious and time-consuming practice to ensure that he was not being observed or followed.

Choosing to walk down a deserted street or alley and waiting to see if someone follows is an elementary precaution for an agent before making a contact with his contact. To lose a 'tail' the agent should never do the expected thing; if he is travelling to an 'assignation' it might not be wise to catch the first train but wait for the next, all the time watching to see if another person on the platform does the same. A perfect illustration of the train trick was shown by Michael Caine in the spy film *Billion Dollar Brain*. In it he has followed a suspect on to a train that stops at a deserted station. The suspect alights and looks along the platform to see who else gets off. There is no one, so the suspect walks away satisfied that he is not being followed. Then, as the train pulls out of the station, it reveals Caine standing on the other side of the track where he has not been seen by his suspect and is able to continue to follow.

There are many tricks to tradecraft, but there are also many tricks to foil the agent who does not want it known where he goes and who he sees and these are practised by 'followers', who generally work in teams. These shadowy figures use the tricks of the KGB and its agents. Blake would have known this as an experienced intelligence officer, and it would have given him some sleepless nights as he continued to feed his handlers with films of documents and gossip from Broadway. It must have been a very uncertain world for him and the prospect of a new and less aggressive existence in the Middle East would have offered an attractive proposition. His KGB masters would not have wanted it, however, as it would have removed him from the centre of the intelligence community.

Blake and his family flew out to Beirut after just over a year or so in London and began to enjoy the pleasant and less hurried lifestyle of the Europeanised Middle Eastern city before its civil war broke out to ruin everything. In my time there, I recall the tranquil air of the whitewashed houses and wide boulevards with sellers of freshly squeezed orange drinks on every corner using fruit recently picked off the trees. Blake must have found the place relaxing after the espionage-thick atmosphere of Berlin, or even the formal and disciplined air of the intelligence community in London. But all was not well for Blake.

Back in Berlin the operations base of the CIA was buzzing with anticipation. For more than two years it had been getting hard intelligence from a double agent who it had named '*Heckenschütze*' (Sniper). Finally, Sniper had decided to defect and give up information about many American double agents – and a couple of British ones as well. The CIA had not briefed MI6 about its catch because he was about to produce evidence identifying the two highly placed double agents operating in the British intelligence community. The defector finally revealed himself as Lieutenant Colonel Michael Goleniewski of Polish counter-intelligence and said he would bring papers to help identify the two spies, and so he did.

He arrived with his mistress and much paperwork to prove to the CIA that there were Soviet agents in many countries, from Israel to Sweden, as well as America. He produced papers to show that a navy man, Harold Houghton, and Ethel Gee, at the Underwater Weapons Establishment in Portland in Dorset, were Russian agents. That led MI5 to uncover a whole spy ring headed by Gordon Lonsdale and aided by Peter and Helen Kroger. All three of them turned out to be 'illegals', Soviet spies who had been living in England under deep cover with assumed names for several years. All of them got heavy prison sentences for their crimes.

The second of the suspected spies was going to be more difficult to trap. The clues were three secret documents that Goleniewski had passed to the CIA that had been brought to the KGB by a Soviet agent. Each one of the stolen secret documents was traced through the hands of every security officer that would normally handle it. Ten of them came under suspicion, including Blake. The careful cross-checking of whose desk each of the documents appeared on proved nothing so the leak was blamed on an unrecorded thief. Blake, who was unaware of Goleniewski's defection, relaxed in distant Beirut. He was in the clear – for the moment.

Back in Berlin, a drinking party was in progress with the Eitners at its centre. This was not all that unusual as they were a convivial pair whose drinking bouts often led Horst and Brigitte to have inebriated rows of gigantic proportions. This one was a bit more vicious than usual and caused Brigitte to go to the local police station and tell them that her husband was spying for the Russians. He only learned about this when he was arrested the following morning. At his interrogation by the German police it became clear that he was a double agent. The interrogation was a shambles with claims of what he had done varying from one interview to the next until he offered to make a statement that would lead the police to a KGB person in MI6.

Eitner's rambling confessions gave police the name of Max de Vries, who had connections with the Soviets, and that made the interrogators wonder about the methods and activities of Blake during his time in Berlin. Further reviews of the evidence made up the minds of the investigators in Broadway that Blake was their man, so it was time to have a serious talk. In Beirut the head of the station, Nicholas Elliott, received the shock of his life when he was told that his long-time close friend, George Blake, was a Soviet agent.

Blake was to be called back to London, but it had to happen in a low-key way in case he absconded before MI6 could question him to find out how much damage he had done. Elliott planned a casual meeting at which he told Blake he would be called back to London to discuss a new appointment. Such a recall was not that unusual, although its timing was odd. The only slightly curious thing for Blake was that instead of staying with his mother at her flat, Elliott insisted that he stay at St Ermin's Hotel where he had booked a room for him. Still oblivious, next morning he boarded the plane to London.

Blake arrived at the personnel department of MI6 in Petty France to be met by his department chief and Harold Shergold, who was one of the department's senior interrogators. They asked him to help them clear up a few matters about his time in Berlin. They began to walk through St James' Park and to 2 Carlton House Gardens, where Blake had worked on his return from Korea, and eventually sat at the table where the first plans for the Berlin Tunnel had been discussed and the questioning began. It lasted for three punishing days, during which time Shergold produced the documents that Goleniewski had brought with him from Poland and wondered how Blake came to be on the distribution list of each one of them.

With all the mounting evidence that Shergold had gathered Blake was being directly accused of being a Soviet spy, which he denied as a matter of course until the third day. Shergold suggested that Blake had been tortured and made to confess that he was a British intelligence officer and then blackmailed, so surely had no choice but to become a double agent? In his account of the interrogation, Blake wrote that the reason for his confession was his rising indignation that he was offered money to betray MI6 secrets to the KGB. When he did confess, he denied that he was tortured or had taken any money for the secrets that he passed, although he admitted that he had approached the KGB himself.

The MI6 interrogation team were taken aback, and continued to be as Blake began to unburden himself by explaining his motives in a most detailed way. He did not have an answer to the most fundamental question, however, why did he not resign from the service and express his views in public without betraying his colleagues and his country in such a blatant way? To that he had no answer, so the police were called in and his confession used as a part of the charges against him in his prosecution in the High Court.

The reaction in Artillery Mansions (and probably in the junior levels of Broadway staff) was that it was all a mistake and a senior intelligence officer such as Blake could not possibly be guilty of a treasonable act. It was true, though, and a message went out to every MI6 and MI5 station that there was a Soviet spy in our midst. It caused a palpably shocked reaction from every corner of the security service.

Someone who had done such damage to such an important department of the British government could expect no mercy. Five charges were made against him and the Crown mobilised a hard-line judge and an even harder-line prosecution barrister to press the damning evidence home and a sentence of the utmost severity was demanded.

Blake got twelve years for each charge and three of them to run consecutively, so he was sentenced to a total of forty-two years' imprisonment – and the papers loved it. Chapman Pincher of the *Daily Express* had a headline of '40 Agents Betrayed', in which that many silhouettes of agents justified the severity of the sentence to the public. A minority felt that the judge was extremely harsh, but the general consensus was that Blake was a traitor and got all that he deserved.

Once Blake was in Wormwood Scrubs jail the KGB deserted him, but he soon established contacts and resources of his own there. He gathered a small group of prisoners, led by a romantically minded Irishman, some of whom were about to be released and who could help from the outside. They assisted him in a successful and audacious escape, which caused much jubilation within the prison. The police search was frantic, checking every Russian ship and associated building and imagining that Blake had escaped with KGB help.

They did not imagine that it had been achieved by a team of amateur ex-prisoners, who kept the fugitive in hiding while a mobile home van was modified to make a hiding place in which to smuggle him out of the country and take him to his old stamping grounds in Berlin. The customs search and ferry crossing from Dover presented no problems to the smugglers, nor did the trip across West Germany and into the Soviet-controlled East.

Blake arrived in Berlin and was welcomed like a conquering hero at Karlshorst by the KGB officer who had acted as his former handler in London, ten years before. He was flown to Moscow and feted again by old friends who had been his handlers and given a luxurious lifestyle. He lived the life of an immigrant in Moscow in the company of Sean Bourke, one of his Irish rescuers, but the two finally fell out. Blake then lived the life of an immigrant with his three fellow KGB double agents as companions, the closest of which was Maclean, but his movements were always restricted to Moscow. He was always under surveillance by the KGB as it was constantly afraid that the Allied security services would spirit him away somehow.

A quarter of a century later a BBC presenter managed to get an unsupervised interview with him, when he was over 90 in his dacha (country house) outside Moscow. In it he defended his record of duplicity and the human cost of so many agents' lives. Blake (and the others) had betrayed their country for the Soviet Union only to see it collapse along with the other repressive regimes of eastern Europe.

Anthony Fredrick Blunt was another double agent, but with a very different kind of career. He too was a homosexual and a most effective recruiter of KGB agent candidates while an undergraduate at Cambridge University. He was the 'fourth man' in the Cambridge Spy Ring and came under suspicion because he was a friend of Burgess. He was exposed by one of his own recruits, Michael Strange, an American whom he had tried to recruit years before. Blunt had a long run, as he confessed to MI5 in April 1964 and gave up several of his recruits from Cambridge, including John Cairncross, so in return for a full confession the security services agreed to keep his espionage career a secret. He was granted full immunity from prosecution and his career as a KGB agent was kept an official secret for fifteen years while he continued the social rounds in London's society and became a guest at the home of Victor Rothschild.

The Queen had been told of Blunt's confession at the time it was made, and although he was Surveyor of the Queen's Pictures he kept the post for another nine years with his record well known by palace staff. He was a leading art historian and knighted as Sir Anthony Blunt KCVO, but one visitor to the palace was told by King George VI's private secretary, Sir Alan Lascelles, as they passed him in a corridor, 'That is our Russian spy'. He was on friendly terms with the head of MI5 and later MI6 and spent Christmas with them and many well-known politicians in Rothschild's house.

With such an open secret it could not last, and a book was published with Blunt's role thinly disguised in it. However, it was picked up by the magazine *Private Eye* and exposed publicly. It was a time of political upheaval and one of its great exponents was Prime Minister Margaret Thatcher, who had taken a stand against a system that covered up unpleasant truths. It was politicians who would decide on policy, not the intelligence community, she decided – and the press agreed. The newspapers began to investigate Blunt and hint at the truth. This caused a social upheaval as well as an embarrassment to the intelligence community, the royal household, et al. The furore that it caused in the press and with the public created a series of witch-hunts, resulting in accusing senior members of the security services of being Russian spies, including Sir Roger Hollis, director general of MI5. Other senior intelligence officers were also accused of being double agents by ex-MI6 spycatcher, Peter Wright, in his book.

There would be yet another blow to the prestige of the service as John Cairncross, who had been working at Bletchley Park during the war, was named, although not with the same high profile as the others in the spy ring. It was possibly because he was *not* a part of the spy ring. Indeed, he was unaware of the espionage activities of the others and thought he was the only valuable KGB working in the British intelligence service.

Cairncross had joined the Foreign Office before the war and was said to be very intelligent, but cantankerous and conceited. He was recruited by an SOE man who was (yet another) communist agent, James Klugman, who became a prominent member of his party after the war. Owing to his difficult personality Cairncross was often moved after a time from one post to another, and from the Cabinet Office he progressed to Bletchley Park, where he worked on the Luftwaffe codes. It was said that he took coded transcripts and even evaluations home in a suitcase (if he was to be believed – and most of the Cambridge Spies did have their flights of fancy).

He was able to warn the KGB, and thus the Red Army, of the intended German offensive at the crucial Battle of Kursk. The Russians were victorious, so he boasted that he had a hand in winning the campaign on the Eastern Front. Cairncross was moved again to counter-intelligence at Broadway, where he worked alongside the members of the Cambridge Spy Ring, but still fondly imagining that he was the only KGB spy in the intelligence service. He was suspected, as already described, but after a document of his was found in a search of Burgess' flat MI6 had him followed and thought he was passing papers to a KGB handler. Although it could not prove it, he was asked to resign.

That would be the end of the Cambridge Spy Ring (we think!) and its association with St Ermin's Hotel. Now the centre of espionage would move on to MI6's purpose-built headquarters on the Thames Riverside and the cryptographers to another purpose-built building in the Gloucestershire countryside.

The changing global interests of Britain were a strain on the resources of her intelligence service but the anxiety of the knowledge that the KGB had

EIGHT

CONCLUSION

penetrated the ranks of the service at many levels was just as big a burden in the early decades of the Cold War. It not only affected the morale of the officers, it also affected the attitude and trust of their American allies in the CIA in Washington. My book has only dealt with the early stages of the intelligence conflict that swirled around the 'Spies Hotel' in the years when I witnessed the drama as a minor spectator.

After that time, in the Cold War's tumultuous struggle the action seemed to move away from me, from Westminster to Korea and even Vietnam as the struggle between communism and capitalism, or autocracy and democracy, progressed. Britain's history of intelligence had started with its service giving the United States a masterclass in the gathering of intelligence and its usage, from which both intelligence communities profited and drew sustenance.

By the 1960s the balance of capability between the two intelligence services was beginning to alter with America's increasing computing capability, which was needed to decrypt signals intelligence transmissions. The vast resources available to America's security services were giving it the edge in the increasing complexity and volume of cryptanalysis. The ability of the Americans to invest in the technology and manpower needed to achieve success was decisive in decrypting an increasing number of transcripts from its vast collection of Venona ciphers. It enabled the CIA to detect a great many Soviet agents working in the Russian spy networks, even though not all of them were clearly identified. It created such a feeling of uncertainty in the Kremlin and its agents that they almost ceased to operate for some time. The cracking of the Venona codes was a triumph for the Americans in the espionage war and severely damaged the huge web of infiltrators who had penetrated into the administrations and institutions of the West. It was a factor in the breaking up and collapse of the Soviet Union.

SECRETS

In the years immediately after the war the British intelligence community was reformed. SOE was disbanded abruptly and MI5, and in particular MI6, picked over what was left of the defunct executive. Experienced SOE personnel, technology and techniques were added to the already considerable capability and reputation of the two agencies, but in the process several Soviet agents were included as well.

MI6 had many shortcomings. A principal one, according to Hugh Trevor-Roper, the historian who served in MI6 during the war, was that during the interwar years its performance was mediocre. He was scathing about 'Six' in the 1930s, 'novels about club land heroes might have given it a fictitious lustre but essentially it remained an amateurish organisation with a slender budget'. The staff were recruited by patronage and the agency acquired some of the characteristics of a coterie, with Menzies, the director of MI6 'giving himself the air of a man that mattered only by making himself the conduit between Churchill and Bletchley Park', to recall Trevor-Roper's words.

From previous passages in this book, aspects of that accusation seem to have some truth, particularly that of a small budget, although the allegations about the director, Major Stewart Menzies, were disputed by some. The effect of the Cambridge Spy Ring changed much of the culture – the budget size had changed and so had the attitude to intelligence methods and the way officers were recruited. It had an effect on me, in that not only were the new recruits put through the positive vetting wringer but also those who had been recruited into the service by a less-than-sanctioned route were also given a going over. I was found wanting mainly because Lennie Brewer, whose protégé I had been, had found himself a better billet in an oil company since he had opted to learn Arabic rather than the Russian that we had all studied. There was no one to speak for me as a result, but then I felt my time with MI6 was coming to an end anyway and I wanted to move on. It found me an opportunity as a columnist in an international newspaper using the connections the service has always had with the press.

I had found intelligence work tedious. A bit like doing a jigsaw puzzle of 100,000 pieces without a picture on the box for guidance, and from the start you know you will not have anywhere near all the pieces to complete it. What is more, some of the pieces will be from another jigsaw entirely and they may have got there by mistake, or been put there with malicious intent by a Russian (or American) doing a jigsaw puzzle of their own. They may (or may not) have been trying to mislead you, and so you cannot depend on having the right pieces in your box. Therefore, you will need to check the same piece two, three or even four times before you can have the confidence to fit the piece into your jigsaw's picture.

A single piece of intelligence from only one source is usually treated as a rumour, and can be of no intelligence value until confirmed over and over again. Any project you are instructed to work on will mean you are a part of a team, within which you are working on a specific task. However, apart from being able to talk to other members of your group socially, you are constrained by a 'need-to-know' policy (and the Official Secrets Act) not to talk to 'them' in the next room about your work. Time is another constraint on the result of your work, so sometimes you have to part with your opus in an unsatisfactory and half-finished state. Added to that, you will probably never see the completed results of your labour because, particularly if you are a fairly junior grade, the 'need-to-know' policy bars you from knowing the results of your puzzle. Any solution or guesstimate you have made may not make any difference to an operation you will probably never even hear about. In addition, the financial rewards are not over generous, so the work is not very satisfying, all of which is not the picture portrayed by James Bond.

There was an enormous plus to our labours, however. I think we all felt that the end product to which we contributed as very small cogs in the slow and cumbersome machinery of government was a factor in determining the policy (and security) of our country. There was a certain pride in that.

CIPHER MEN

I had little to do with cryptographers. They were strange beings from another planet (or at least another floor) who were constantly trying to solve codes that seemed to equate to fiendishly complicated crosswords that the designer was determined they would not solve. I had fancied myself as a crossword solver at the time, but what little I saw of their exercises completely defeated me, mainly because seeking to 'find a way in' to a code was immeasurably more boring than doing an intelligence jigsaw.

Codes touch our daily lives in the developed world, even if we do not know it, and can be found as an integral part of computing and related technology involved in the internet, but in the early days of the Cold War it was different. The effect of breaking the Venona cipher was making an impression on the cryptographic community, as they were beginning to feel that no coding system was safe from the hackers. GCHQ and its massive computer capability was being used to attack the most complex codes and ciphers.

The situation created a major effort in cryptographic research, and resulted in two advances in the technology, both in industry and government-sponsored research in universities. The first was the proposal of an encryption standard by IBM. It was adopted by the Federal Government of the United States as the first publicly acceptable cipher (if you are puzzled by the notion of a publicly available code, then so am I). It was approved by the American NSA – and if you want to know more see http://csrc.nist.gov/publications/fips/fips46-3/fips46-3.pdf. This was integrated into the systems of major military and business organisations, although it turned out later to be insecure. The second important advance was the 'public key' encryption (see www.citeseer.nj.nee.com/340126html) which changed the 'symmetric code', in which the sender and the recipient both need to share the 'secret key' to decode their message, into an asymmetric code. The public key uses an asymmetric key so the sender and the receiver have mathematically related keys but do not need to share the secret key. One of the keys is public and the other secret so the recipient does not need to know the secret key of the sender. Therefore the controller does not need to get involved in the messy business of having to personally distribute code keys to agents – read the web pages if you want to understand it further.

Organisations such as the NSA and GCHQ were alarmed as they want things both ways; they wanted to be able to crack other people's codes but did not want others to read their own communications. Advanced encoding techniques have been discouraged by governments in legal and other ways, so published technical literature on the subject is hard to get and, in my experience, hard to understand if you can get it.

That is enough of codes and ciphers so let us go on to something else.

COMMUNICATIONS

There are different aspects of intelligence communications, both secretly coded and publicly open broadcasts to the public on the radio. I am old enough to remember the bizarre and mysterious messages sent over the radio to Resistance members in Nazi-occupied Europe during the war. The line of a poem, 'the sobbing violins wound my heart', broadcast on the European Service of the BBC in June 1944 alerted French Resistance agents to the fact that the next day would be D-Day. The tradition continued into the Cold War with the use of specific pieces of music played by Radio Moscow to indicate to their spies in Britain which of their dead letter boxes had a message in it for them.

Short-wave radio is a more restricted form of transmission than public broadcasting, and this became an established transmitter of coded messages by and for agents during the war. However, the advent of the Cold War changed the content of those transmissions. The messages that are sent in different forms of code from 'number stations' today are still carrying coded instructions to agents in the field and can still be overheard by the committed listener today. These openly transmitted coded messages are monitored by Enigma 2000 on a daily basis and a closely typed listing of transmission details can run to eighty plus pages a month. A message invariably consists of streams of numbers – hence the name 'numbers stations'. They are generally in groups of five digits. One station regularly read out the meaningless string of numbers in a somewhat tinny woman's voice from what was obviously the Stasi East German secret police at the height of the Cold War.

Morse code is still the preferred mode for some stations to transmit their strange stream of five-number groups, and locations of these stations can be found all around the world. They broadcast from Europe, Russia, the Middle

East and, increasingly, Asia although no government has ever admitted to their transmission.

In spite of that, the style and presentation of many stations gives clues to their origin. Numbers stations are often given a nickname that reflects a distinctive aspect of the station, such as the way they sign off. The format can be 'End of Message', '*Ende*', '*Fini*', 'Final', or some stations thought to originate from the former Soviet Union end with groups of zeros '00000'. Other stations begin or end their transmissions with a signature tune; a well-known one was the tune of 'Lincolnshire Poachers', so it became known by that nickname. The station was located by a direction finder as being based in the RAF station in Akrotiri in Cyprus and almost certainly run by the British SIS. The station was closed down in 2009 leaving its sister station, nicknamed 'Cherry Ripe', to transmit its number messages to the Far East and Australia. The German Federal government's *Bundesnachrichtendienst* (BND) intelligence agency used to run a numbers station known as 'Hotel Kilo' and transmitted on a particular frequency until it was jammed with malicious transmissions from Moscow.

These secret messages use technology that is growing increasingly ingenious, with images or tones being used to send the numbered messages. Some of the images and tones are quite beautiful and their message becomes even more impenetrable. The transmissions of numbers are decreasing, probably in favour of newer and more secure technologies such as the Broadband Global Area Network (BEGAN), which is a device much used by journalists worldwide. They use it to transmit their piece back to London from remote locations via the internet. Messages destined from agents to their controllers and vice versa can be passed just as easily. Devices such as these can transmit their coded messages with great ease and such technology has greatly enhanced the world's communications methods. The same technology can also be used as a radio signal locator to find transmissions by covert operators – so a young James Bond today needs to be a computer expert.

In the Cold War, secrets played an important part in the Great Game. Each side tried to find out what the other side was doing but at the same time endeavoured to keep their own activities from being known. Once the secrets had been discovered, however, they were sometimes treated in very strange ways and none stranger than the secret of the Berlin Tunnel telephone tap that had been betrayed by the double agent George Blake.

The KGB knew about it and did nothing – why? There are many theories about the reason, from the possibility that the Russians faked thousands of telephone calls to mislead the Americans, to the possibility that the KGB let it happen to reassure the Allies that they had no warlike intentions. With the first option, how do you get thousands of people involved in faking all those conversations without the secret becoming common knowledge? The more likely reason was that the KGB knew the Cold War could not carry on and was letting the West know that there were no preparations for attacking the Allies. This implies that it had little faith in the Soviet leadership, but it did not seem to be the only one. The American people grew sick of the McCarthy witch-hunts on the TV and they rebelled against the whole charade.

On the other side of the Iron Curtain the Russian people began to feel even more strongly about the authoritarianism of the Brezhnev Doctrine, which tried to maintain the tyrannical Stalin-like policies. Mikhail Gorbachev, who was president of the Soviet Union, felt that his country could stand the pressure of the arms race no longer and so he went to New York to address the assembly of the United Nations and made an astounding speech. It put an end to the Cold War when he announced that Soviet satellite states would be free to make their own plans for the future and the Red Army would cease to arm itself. Uncertainty swept through the unprepared leadership of the Soviet-controlled Warsaw Pact countries as their intelligence network had failed to foresee the end coming – but then, nor did any of the Allied agencies. The Cold War that had begun with the Berlin Blockade in 1947 had come full circle and the people of satellite countries began to flex their democratic muscles, starting in 1980 with a revolution in Poland led by a Polish welder, Lech Walesa, in a shipyard in Gdansk. The changes took the communist leaders in the satellite countries by surprise; they were deposed by various methods, one by one, as the people of eastern Europe took control of their own destinies.

A newly elected president of the United States, George W. Bush, thought it was all too good to be true and so did his advisors and military men. What were the wicked communists up to and was it a trap laid by the devious Soviets for an unsuspecting United States? The new president's suspicions were put to rest as the Polish welder's revolution spread to East Germany. The dramatic fall of the Berlin Wall spelt out in letters of fire the fact that the Union of Soviet Socialist Republics had lost its grip. On 10 November 1989 thousands of East Germans marched to the wall and started to hack at its structure to pull it down, helped by the guards, until the border between East and West Berlin ceased to exist.

Communism may have been dead, but it was not about to lie down as Soviet hardliners became disillusioned when the harsh realities of democracy's market began to bite. Tanks moved on to the streets of Moscow once more, at the command of an 'Emergency Committee' who announced that Gorbachev was held at his dacha for 'treatment', and worst of all the scheduled television programmes were replaced by recordings of the ballet. It was clearly a national emergency and so 'cometh the hour, cometh the man', as groups of the Emergency Committee's militia were attacking the White House, home of the Russian Parliament. It was stoutly defended by others led by Boris Yeltsin, who stood on a tank and urged his people to resist and overcome the opposition to the reforms that the country demanded. Later Yeltsin became the president of the Russian Republic and formally ended the Soviet Union and replaced it with the Commonwealth of Independent States. Gorbachev may have killed the Communist Party in Russia but Yeltsin buried it and went on to be its president.

THE COLD WAR AND OUR CULTURE

Many lives have been shaped, changed and even taken by a battle of ideologies. Many of these were in Korea, Vietnam and other places, but the main arena for the conflict was always Europe, and mainly Germany. It was here that the Cold War played out, with the use and misuse of spies and spying in what Winston Churchill described as 'The Battle of the Conjurors', although the effects of the contest did also stretch across the Atlantic. The American 'special relationship' with the British intelligence community was deeply marred by the series of leaks and the disaffection of senior intelligence staff.

The British public seemed to share America's view that our whole security services were severely damaged and ineffective after the many newspaper reports about KGB agents in MI6, so the government decided to do something about it. They encouraged a senior MI6 officer, F.W. Winterbotham, to publish a book, *The Ultra Secret*, in 1974, about the glory days of Bletchley Park. This began to change the public view about our intelligence services, although it did not necessarily affect the opinion of the CIA.

Winterbotham had been responsible for supervising the distribution of Ultra intelligence evaluations during the war and his first-hand knowledge of the subject aroused the interest of the public (and the book publishers) to today's level. Any publication to do with Bletchley Park began to sell well, until there are now more than seventy books that have been published on some aspect of the 'Park' – a couple of which are mine.

Some authors of pseudo spy books did have experience of operating in the espionage world, particularly Ian Fleming, whose Bond books sold millions and whose accounts of events in his books can sometimes be traced back to events in which he was actually involved during the war. John Le Carre also did some time in the service, although not as much or as dramatically as Fleming, but his experience of the service shines through in *The Ipcress File*. In the film version, actor Michael Caine is seen arguing with his superior officer about his expenses, and the routine ordinariness of espionage is emphasised. The KGB double agent George Blake used to take the commuter train from Bromley to Victoria every morning when he was working in Artillery Mansions, just like other business people who worked in the area. To be honest, life in the secret service is generally fairly routine, but if that became generally known the book market would crash and they would probably never make another film about 'spooks' …

Films have been a major factor in creating an image of life in the underworld of espionage. Although the treatment of the Bond films is wildly unrealistic it does seem to have touched the public's consciousness. The 'baddies' image introduces a series of characters that the viewer can recognise as hateful, such as Ernest Blofeld, with a sinister Germanic air, or Doctor No, whose film was launched during the Cuban Missile Crisis and was President Kennedy's favourite. A series of evil geniuses were portrayed as Bond's enemies and reflected the current international tensions starting from the East–West conflict through to the drug trade and the use of nuclear bombs to rob Fort Knox, as well as occasional themes in intelligence. I particularly like the Bond film where 'M' (it was 'C' in real life) was a woman played by Judy Dench, probably because the head of security at the time was also a woman – Stella Rimington (some of the old guard in the service would have been turning in their graves). Rimington later wrote a book about her experiences in the service and that would have made the old boys positively spin as the usual secret service rules were breached.

However, times change, even in the world of intelligence. Its landscape certainly changed the morning that two hijacked aircraft crashed into the World Trade Center in New York. It meant that the war against Islamic terrorism went into overdrive. GCHQ doubled the size of its counter-terrorism team almost overnight, although it had considerable trouble with recruiting Arabic-speaking staff who would be able to pass the security tests needed. Interception of signals intelligence was being made difficult by the fact that Al-Qaeda operators were beginning to practise their own form of radio transmission discipline. They were advising their agent operators to move from place to place when sending messages to avoid detection. The same advice would have been given to an agent in German-occupied Europe during the war when the Resistance was transmitting messages back to its controller in London. In either case, brevity of transmission is still the watchword.

NEW ENEMIES AND FRIENDS

The mood among the intelligence community after 9/11 seemed reminiscent of the early days of the Cold War when the conflict against communism suddenly became apparent with the Berlin Airlift. They both had the same effect as the Islamic terrorism act in New York – panic.

The end of the Cold War had caused a relaxation of the intelligence effort so the sudden switching of target to transmissions in Arabic in new and burgeoning audio technology found an inadequate supply of speakers of the language. A review of recordings did identify some significant phrases (at least in retrospect) that, had they been intercepted and understood as 9/11 went into action, might have changed things but they were not sent for translation until the following day.

The result has been that the old alliances that were beginning to flag did spring back to life against a foe that was generally little understood and beginning to operate a form of guerrilla warfare. Old alliances began to shift into new patterns because the old Anglo-American intelligence alliance had never been universally accepted in Europe as so many states were excluded from its intelligence sources and evaluations to one degree or another. France was a principal one, which had a lot to offer, but the sinking of the Greenpeace vessel *Rainbow Warrior* by agents of the *Direction Générale de la Sécurité Exteriéure* (DGSE) set back its acceptance. The attack in Auckland, New Zealand, in 1985 hit a low point for French intelligence when it used explosives to sink a vessel about to sail on a voyage of protest against French nuclear weapon testing in the Pacific. Two agents of the French foreign intelligence service were arrested by the New Zealand police and convicted of the crime and the French defence minister, Charles Hemu, had to resign.

French intelligence began to march out of step with her American and British counterparts and it took a few years for DGSE to recover its poise, but it soon realised it was lagging behind with intelligence facilities. During the Gulf War of 1990 the French military engaged the enemy in action without adequate intelligence, causing it to depend on others for the information it needed about the enemy. As a result, French expenditure on intelligence during the 1990s escalated while the rest of the world was paring back and enjoying a 'peace dividend' at the end of the Cold War. The French built a satellite base with military surveillance capability in French Guiana, sharing the cost with Belgium, Spain, Italy, Germany and Greece. It had the capability of launching Ariane rockets carrying Helios satellites with high-resolution imaging cameras to monitor crisis points that concerned France, such as the Ivory Coast, Iraq, etc. A 'situation centre' was built in 2000 by the DGSE to handle the increasing flow of images from the satellite so the media in France boasted of its intelligence achievements in satellite surveillance technology.

France's cost-sharing initiative became the centre of several debates in the European Parliament in 1990 about an EU-wide intelligence service modelled on similar lines to the CIA but distancing itself from the Anglo-American intelligence accord. The terrorist bombing in Madrid in 2004 intensified the demand for an intelligence capability, particularly from Austria, Belgium and Greece, although Britain's Tony Blair remained committed to his country's 'special' American alliance.

The EU intelligence co-operation between member states continued, however, as a result of the poor intelligence practices of the Bush administration over 9/11 and the Iraq controversies. The American-dominated intelligence system also showed a disregard for civil liberties, both at home and abroad, that disturbed several European countries. There was resentment in the UK at the threat made by the Bush administration that the USA would deny anyone (including the UK) intelligence data if they did not toe the American line.

In the case of Binyam Mohamed, a former Guantanamo Bay detainee, the British government was requested to withhold intelligence documents that might assist Mohamed's defence. The issue caused enough heated debate for the American Embassy in London to call off an event entitled 'A Special Relationship: 60 Years of Formal UK/US Defence Intelligence Co-operation'. At the same time, aspects of intelligence had begun to change with the use of 'data mining' techniques used on public domain information such as Facebook or Twitter, etc., giving rise to concerns about personal privacy. Relations with washington became strained.

Britain took on the responsibility for EU Justice and Home Affairs, enabling the creation of Europol and the Common Foreign and Security Policy (CFSP) to be opened up to the need for independence of intelligence in Europe. Many had begun to doubt if the flow of American intelligence could be relied on now the Cold War had ended.

The Bosnia-Herzegovina War in 1992–95 was a crisis in which the EU gratefully accepted the intelligence capability that America offered, but the situation heightened awareness of the lack of a home-grown agency. An organisation entitled the Western European Union (WEU) that had been in abeyance for some years was revived and given the capacity for analysis of situations, sources of intelligence and a 'capability for relevant strategic planning' by Tony Blair.

Since then, Britain has voted to leave the EU, which or may not change its relationship with European, American and even Commonwealth intelligence communities. Nonetheless, developments in the EU will remain of importance in global intelligence matters.

In 1999 the Balkans flared up again and a NATO bombing campaign was largely directed by American intelligence, but it led to a reinforcement of EU satellite intelligence capability with the establishment of a European Satellite Centre (SATCEN). It had been set up just outside Madrid using an imaging system called Galileo at the cost of €20 billion, which considerably extended the existing French satellite surveillance system. The new spy in the sky cameras freed member states from having to purchase images from the USA, Russia and China, who could have shut their image feeds down in a time of military or economic crisis. The Galileo service was made available for civilian intelligence and information as well as the military one for all EU states and as an independent intelligence facility it is proving to be a prodigious asset.

SATCEN and its Galileo system are a part of the expanding EU intelligence facility with Norway and Switzerland co-operating in an intelligence exchange forum called the Club de Berne, along with the EU Military Staff Intelligence (EUMS INT) organisation, which it shares with a civilian Joint Situation Centre (SITCEN). The three facilities, SATCEN, Galileo and EUMS, have come together in gathering intelligence to feed it into SITCEN for evaluation although there is, as yet, no signals intelligence (SIGINT) capability such as intercepted wireless transmissions or human intelligence as provided by spies such as Kim Philby (HUMINT) available to the European Union (as far as we know). Charles Clark, the British Home Secretary (2004–06), stated in 2005 that SITCEN monitors and assesses events and situations on a twenty-four-hour basis with a focus on potential crisis regions, terrorism and the proliferation of weapons of mass destruction for its twenty-seven members. At that time, the centre only had seven analysts but three years later the number had increased to more than 100 devoted to those tasks, of which forty were working on open source material.

Europe's relatively small but growing intelligence bureau did not involve itself in covert operations (as far as we know) but monitored such matters as piracy activities around the Horn of Africa, largely by Galileo imagery. It was probably involved in the deployment of the European Naval Force that raided dumps of pirates' stores in Somalia in May 2012. Georgia's disputed boundaries are being watched by the EU, with 300 people there on the ground, as evidenced before the House of Lords in 2010 by William Shapcott, the first director of SITCEN. A senior EU official discussing Galileo's imagery stated that it might be primitive compared with what the Americans could do but as their images are not being easily shared it was necessary for the Europeans to fall back on their own resources – which were improving with use.

The future shape and function of an EU intelligence centre is currently being fiercely and often critically debated by their intelligence functionaries. One school of thought wants to model a new European intelligence bureau on the format of the American CIA, at least as the agency was in its early days. A European agency with multiple sovereign nations partners does, however, raise the difficult question about the quality of co-operation, which the Americans do not have to dela with. Acceptability of intelligence evaluations from inputs coming from so many sources raises the age-old problem – who can one trust? Are the partners (in any intelligence partnership) holding back, editing or even purely inventing aspects of their findings for their own purposes?

National sovereignty interests and how they might affect the quality and value of intelligence information and how it is shared is a prickly problem. It was addressed by the European Parliament in 2002 was how to maintain oversight of the burgeoning EU intelligence community. A Select Committee of five MEPs was appointed to review secret information, including sensitive data from foreign intelligence bureaus, to ensure that 'Top Secret' material was not being betrayed.

The EUs 'External Action Service' is viewed with reserve by the British government. Listening to what politicians say in public is one thing, but what they do is another. The fact that London has secured a remarkable number of high-level security and intelligence appointments for British people in Brussels is of interest. Jonathan Faull has followed Adrian Fortescue as director general of Justice Affairs; William Shapcott is heading SITCEN; Robert Wainwright is director of Europol and Aled Williams is the president of Eurojustice. The slightly surprising appointment of Catherine Ashton at a high political level as High Representative for Foreign and Security Policy has topped off the British cadre of officials. Each of the positions is related to the EU security and intelligence portfolio, but all of these positions will be lost with Brexit. Such appointments would have needed much lobbying by London to have gained that much success. But they indicated commitment to the formation of a Europe-wide intelligence agency.

So what does that have to say about the Anglo-American intelligence axis? The intention of the emerging European intelligence community is obviously to hive off from Washington's global intelligence policies, particularly with the uncertainties arising from a presidential election. British intelligence policy is therefore in disarray and will probably be so for some time. The American people's choice of Trump or Clinton will soon define future intelligence policy towards Britain, EU and the wider world. Clarification of the relationship between the emerging EU

Common Foreign and Security Policy and our own security services will undoubtedly take longer. The British Secret intelligence Service is about to go through as difficult a time as it did in 1940.

BIBLIOGRAPHY

There are two kinds of book author, the academic and the journalistic one, and I come via training and experience from the second of these traditional values. The academic will notate all the sources of his reading, often down to the page number, whereas a journalist such as myself tends to keep his sources confidential. I will opt for a middle course and of the fifty or so books that I have read in researching this book I will comment on the ones that have made the most contribution to a specific chapter. I cannot see the reason for a specific citation. It would be unrealistic, as I read each book holistically and think that a single reference could destroy the story for you, so get the book that I mention out of the library and read it for yourself, if you will.

I   THE FIRST WORLD WAR

The period piece before and during the war, *Huns and Englanders* by James Hawes (Simon and Shuster, 2014), illustrates how the newspapers talked the British people into war. Then *When the Lamps Went Out*, by Nigel Fountain (Guardian Books, 2014), recounts how the politicians struggled to hold back the inevitable. In *Whitehall* by Colin Brown (Simon and Schuster, 2009), the scene is set at the Admiralty for *Room 40* by Patrick Beesly (Hamish Hamilton, 1982). It tells the incredible story of the beginning of the golden years of British intelligence in 1914, which laid the foundations for Bletchley Park's achievements almost three decades later.

Counter-intelligence that foiled the Kaiser's spies is described in Chris Northcott's *MI5 at War*, showing the beginnings of the agency.

2 THE INTERWAR YEARS

The *Encyclopaedia of Espionage* by Ronald Seth was published in 1972 before Bletchley Park went public and has details of spies of the First World War of whom I have never heard, and is the more fascinating for that.

A very different book set in the interwar years is *Conjuring Hitler* (Pluto Press), in which Guido Giacomo Preparata describes how British and American money financed the rise of Nazism, guided by the future CIA spymaster Allan Dulles. A fascinating book, although I am able to fault some of Guido's research.

Information about the development of coding machines came, to some extent, from *Voices of the Code Breakers* by Michael Harris (David and Charles), but much of the research was made in the Imperial War Museum. The use of ciphers and codes in signals intelligence or SIGINT had been important but message security was becoming less certain as the Cambridge University Press book, *Delusions of Intelligence* by R.A Ratcliff, explains in an analysis of German blindness to Enigma's compromise.

3 THE WAR'S BEGINNING

There are many books about the derring-do of the Special Operations Executive, formed in the most desperate early days of the war, but none better than *SOE in France*, massively researched by M.R.D. Foot (Whitehall History Publishing, 2014).

Others pay homage to Winston, who was the instigator of SOE and many other devices to do mischief to the enemy, so *Churchill's War Lab* by Taylor Downing reviews his career and innovations. *Churchill's School for Saboteurs* by Bernard O'Connor tells the story of one of the SOE training schools, and *Churchill's White Rabbit* by Sophie Jackson (The History Press) relates the exploits of Forest Yeo-Thomas, alias 'White Rabbit', who became a legend in SOE. His exploits in occupied France were such that he was able to get a meeting with Churchill and persuade him to increase SOE support for the Resistance, but on his last clandestine visit Yeo-Thomas was betrayed to the Gestapo.

Women were also recruited into SOE and one of the first was a Polish woman whose deeds, described in *The Spy Who Loved*, match any of the many others recorded in the executive. Numbers of other women active in the French Resistance have their stories told in *Sisters in the Resistance* by Margaret Weitz (John Wiley, 1995), telling of their individual heroic struggles.

A woman with a less dangerous story to tell, but just as demanding, was Noreen Riols' book *The Secret Ministry of Ag and Fish* (Macmillan), in which Noreen gives an inside story of life in SOE, in London and in the field (occupied Europe).

Finally, to celebrate the heroism of the RAF pilots who provided an air taxi service for agents coming and going into France under the noses of the Nazis there is *Airbourne Espionage* by David Oliver (Sutton Publishing).

Although not strictly a spy book, I include *Ian Fleming's Commandos* (Faber and Faber) in this chapter, as it was not only quoted in the Dieppe Raid but aspects of his real-life exploits appear in the books about the world's most famous spy – James Bond.

NOTE – I have used no publications for the story about Operation North Pole as I did the research for the SOE disaster in Holland for my previous book, *SIGINT: The Secret History of Signals Intelligence in the World Wars*, among the Dutch people.

4   D-DAY

The preparations for the landings, a huge deception, are described in *Double Cross* (Bloomsbury) by an ill-assorted team of only five people. I have tried to maintain a balance in accounts of the great event and so the book *Normandie Front* by Vince Milano (The History Press) gives that through German eyes. Comparing it to the Antony Beevor classic *D-Day*, you would think they were two different battles.

Voices from D-Day (Robinson), gives no balance but it does give colour and *The Normandy Campaign 1944* (Pen and Sword) describes the follow-through of the Allied forces in the battle. An important part of the assault is given in two books – *Code Name Mulberry* by Guy Hartup (Pen and Sword) and *A Harbour Goes to War*, edited by J. Evans (Brook House Publishing) gives accounts of its construction, to which I can add reminiscences of those who I knew.

The culmination of the battle in France is celebrated in *Eleven Days in August*, recalling the liberation of Paris.

5   THE COLD WAR

The small teach yourself book, *The Cold War* by C.B. Jones (Bookprint Ltd), was invaluable to check on dates and the tumultuous progress of events after the war. *Six Months in 1945* by Michael Dobbs (Arrow Books) described the descent into a new conflict.

Following that, the first real move by the Soviets is depicted in more than 500 pages of *The Berlin Blockade*, which not only tell of the part played by the huge fleet of aircraft that supplied the city but also the courage of the Berliners in facing unimaginable hardships for just under a year of the siege.

6   BERLIN

The chapter on Berlin is mainly concerned with intelligence and dirty tricks, and there is no better account of the efforts of both the KGB and the CIA than *Battleground Berlin* (Yale University Press). It was written jointly by David Murphy of the CIA and Sergei Kondrashev of the KGB, both of whom were involved in espionage operations in Berlin and later co-operated to produce this 500-page magisterial study of the early days of the Cold War.

A major part of the CIA's effort to spy on the Germans was through the Gehlen Organisation, but *The Gehlen Memoirs* (Collins) gives very little away, while two others do: *Gehlen – Spy of the Century* (Hodder & Stoughton) is a laudatory account of the general's career by E.H. Cookridge, while *The General was a Spy* by Heinz Holne (Pan Books) is a warts-and-all account of his contribution to intelligence in Europe.

7   LONDON SPIES

Now on familiar ground, the story of *Kim Philby* (Biteback), by his friend Tim Milne, is a fairly impartial account of their relationship considering Philby betrayed his friends and country.

The account of the life of Guy Burgess in *Stalin's Englishman* makes no apology for being a laudatory study of another of the Cambridge Spy Ring. It creates a surprisingly kind picture of a drunken, philandering double agent who finally brought down all the members of the ring.

George Blake's life as a double agent is recounted in *The Greatest Traitor* (Aurum Press), which tells the story of his betrayal, detection and forty-two year sentence in jail, from which he escaped and fled to Russia.

The last of the spies was, thankfully, a British one. The father of Peter Ustinov was a most effective agent according to Peter Day's account in *Klop* (Biteback). Klop would have recognised the story in *Deception* by Edward Lucas (Bloomsbury), which tells of how Russia duped the West, first with the KGB and now with today's agency, the FSB.

8 CONCLUSION

The story of recent Western intelligence developments is told in detail in Professor Aldrich's *GCHQ* (Harper Press), which gives an understanding of the intelligence challenges facing the present day. *In Spies We Trust* by Professor Rhodri Jones (Oxford University Press) looks towards the future patterns of intelligence and comes to some surprising conclusions.

Last, and definitely not least, is the 'Guidebook of the Imperial War Museum', which has made inputs into all aspects of this book from the contents of the museum's galleries and its research department.

GENERAL REFERENCES

My own book, *SIGINT: The Secret History of Signals Intelligence in the World Wars*, was published by The History Press in 2013 and the research that I did for it has shaped this book – or at least the first half of it.

The second and most valuable contribution was made by *The Insider's Guide to 500 Spy Sites in London*, complied by Mark Birdsall and Deborah Plisko of *Eye Spy* magazine. That 500-page publication not only records the major espionage events of the decades but also illustrates them in a way that was most helpful to me.

PLACES OF INTEREST

THE IMPERIAL WAR MUSEUM (IWM)

I have had a long and interesting relationship with this institution and give regular talks there to invited audiences about wartime experiences. I therefore know my way around the museum's exhibits and services, which helped greatly in writing this book. Readers may be interested to know about some of the exhibits; particularly the museum's Secret War Gallery, illustrating the clandestine world of espionage, covert operations and the work of Britain's Special Forces from the development of MI5 and MI6. Exhibits range from First World War items through the Second World War to the Cold War and its intelligence conflict. Some of the displays I mention in my books so that readers who visit the museum and its Secret War Gallery may see them for themselves. The main building is in Lambeth, but the museum maintains two others in London where you can experience the atmosphere of espionage.

IMPERIAL WAR MUSEUM LONDON

Free admission.
Open seven days a week – 10 a.m. to 5.45 p.m.
Free audio guide in five languages.
Telephone 020 7416 5000.

The museum tells the story of the people whose lives have been shaped by war and the weapons they used, from the First World War through the Second and up to the present day. The IWM London's major refurbishment recounts the lives of 'A Family in Wartime' and the award-winning Holocaust Exhibition.

CHURCHILL WAR ROOMS

Charge for admission.
Open seven days a week – 9.30 a.m. to 5.00 p.m.
Free audio guide in five languages.
Telephone 020 7930 6961.

The original Cabinet maze of War Rooms in which Churchill and his inner circle worked in secret at the heart of government for victory is preserved for you to walk its corridors, which remain as they were when the lights were turned off in 1945. This trip into the wartime past beneath the streets of Westminster is only ten minutes' walk from the 'Spies Hotel'.

HMS BELFAST

Charge for admission.
Open seven days a week. 10 a.m. to 5 p.m. March–October and 10 a.m. to 4 p.m. November–February.
Free audio guide in five languages.
Telephone 020 7940 6300.

The Royal Navy's heavy cruiser that saw much action in the Second World War is moored in the Thames just upstream from Tower Bridge on the opposite bank to the Tower of London. Immerse yourself in the 'Gun Turret Experience' featuring the guns that were some of the first to fire on German defences on D-Day seventy years ago.

IWM DUXFORD

Charge for admission.
Open seven days a week – 10 a.m. to 6 p.m.
Free audio guide in five languages.
Telephone 01223 835000.
This historic airfield is not in London but in Cambridgeshire (postcode CB22 4Q2) for those who are interested in a unique collection of famous aircraft of the past. It has exhibits describing the Battle of Britain, American bombing of Germany and the Berlin Airlift, as well as many other aerial actions. It is best to telephone first to see if any particular display in which you might be interested is open to the public as exhibits are often being rearranged for improvements.

ST ERMIN'S HOTEL

Address: 2 Caxton St, London SW1H 0QW
Website: www.sterminshotel.co.uk
Telephone: 020 7222 7888.

Nestled at the end of a tree-lined courtyard in the heart of Westminster, St Ermin's Hotel is an independent four-star deluxe hotel and the only publicly accessible establishment in London closely associated with the history of British espionage. With many of London's top historical attractions on the doorstep and its close proximity to St James's Park underground station and Victoria station, St Ermin's Hotel is the ideal destination for both business and leisure travellers, offering excellent service, award-winning dining at the Caxton Grill, eclectic styling and a relaxed, welcoming atmosphere.

INDEX

If you enjoyed this book, you may also be interested in…

Sigint: The Secret History of Signals Intelligence in the World Wars

PETER MATTHEWS

978 0 7524 8734 2

"SIGINT is a fascinating account of what Allied investigators learned post-war about the Nazi equivalent of Bletchley Park. Turns out, 60,000 crptographers, analysts and linguists achieved considerable success in solving intercepted traffic, and even broke the Swiss Enigma! Based on recently declassifed NSA document, this is a great contribution to the literature."

The St Ermin's Hotel Intelligence Book Of The Year Award 2014.

Spycraft Secrets: An Espionage A-Z

NIGEL WEST

FOREWORD BY GENERAL (RET.) DAVID PETRAEUS

978 0 7509 6608 5

Tradecraft is the term applied to techniques used by intelligence personnel to assist them in conducting their operations and, like many other professions, the espionage business has developed its own rich lexicon.

In the real, sub rosa world of intelligence-gathering, each bit of jargon acts as a veil of secrecy over particular types of activity, and in this book acclaimed author Nigel West explains and give examples of the lingo in action. He draws on the first-hand experience of defectors to and from the Soviet Union; surveillance operators who kept terrorist suspects under observation in Northern Ireland; case officers who have put their lives at risk by pitching a target in a denied territory; the NOCs who lived under alias to spy abroad; and much more.

Turn these pages and be immersed in the real world of James Bond: assets, black operations, double agents, triple agents ... it's all here.

Agente: Female Secret Agents in World Wars, Cold Wars and Civil Wars

DOUGLAS BOYD

978 0 7509 6694 8

Forget the adventure stories of James Bond, Kim Philby, Klaus Fuchs and co. – espionage is not just a boys' game.

As long as there has been conflict, there have been female agents behind the scenes. In Belgium and northern France in 1914–18 there were several thousand women actively working against the Kaiser's forces occupying their homelands. In the Second World War, women of many nations opposed the Nazis, risking the firing squad or decapitation by axe or guillotine. Yet, many of those women did not have the right to vote for a government or even open a bank account. So why did they do it?

This revealing history explores the lives and the motivations of the women of many races and social classes who have risked their lives as secret agents, and celebrates their intelligence, strength and courage.

The destination for history
www.thehistorypress.co.uk